Tom Knoblock

Goldfish Pools
Water-Lilies
and
Tropical Fishes

BY DR. G. L. THOMAS, JR.

Distributed in the U.S. by T.F.H. Publications, Inc., 211 West Sylvania Avenue, PO Box 427, Neptune, NJ 07753; in England by T.F.H. (Gt. Britain) Ltd., 13 Nutley Lane, Reigate, Surrey; in Canada to the book store and library trade by Beaverbooks Ltd., 150 Lesmill Road, Don Mills, Ontario M38 2T5, Canada; in Canada to the pet trade by Rolf C. Hagen Ltd., 3225 Sartelon Street, Montreal 382, Quebec; in Southeast Asia by Y.W. Ong, 9 Lorong 36 Geylang, Singapore 14; in Australia and the South Pacific by Pet Imports Pty. Ltd., P.O. Box 149, Brookvale 2100, N.S.W. Australia; in the British Crown Colony of Hong Kong, in South Africa by Valid Agencies, P.O. Box 51901, Randburg 2125 South Africa. Published by T.F.H. Publications, Inc., Ltd.

Published by T.F.H. Publications, Inc. Ltd., The British Crown Colony of Hong Kong. Manufactured in Hong Kong.

BY DR. G. L. THOMAS, JR.

Library of Congress Catalogue Card No. 58—11116

Acknowledgment

Grateful acknowledgment is hereby given to all who have contributed to the development of this book, especially to our friends and customers from far and near—who, loving goldfish, water lilies, aquatics, and tropical fish—have sought answers to their many questions and have provided constant stimulation: to Ralph Reppert, Baltimore newspaperman and water gardener, for valuable help in assembling and presenting the material; to A. Aubrey Bodine, F. P. S. A. of Baltimore, for exceptional photographs for this book; to Miss Helen L. Smith of Old Braddock, Maryland for the excellent line drawings; to Dr. Herbert R. Axelrod for editing that portion on tropical fish, providing all transparencies for them, and for art direction and layout; to Mrs. E. Delue Crawford and Mrs. Barbara L. Sexton for seemingly endless but necessary typing; to Dr. George H. Pring of the Missouri Botanical Gardens, probably the world's foremost authority on orchids and tropical water lilies, for patient and vital consultation.

Particularly, I gratefully thank my parents, my wife, our sons and their wives for unfailing encouragement and understanding.

Dedication

To our grandchildren, George Leicester Thomas IV, Margaret Mary and Virginia Jeannette Thomas, who we hope will carry on the tradition of their great-grandfather Thomas . . . for the great love of flowers this book is lovingly dedicated.

Foreword

For a century or more the growing of water-lilies has delighted American gardeners—that is, a certain number of them. These have sung the praises of the exquisite and opalescent blossoms and emphasized the easy culture in tub, pool, or pond. Unfortunately they haven't always been believed—about the "ease," I mean, not the beauty. Anyone who has ever seen a water-lily readily admits that it is among the loveliest of flowers.

But pools are hard to build, some argue; pools take up a lot of room; they leak; they get scummy; they're for the fellows with lots of time and money.

But at Lilypons near Frederick, Maryland, the Thomas family keeps proving these criticisms are unjustified. They have built up a vast business on aquatic plants (and tropical fish), and there isn't a question on water gardening that their customers haven't asked and they haven't answered—successfully. It doesn't cost much, they demonstrate; it is simple, and it doesn't take much time.

It should all be in a book, we decided, so that this easiest of gardens could be enjoyed by all the busiest of people, the ones who don't want to dig, hoe, spray, dust, stake, and trim; the ones who like to sit and enjoy. For them a clear pool, a few lilies, the flash of fish, and the relaxed attitude are the thing.

This ever-increasing multitude can find in this book all they will ever need to know about easy gardening, that is, *water* gardening in a tub, in a prefabricated pool, in a concrete pool they can make in a day, or in a quiet pond, if they are lucky enough to have one.

And the dedicated gardener, the enthusiastic one for whom nothing is too much trouble, will find here a thorough discussion *not elsewhere available* on every aspect of water gardening. Every type of pool is considered. Every available water-lily and other aquatic plant is described. All possible advice is offered as to appearance, culture, and propagation, on how to plant the water garden "inside" for balance of life, outside for beauty of setting.

Then about fish. If you have a few now, you will soon have a multitude; first you won't lose an expensive favorite through ignorance after getting this advice, and then you will find it almost impossible to resist further collecting.

This is a grand book, I think, simple and delightful in style, sound down to the last detail. When I visited Lilypons, I saw the pools and water-lilies in vast numbers and talked at length with Dr. and Mrs. Thomas (actually a husband-and-wife collaboration is responsible for this book), and I met their two boys who are now sharing the responsibility and work at Three Springs Fisheries. A wonderful American family has developed this business, and from it has come this delightful and most American book.

Helen Van Pelt Wilson

This 1965 edition brings the book up to date since the original—and very successful—1958 edition was published, and it includes a fascinating new chapter on Tropical Fish.

H. VAN P. W.

Contents

Visit to Lilypons

Here at Lilypons, ten miles south of Frederick in Maryland, we look out upon a vast area spotted with shallow ponds, most of them staggered at hillside levels like Chinese rice paddies. Crews of men with steam shovels and bulldozers are forever pushing earth around among the ponds and every man works with a loaded shotgun close at hand. Now and then, throughout the day, the sound of gunfire rolls in to us from across the water.

An aerial view showing some of the water-lily and goldfish ponds in which the author has produced millions of fish and lilies.

In the center of this strange countryside is Lilypons, a community of some thirty families living on scattered farms. Lilypons is the home of our business, the Three Springs Fisheries, which has become the largest source of ornamental fish and exotic water plants in the world.

Tourists drive out to see us, stroll among the ponds, and are delighted with the contradictions they find. They peer through coarse plantings of cat-tails to view the sunken beds of Egyptian lotus, tall, elephant-eared flowers with dewy pink blooms larger than a man's hat. They look through screens of bulrushes and come upon the breathtaking sight of hardy and tropical water-lilies—glossy whites, brilliant yellows, pinks, blues, red-golds, crimsons, deep reds.

Sometimes visitors just follow their noses, for many water-lilies have far-reaching scents, varying from the delicate fragrance of lily-of-the-valley to the rich, ripe smell of newly picked apples. The mingled scents of a galaxy of water-lilies, particularly after an early shower, offer a never-to-be-forgotten experience.

We enjoy explaining the place to visitors. The men with the earth-moving machinery are shaping dikes to form ponds. We fill the ponds with water, and in them we grow our "crops," the some 70,000,000 or-

Workmen thin out a pond and gather blossoms which are sold for about $3 per dozen when in season.

namental and bait fish, and the hundreds of thousands of water-lilies and other aquatics which we ship out to a multitude of markets every year. Everyone is impressed by our freedom from mosquitoes. With 400 of our 1,800 acres under water, the place would seem a veritable paradise for water-bred insects. The answer is: the fish eat them.

Fish hawks give us a lot of trouble, which explains the shotguns. From a high, smooth glide, a hawk spots a big, slow-moving fish, goes into a power dive to get it, and then flaps away with his meal. This may be a pretty sight for a bird-lover, but it is an expensive proposition for the Fisheries. Chances are that the fat, slow-moving fish the hawk chooses will be one of our high-priced five- or six-year-old brood fish. It piques me to see a bird get away with a two- or three-dollar meal at my expense. That's more than I usually pay for my own lunch.

Kingfishers, sea gulls, blue cranes, white cranes, and fish ducks also take their toll of fish, and would soon deplete our ponds if not driven away by gunfire. Muskrats and crawfish present problems too. They burrow into the dikes and so drain the ponds. A bounty program, which we inaugurated years ago, keeps these pests pretty well in check.

The Hobby That Grew and Grew

The present expanse of pools, ponds, and canals which is now Lily-pons is a development begun as a hobby in 1917 by my father. Father undoubtedly came by his love of water gardening from his mother, who always had a water garden of some sort. First it was a sunken tub, then some half-barrels, and then a whole series of sunken tubs, and finally a pool. I remember two water-lilies which always did especially well for her. One was white, one yellow, and both were delightfully fragrant. She never had visitors who didn't admire them. Years later, when we produced a new hardy variety, a most fragrant and beautiful pink, we named it for her—the Mrs. C. W. Thomas water-lily—and her pleasure was unbounded.

Father bought the Three Springs Farm, then a 360-acre spread, at the turn of the century, when he was just out of Franklin and Marshall College and teaching school. To beautify the place, he converted fifteen acres of lower ground into ponds and stocked them with brood goldfish and water-lilies. He gave away a lot of fish in the early days and then, rather reluctantly, began to sell them as the demand grew. Almost without realizing it, he became a fisheries operator on a full-time basis.

Lily Ponds, Lily Pons, and Lilypons

The business grew, particularly after the dime stores began stocking goldfish. Soon father had to look around for more convenient shipping arrangements—more convenient for him and for the U. S. Post Office Department. Postal authorities agreed to establish a branch at the Fisheries and advised him to choose a single, descriptive, easy-to-remember name. It was a postal official who suggested the name Lily Pons—well known, and certainly descriptive. So Lilypons it was. It became official in 1932.

Miss Pons, bless her heart, was delighted. She paid her first official visit to Lilypons in 1936. Her many commitments have made frequent returns impossible, more's the pity, but she often has her Christmas cards and gifts mailed from her namesake post office, and she writes to us and also sends us albums of her latest records.

Although Miss Pons gave our address a touch of glamor, the fisheries area was already a pretty well-visited place. For one thing, our ponds, when frozen, make excellent skating rinks and draw skaters from all over Frederick county. Also, in the early days, when father processed his own goldfish food from hard-boiled egg yolks, there were gallons and gallons of raw egg whites to give away. People came for it regularly with fruit jars. Angel-food cake, the thirteen-egg kind, became something of a tradition in our part of the country.

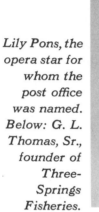

Lily Pons, the opera star for whom the post office was named. Below: G. L. Thomas, Sr., founder of Three-Springs Fisheries.

Today my sons and I operate the business along lines similar to those organized by my father. To be sure, we have installed systems of tile and piping so that we can now drain, refill, and otherwise control our vastly grown expanses under cultivation, which now number some 800 ponds. We have worked out systems, and trained employees to follow them, for keeping exact genealogical records of all our family strains of fish and plants. We experiment with new types of pools, new pool equipment, and new pool supplies. Recommendations to our customers are therefore based on practical experience.

We have a research program which has produced some interesting information. For instance, we know that eighty-five out of every hundred goldfish we breed will color up properly. Once we sold the drab, uncolored fifteen per cent for bait, and considered ourselves lucky to find such a market. Then the demand for the bait fish increased to such an extent that, through research, we developed a noncoloring strain of fish to satisfy the special market.

Another of our research programs resulted in what we believe to be the finest conditioning method for goldfish in the country. Before we ship, we route the fish into a number of spring-fed pools of hard, cold, clear water. A few days of "hardening" in these pools gives fish robust and lasting health so that casualties during shipment have been practically eliminated.

With my sons' help, we are moving ahead in other phases of water gardening.

George Leicester Thomas, III, is traffic manager. Charles Brosius Thomas is sales manager. All of us work together in production and experimentation.

One of our more successful efforts has been in the development of a vastly improved system for shipping fish.

There was a time when shipping fish to a distant city entailed the cumbersome business of loading and transporting our orders in heavy, slosh-proof metal cans. It was a clumsy business for both shipper and customer. It was also expensive, for the heavy containers had to be either returned or paid for.

Now we ship boxes of living fish around the world as casually as we ship boxes of fish food. The device which makes this possible is our patented method by which our fish travel in sealed polyethylene bags filled with oxygenated water, the bag encased in a conventional corrugated cardboard shipping box. It is clean, comfortable for the fish, and safe. And there are no containers to return.

Recently we added facilities to handle tropical fish. To learn something of these fishes—where they originate, how they are captured, how they should be cared for—Charles Thomas studied methods with dozens of native fishermen in South America and the Far East. These native suppliers, who ship to us by air, have come to know us, and they trust us with their best.

By dealing directly through our own supply network, which now extends to countries all over the world, we are able to obtain exactly the fish varieties we want, and to market them at lower prices than we might if we dealt exclusively through tropical fish brokers.

As we have worked out our own problems with plants and fish, we have passed on our findings to amateur fanciers. It seems that almost everyone who has ever ordered plants or fish from the 75,000 catalogs we mail out every year has written in at one time or another with some sort of problem: a woman in California wants to illuminate her pool from beneath the water; a man in Alabama needs a prolific water-lily to cover a farm pond in one season; another man wants us to recommend a substitute for cinders in this diesel age, and I expect a hundred customers have written to ask where in the *world* a city dweller can go to get cow manure.

This book, to a large extent, is a product of all those questions. I shall try to offer at least one good, practical solution—and an alternative wherever possible—for all the questions a water gardener might encounter.

I'll try to do the job impartially, free of my personal enthusiasms. I'll *try*. Water gardening, you see, isn't only my business. It's my *hobby*, too.

Three Springs Fisheries
Lilypons, Maryland 21717

PART I *POOLS,*
PONDS, AND
PLANTS

CHAPTER ONE · *Planning for Your Pool*

A water-lily pool, together with the variety of plants used for decorating its margin, offers a quick and rewarding means of "landscaping" a new place. Under fair conditions, a pool of average size can be visualized in the early summer, constructed, "cured," planted, and brought into full bloom in four to six weeks. What a refreshing sight a pool is for a family in a new home while they wait for grass and shrubbery to take hold.

Plate 1. The refreshing expanse of reflected color on Senator Andrew J. Sordoni's farm at Wilkes Barre, Pennsylvania, shows what can be accomplished in a farm pond by the wise placement of just a few hardy water-lilies.

The Versatile Water Garden

Pools are remarkably varied and adaptive. A "pool" may be a farm pond, big as a city block, with free-growing species of water-lilies scattered over it like a sky full of stars. In the suburbs or city a pool may be roughly the size of a living-room rug, a sunken affair of concrete in the side, front, or back yard; or it may be really tiny, a garden spot taking up no more room than a lawn chair—a little living bouquet, all the more beautiful for its small and intimate setting.

A pool in a new landscape can become the center of interest around which the rest of the garden is designed. A new pool placed in an old and loved garden will bring added magic by reflecting and complementing the flowers already there. And, speaking of magic, I think a shimmering water surface set into a garden is the best possible way to bring a patch of sky down to earth and make it part of the landscape. From a picture window, a pool of water-lilies is a lovely, refreshing sight and colorful for a long season. By the strategic placement of a pool just outside a window, a gardener can bring the beauty and serenity of water-borne flowers right into the house.

The Time, the Trouble, and the Cost

Expensewise, water gardening also is widely varied. With a tub, half-barrel, or similar container, a man can sink a miniature pool in his yard—and plant it with practically any water-lily he wants—for less than he would spend for a new hat. With only average handiness with tools, he can build a concrete pool big enough for the whole neighborhood to enjoy for as little as fifty dollars.

The maintenance of a water garden requires practically no work at all. There is no hoeing, no weeding, no watering. Given a fair chance, water-lilies will not only grow and bloom—they will thrive. There are few diseases and insect pests that affect them, none that destroys them.

I hope I am not dwelling too long on the practical aspects of water-lilies. I would want you to consider that, with the possible exception of their wonderful therapeutic value and the satisfying outlet they provide for artistic expression, water-lilies have no practical use whatsoever. They are a sheer, out-and-out luxury, existing solely and completely for whatever pleasure their beauty and fragrance may give you.

Types of Water-Lilies

There are only two basic types of water-lilies—hardy and tropical. They are cousins, so to speak, but nobody so far has been able to cross-breed them.

Plate 2. A planted tub installed in a corner of an old-fashioned garden brings a flash of sunlight into the corner and complements the surrounding flowers by reflection. A few goldfish in the tub provide additional interest.

A. AUBREY BODINE PHOTO

Plate 3. A formal water garden with flagstone rim which looks well with the fieldstone construction of the A. E. Duncan home in Baltimore, Maryland. The restrained planting permits reflection to become part of the decorative scheme.

A. AUBREY BODINE PHOTO

Hardy water-lilies are, for the most part, perennials which propagate themselves without any help from the gardener. Once planted and left undisturbed, even though ice covers the pool in winter, they will burst into new life from the original root each spring for several years.

Hardy lilies, some no larger than the face of a pocket watch, some a foot or more in diameter, come in many tints and shades of every color except blue. Some of them float upon the water among their round, smooth-edged leaves. Others, reaching for the sun, stand above water. Many are fragrant.

The "hardies" open their flowers to the sun in the forenoon and stay open until late afternoon. They begin blooming in May in most parts of the United States and continue until frost.

"Tropicals" might be called annuals, for they are so handled by most casual water gardeners. They differ in many ways from the hardies. They require more pool space because they grow bigger in both blossoms and leaves, which are frequently scalloped or frilled along the edge. They must be planted outside a bit later than the hardies, but they grow rapidly and their blooms open by midsummer and continue to appear long past the time when September frosts put the hardies to sleep for the winter.

Tropicals come in many shades and tints, including blues and purples, but there are few yellows. Yellow is comparatively rare in *any* type of water-lily. Tropicals bear their blossoms on stiff, strong stems which carry most of the blooms well above the surface of a pool.

Plate 4. The Honorable Theodore R. McKeldin of Maryland stands by a formal pool which reflects the white window frames in an attractive way.

A. AUBREY BODINE PHOTO

Day Bloomers, Night Bloomers

Tropical water-lilies are of two kinds—day bloomers and night bloomers. Day bloomers open their flowers, like the hardy lilies, in the forenoon, closing them in the late afternoon. Practically every day-blooming tropical has a fine fragrance.

The night-blooming tropicals open their blooms around 6 to 7 o'clock in the evening and close them about 11 o'clock the following morning. In dull weather, particularly in the East, they will stay open all day. This blooming pattern, which enables even the busiest commuter to see them at their best twice a day, has caused them to be called "the businessman's flower." Only a few of the night-blooming tropicals are fragrant.

Selecting the Site

The selection of a site for your pool usually amounts to deciding where it will look best; actually, however, there are few places where a pool won't look and do well. The only limiting factor to any site is the amount of sunlight that falls upon it. Hardy water-lilies require a minimum of four hours of sun a day. The more they get, over and above that, the more vigorously they will grow and the better they will bloom, but in any spot where they get the four-hour minimum they can be depended upon to give satisfaction. The tropicals won't do their best with less than five or six hours of sun daily.

Night-blooming tropicals require as much sunlight as any of the others. Contrary to what seems to be a popular opinion, they draw only moral support from the moon.

Checking the Site

For Sunlight

If you are doubtful about a site, check it, by all means, before you get started. If you have a spot in mind and there are other flowers there now, rest assured that water-lilies will do as well or even better.

Otherwise, stretch out a length of garden hose or clothesline in a figure the size and shape you want for your pool and in the place you have selected. Then check the spot several times during a day when the sun is shining, and you will know all you need to know about sun requirements. If the shifting shade of a tree barely edges out the needed amount of sunlight from an otherwise desirable spot, a little judicious pruning may let in enough sun to allow you your preferred location.

23

OVERHANGING TREES

A word of warning about trees. I tell customers every year that a water-lily planted under a tree will not bloom. It will produce foliage, but it will not bloom. At least once a year somebody sends in a letter that makes a liar out of me. Often the letter is accompanied by a snapshot of a water-lily blooming beautifully from a tub or barrel in the deep shade of a spreading tree. All I can say, into the teeth of such challenges, is that these are freak blooms that just happen, like the dandelions that sometimes come up in February. Believe me, there is no such thing as a "shade" species of water-lily. If there were, and I had access to it, I could retire comfortably after one season of selling it.

A pool directly under a tree is, therefore, out of the question. Even a pool *partially* under a tree is to be avoided if possible. Leaves and other matter dropping from a tree generate gas as they decompose in the pool, and this gas retards—frequently kills—fish. Oak leaves, probably the worst of the lot, give pool water a strong acid content within a few days.

COLD WINDS

If it is practical for you to locate your pool so that it is protected from the north by a building, a line of trees, a hedge, or similar windbreak, I would advise you to do so. Shelter from northerly winds, particularly

Plate 5. At the home of Miss Pauline Roetling in Baltimore, an informal pool of irregular shape has a natural appearance due to the judicious placement of marsh and bog plants. Each approach to the pool presents a different view.

A. AUBREY BODINE PHOTO

Plate 6. This free and natural looking retreat at Kay's Toll House Tavern, Silver Springs, Maryland, is man-made and didn't just grow, although that impression is cleverly established by the arrangement of the border planting. An overhanging willow is open enough to allow water-lilies at least half a day of direct sun.

A. AUBREY BODINE PHOTO

in early summer, will give your water-lilies a better chance for an early, healthy start. I would recommend only a *casual* effort to provide this protection, however. I don't think I would go to the trouble of planting a windbreak if I had none.

DRAINAGE

The only other consideration in selecting a site is that of filling and emptying the pool. Filling it entails only the business of running a garden hose out to it from the nearest water tap. Emptying isn't much more difficult. Since we shall discuss drainage in detail later, let it suffice at this point to say that the closer the site is to lower ground, to or through which water might be emptied by gravity, the simpler the drainage arrangement of a pool can be.

A natural, flowing body of water usually is too active and too cool for good water-lily growth. Water-lilies do best in still water warmed by the sun. They will sometimes produce foliage in cool water, but they rarely bloom.

Formal and Informal Pools

Aesthetically speaking, there are two types of pools—formal and informal.

A formal pool may be practically any severe and regular shape. Obviously it should suit a man-made decorative scheme. Formal pools can be very beautiful, as our illustrations show, but they should not be attempted if there is little space. The slightest suggestion of crowding ruins the effect of a formal pool.

The informal pool may have just about any kind of outline, although a regular, or at least uncomplicated, shape is likely to be the most pleasing. Through the clever arrangement of marginal plants, the informal pool appears to be a work of nature.

There is also the completely natural pool, the spring-fed pond where you have only to plant water-lilies to convert the site into a garden. The natural pond is rare and stands in a class by itself. I will discuss its possibilities in more detail in Chapter 8 on planting.

Whatever the style of pool decided upon, I strongly recommend a simple shape. Stars, triangles, extreme kidney and crescent shapes and the like are bad. By no stretch of the imagination do they fit in with any kind of formal landscape, and it is next to impossible to give them the natural appearance an informal pool should have. Moreover, the more intricate the pool form, the more difficult it will be to build.

Building Materials for Pools

REINFORCED CONCRETE

For pool construction, above all other types I recommend a simple, reinforced concrete structure, poured into wooden forms. It is oblong or square in shape and is sunk squarely into the ground. Such a pool is easy and inexpensive to build, easy to plant, and easy to clean. Once it is constructed, it is sturdy and watertight, and a pool that a man can maintain with very little attention for the rest of his life.

Another type of reinforced concrete pool is constructed by a technique called "puddling." Such a pool is usually made in an irregular shape, without forms. It is not as practical as the first type pool, but the next best. We will go into construction details for both types later. (See Chapters 2 and 3.)

CONCRETE BLOCK

Although a pool can be built of concrete block somewhat more cheaply, I advise against it. Even with an experienced mason doing the work, such a pool can hardly compare with reinforced concrete for structural strength, and it is far inferior in its ability to hold water.

There are preparations on the market which are guaranteed to make concrete and various types of composition blocks impervious to water, and under certain tests the manufacturers prove their claims impressively. However, as far as I am concerned, this is just another case of the operation being a success, with the patient dying. Practically everyone I know who has built a concrete block pool has had, and is still having, trouble with it.

The ideal depth of a miniature pool is 18 inches. That allows 4 inches for the box or pan of soil in which the water-lilies are to be planted, 12 inches of water to cover the crowns of the roots, and 2 inches to spare. A pool filled to brimming is not as attractive as one filled to within a few inches of the top—hence this 2-inch allowance. When the pool is sunk into the ground, an inch of rim should extend above ground level

Plate 7. An interesting example of controlled profusion, at the J. G. Paul home in Baltimore, Maryland. The blooms and leaves of hardy water-lilies usually float, but they push themselves up above the water when plants become crowded.

A. AUBREY BODINE PHOTO

to prevent surface water from draining in every time it rains. The rim can be banked with stones or sod to give the setting a natural look.

Water-lilies planted in tubs, half-barrels, and other containers placed on top of the ground will produce foliage but seldom bloom. For some reason—one having to do with consistent temperatures, I suspect—water-lilies do best in sunken containers.

Drainage arrangements need not be planned for any of these miniature pools. They are small enough for water to be bailed out with a pail in a few minutes whenever emptying is necessary for cleaning or re-planting.

There are scores of lilies which *will* grow in miniature pools. Among them are several forms especially developed for miniature pools, and these do best of all. (Water-lilies appropriate for miniature pools are listed in Chapter 12.)

Plate 8. A formal pool need not be very large, although is does require more space than an informal water garden. This small formal pool occupies a lawn section at the home of F. W. Zeller in Baltimore, Maryland.

A. AUBREY BODINE PHOTO

BRICKS

Pools constructed of bricks have the same disadvantages as those made of concrete blocks, only more so. It is impossible for anything with that many mortar joints in it not to have a few leaks. However, if it's the brick *appearance* you like, by all means trim the edge of your pool —or the outside surface of a raised pool—with brick.

PREFABRICATED POOLS

There are on the market a variety of prefabricated pools, constructed of both metal and plastic, and turned out in a variety of sizes. A man has only to dig a pit to fit the shell of the pool, set the shell in, fill it up with water, and then plant. The manufacturers of most of these pools checked carefully with water-lily and goldfish culturists before designing them, and so have come up with both practical and attractive designs. They work out very well and are, of course, the very least trouble "to build" of any kind of pool.

Miniature Pools

Various new or used receptacles can be adapted prettily to the construction of sunken miniature pools. A few prerequisites apply to *all* of them, however, regardless of their shape or material.

POOLS FROM TUBS, TANKS, AND KETTLES

Wooden tubs and half-barrels sunk into the ground fit beautifully into small spaces and provide a pleasant focal point in any yard. But remember that new wood is injurious to fish and water-lilies and a certain amount of aging is necessary. Any receptacle that has been out in the weather through the winter will do nicely as is. A new receptacle can be aged quickly by filling it with water and slaking a chunk of lime in it for three or four days. It can then be rinsed out and put into service.

This same quick-aging technique should also be applied to any tub or barrel which has previously held whisky, vinegar, molasses, or other liquid.

Wooden receptacles which have ever been filled with gasoline, oil, tar, roofing compound, wood preservative, or other oily substance are out of the question. No amount of treatment will completely cleanse the wood, and neither flower nor fish will do well in containers so tainted.

If you are buying a new tub in which to plant your miniature garden, buy one of white cedar. The only aging this mild wood needs is a night's soaking in cold water.

Steel tanks, iron kettles, and old bathtubs can be used quite effectively as sunken miniature pools. Be sure to coat the inside with a good rubber-base paint, which can be purchased from any fish or water-lily dealer. As far as the bathtub is concerned, painting is merely in the interests of beauty. For the tanks and kettles, it is an absolutely necessary protective measure, as their unpainted surfaces will rust and discolor the water.

Do not use oil or lead-base paint. It will not hold up for long and it will poison fish.

Sheet-lead tanks, set into brick or stone masonry, do very well for miniature pools. These, also, must be coated on the inside with rubber-base paint.

Containers made of copper cannot be used, for copper poisons fish.

Plate 9. The refreshing sight and sound of splashing water is the motif in this water garden at the home of Judge Harold Hartwell in Worcester, Massachusetts. Fountains with strong streams keep water too cool for good water-lily development, but not for border plants.

A. AUBREY BODINE PHOTO

CHAPTER TWO

How to Construct a Concrete Pool

A glance at the various pools illustrated will show you many designs from which to choose. Some are simple, straight-sided affairs without any fixed arrangements for planting; others are a bit more elaborate with plant receptacles built into the concrete. Some are sunk into the ground; others are raised above ground level or are only partly submerged. I prefer a raised pool. The rim of it makes such a nice place to sit while you enjoy the water-lilies and goldfish.

As for planting arrangements, I do not advise permanent, built-in receptacles. Planting boxes of wood, which can be moved around as you wish, are superior in many ways. I will tell you more about them in Chapter 8.

Building a Typical Pool

It is unnecessary, I am sure, for me to outline construction procedures for all the different kinds of pools. Directions for the basic types will suffice, since these include all the know-how needed for any pool you may have in mind. Let us consider first a simple, straight-sided pool of average size for the back or side yard, say a pool 8 feet wide, 10 feet long, and 2 feet deep, with floor and walls 6 inches thick.

It is a good idea, here in the beginning, to decide whether you will use ready-mixed concrete or mix it yourself. In most localities, concrete already mixed costs very little more than the separate ingredients. If you count your own labor as worth anything, the ready-mix is far cheaper, for manhandling concrete is a job that is even harder than it looks. Two cubic yards of concrete, says a friend of mine who is in the business, is all a good man can mix and pour in a full day of work.

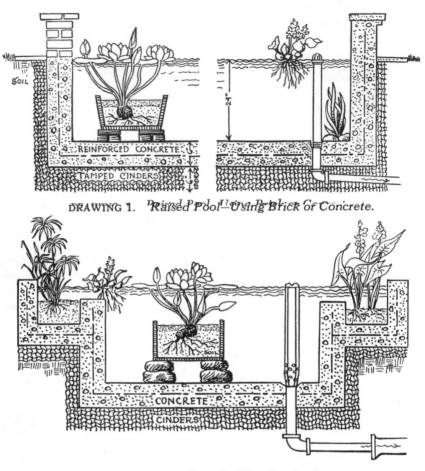

DRAWING 1. Raised Pool—Using Brick or Concrete.

DRAWING 2. Built-in Planting Ledges.

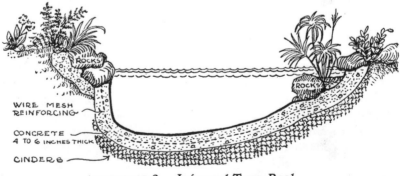

DRAWING 3. Informal Type Pool.

If you decide on the ready-mix, give your dealer the dimensions of your pool. Then he can determine the amount you need.

ESTIMATING THE MATERIALS

If you plan to mix and pour the concrete yourself, first figure the cubic feet of fill required for your forms, and then divide by 27 to see how many cubic yards you need. A cubic yard of concrete consists of seven sacks (7 cubic feet) of cement, 14 cubic feet (0.52 cubic yard) of sand, and 21 cubic feet (0.78 cubic yard) of gravel. Allow some margin. It isn't too expensive a proposition to have some sand and gravel left over, and you can get a full refund for every unbroken bag of cement you don't use.

Before ordering lumber, consider your many needs for wooden planking, over and above that required for the concrete forms. You may have to build your own platform for mixing concrete. You will need a number of pieces for bracing, and probably you will want to lay out a plank track for the wheelbarrow to protect the lawn.

You will need cinders, and they are awfully hard to find in these days of diesel and electric power. Any industrial plant that burns coal for power probably will have a load it will sell you reasonably enough. In estimating the needed amount of cinders, plan to cover the entire pool floor with a foot of them, and then tamp them down to a 6-inch thickness.

If you can't get cinders, then crushed limestone or gravel—which are somewhat more expensive—will have to do. With these, allow a 7- or 8-inch thickness on the pool floor, before tamping.

WHEN TO BEGIN

Once I would have told you the most practical time to build a pool was the fall of the year. The soil is easy to work then. A man's lawn, flower, and vegetable gardens make few demands upon his spare time, and the weather is cool enough for him to do heavy work in comparative comfort. These advantages still hold.

My principal reason for recommending pool building as an autumn job would have been in the interests of curing the pool. A tremendous amount of free calcium in newly formed concrete dissolves in the water when the pool is first filled, making it fit for neither flowers nor fish. We used to wash away this free calcium by filling the pool with water, allowing it to set for two or three days, draining it, and then repeating the process up to a dozen times. When a piece of litmus paper dipped into the water finally told us it was no longer alkaline, the pool was at last considered cured. You were lucky if you finished the business in six weeks.

A simpler system was to build the pool in the fall, leave it uncovered, and let the winter weathering take care of the curing—which it did very well.

A few years ago, however, we worked out a system for curing a pool, quickly and surely, within a few days. This system reduced the work of pool preparation to a fraction of what it once was and enables a man to start building a pool in midsummer and bring it into bloom for a good part of the remaining season. In Chapter 4, this matter of curing is discussed fully.

Excavating

The amount of work you will have to do depends upon the texture of the soil in which you sink your pool. If the soil is firm enough for an excavation to hold shape—a heavy clay, perhaps—you will need to build only one form, the inside one, to hold the concrete. The faces of the excavation can serve as the outer form.

If the soil is crumbly, possibly with a lot of sand or gravel in it, you will have to build both inside and outside forms. In either case, it will be wise for you to lay planks along the edges of the excavation as you dig so they will hold up cleanly under your weight.

The length, width, and shape of the pool are up to you, but ideal conditions for growing water-lilies—ideal for their well-being and for your convenience—call for a water depth of 2 feet. This allows about a foot for the containers of soil in which the lilies will be rooted and a foot of water to cover crowns of the plants. A pool this deep will allow flowers and plants to grow comfortably, and yet it is not so deep as to make the business of climbing in and out of it to plant, to rearrange flowers, or to clean, a difficult or awkward job.

Add another 2 inches to the height of the walls, because pools look best when the water level is about 2 inches short of the brimming point. Allow up to an inch of side wall to extend above ground level so as to keep surface water from draining in during rainstorms.

Save the sod when you make the excavation. Set it out of the way and give it a good watering now and then. It will be handy for patching up or for edging the pool when you are finished.

Depth

For a pool 2 feet deep, excavate to a depth of 3 feet. Six inches of that extra foot are to be filled with hard-tamped cinders, gravel, or fine crushed stone. The other six, of course, will be the layer of concrete which forms the pool floor. An ideal thickness for walls is also six inches.

When you get the excavation down 2 feet or so, take pains as you progress to keep the floor as level as possible. Slight irregularities in an off-level pool bottom are easily covered over by the concrete. A big irregularity is another matter, indeed.

An excavation made too deep, and then corrected to the desired depth by refilling with tamped earth, is dangerous business. Replaced earth, no matter how hard it is tamped, is not as solid as it was originally. Thus, a concrete pool built into a half-true, half-refilled excavation, sets upon a half-soft, half-hard foundation.

Water weighs more than 62 pounds to the cubic foot. In an 8- by 10-foot pool, 2 feet deep, the water mass weighs 5 tons—enough weight to break a pool shell in two as easily as you would crack a yardstick over your knee.

CHECK PEG

A check peg is as good a device as I know for assuring a level excavation.

A few feet away from the pool site, where it will be out of the way, drive a stout stake into the ground and mark some arbitrary point upon it, say a point a foot above ground level. That will be your check point.

DRAWING 4. *Method of Using a Check Peg.*

Now drive a long stake into each corner of the excavation. Run a string level, or a straight board with a carpenter's level secured to it, from your check point to each of the corner stakes and mark each stake accordingly. Now your excavation is marked in all its corners with points which are level with each other, and you can measure downward from these points to establish a truly level excavation.

DRAWING 5.   *Overflow and Drainage.*

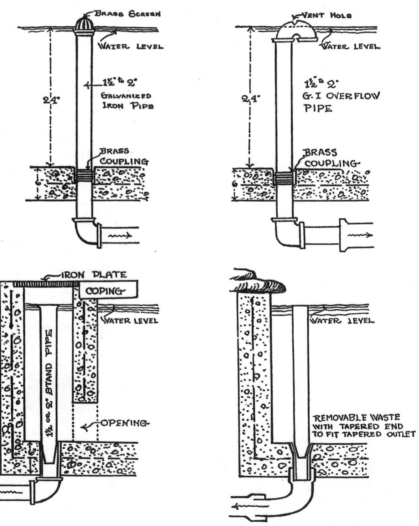

Drainage Arrangements

From this point forward, you move in one of three ways, depending upon the type of drainage arrangement you prefer for your pool or whether, indeed, you want any at all. Whatever arrangement you decide upon must be provided for now, and, if pipe lines are to be used, they must be placed before any concrete is poured.

To Drain or Not to Drain

Some pools have no drainage at all. The principal point in favor of a drainless pool is that it is slightly easier to build. In all fairness, the average pool has to be drained for cleaning only once a year, and some water gardeners clean only once every other year. This can be done by siphoning out the water, with a garden hose, to some lower location—to a gutter, to a sewer outlet in the basement, or to some lower area of ground where the water can spread and evaporate. It is an overnight job which does not require watching. Simply fill the hose with water, double over the ends to keep it full while you put it into siphoning position, and then let it go.

Unfortunately, you may see the drawback of drainless construction all too graphically after the first exceptionally heavy rainstorm fills the pool to overflowing. Probably you will lose some goldfish, and the excess water will make a mess of the whole area.

DRAWING 6. *Siphoning Water from Pool into Basement Drain.*

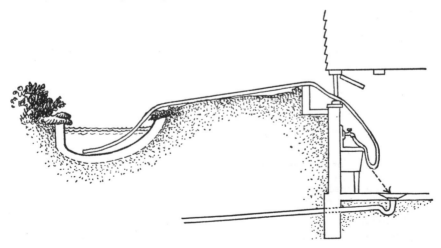

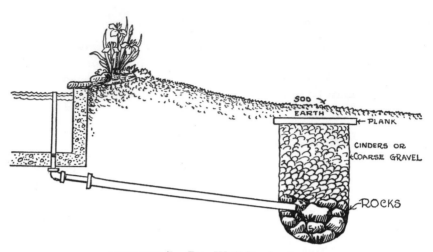

DRAWING 7.   *Dry Well Drainage.*

DRY WELL

A dry well installed within a few feet of the pool will take care of overflow through any season of normally heavy rainfall. Excavate a cubic yard of earth, making sure to excavate lower than the pool, as illustrated. Fill the excavation to within a few inches of the top with rocks or cinders, and tamp them down. Run an overflow pipe from the pool to the dry well as shown, and cover the well, first with planking, then earth, and finally with a layer of sod.

COMPLETE DRAINAGE

Far more practical, if you have access to some gutter, sewer outlet, or lower point of ground into which the overflow pipe can empty, are various drainage arrangements. Use galvanized iron pipe, 1½ or 2 inches in diameter, for the drainage system. Set the coupling, of brass, which will not rust, into the floor of the pool. The pool will drain more efficiently if the coupling is set an inch or so below the surface of the floor so that the surrounding area will slope down to it.

Forms for the Concrete

If you are building your pool in soft ground which requires both outside and inside forms, the outside structure need be constructed only tight enough to hold back the sides of the excavation. Two-by-four stakes driven into the ground around the perimeter will do nicely as

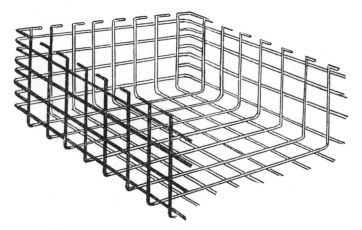

DRAWING 8. *Placement of Reinforcing Steel for Pool Forms.*

supports. To these, you can nail the planking which comprises the outer form. This form need not be removed after the pool is finished.

The inner form requires neater work, for the outside of this form will mold the inside of the pool shell and the surface will show. One-inch lumber, new or used, is best. Forms made of thinner wood will bulge

DRAWING 9. *Wooden Forms for Concrete Pool.*

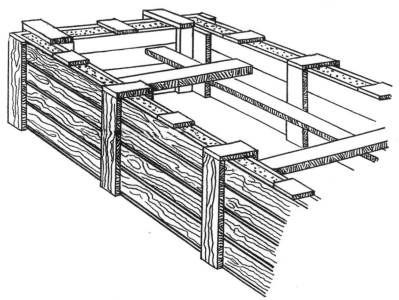

with the weight of the concrete. Wood thicker than an inch makes for heavy, clumsy handling. Even with sturdy forms of 1-inch lumber, guard against bulging by using two-by-four cross-braces every 3 or 4 feet along the length of the pool.

Build the form as you would build a bottomless box. Remember that for a pool which is to have a water depth of 2 feet, the form will have to have a depth of 2 feet and 2 inches. When the pool is filled to a 2-foot depth, the water won't be lapping over the brim; there will be a 2-inch margin of dry wall extending above water level. Be sure to set the form so that the rim of the pool will be slightly above ground level (up to an inch) to prevent seepage of surface water.

If you plan an ornamental rim for the pool, perhaps a surfacing of brick or flagstone, you still extend the concrete walls to a point just above ground level, a half inch or so. Remember that with *any* kind of material, it is extremely hard to get a watertight seal between it and the rim of the pool. Say, for example, that you have a brickwork rim. If you fill the pool to the top of the bricks, pool water will leak out. If the brick rim is below or at ground level, surface water will leak in.

When the inner form is completed, square off each corner and nail a temporary brace across it to hold it true.

PLACING THE FORMS

There are two ways of setting the inner form into position. One school of pool builders advises lowering the form into the excavation and chocking it up into position by wedging rocks under it. If you do this, be sure to use rocks large and heavy enough not to be knocked out of position when the concrete is poured. Be sure, also, that you take particular care in working the concrete in solidly around the rocks, or the pool floor will not be watertight. Hold the forms in place with temporary braces running from them to sturdy stakes driven into the ground nearby.

A more workmanlike method is to suspend the forms from two-by-four supports.

Whichever approach you take, remember that placing the forms is the most exacting phase of the work. When the forms are in place, check them, and check them again with a carpenter's level secured to a straight board. If they are off-level, don't try to balance the corners with each other. Work from one corner only, bringing the others to a level with it.

A transparent garden hose, partially filled, is an excellent device for determining where the water level will hit at different points around the pool.

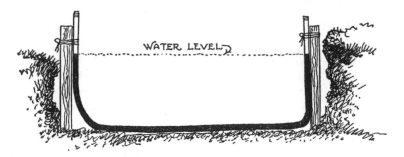

DRAWING 10.   *Method in Using Garden Hose as a Level.*

Before you fill the forms with concrete, paint them with a coat of used motor oil, which any filling station will supply without cost. Untreated wooden forms are often difficult to pull away from the concrete.

Reinforcing with Steel

You can buy reinforcing steel for concrete, or you can use scraps of iron and steel that you have on hand. Scraps of pipe are good if they aren't more than 1½ inches in diameter. Materials no larger than coat-hanger wire do not add enough strength to concrete to pay you for bothering with them. A coat of rust on the scrap won't hurt, but scrap with paint on it must be scraped or burned down to the base metal befor it can be used.

Any concrete dealer will have for sale, or will tell you where to buy, reinforcing steel, either in pencil-rod form or in sheets of highway mesh in which the rods are joined to form a 6- or 8-inch mesh.

Line the pool excavation with reinforcing steel so that the concrete walls and floor will envelop it evenly. The reinforcement can be held in place along the floor by stones.

If you use scrap steel for reinforcing, imitate as closely as possible the 6- or 8-inch crisscross pattern of commercial reinforcing steel. Before pouring the concrete, lay the pieces of scrap into position on the pool floor, and wire them together wherever they cross.

Use the same crisscross pattern of reinforcing in the walls. Thrust in the pieces of scrap perpendicularly and lay them horizontally into the wet concrete as the pouring progresses.

Concrete structures need reinforcing most at the corners where wall meets wall and where wall meets floor. Reinforce these places with pieces of scrap about 4 feet long, each bent to form a right angle. These can be seated in the wet concrete as you pour.

41

Use only Portland cement. Buy a clean, well-graded sand with particles which range from ⅛-inch coarseness down to fine. This varied particle size will give you a stronger, denser concrete than sand which is all coarse or all fine. Dusty sand makes weak concrete that sets poorly. Use crushed stone or pebbles that are free of foreign matter.

Concrete mixes which make use of bank-run gravel seldom are satisfactory, principally because the sand and gravel are not in proper proportion. Usually there is too much sand in the natural mixture as it is taken from the gravel bank, and that produces an overporous concrete. It can be used, however, by separating the sand and gravel by screening, and then adding each in proper proportion.

Easy with the Water

The best concrete mixture for pools consists of one part cement, two parts sand, and three of gravel. If the sand and pebbles are bone dry, a one-sack batch of concrete (all a man can mix really thoroughly at one time) will require 5½ gallons of water. Use only water that is clean enough to drink. If the sand and pebbles are damp (damp enough to be formed into a ball of sand in your hand) use 4½ gallons. If they are wet, use 3½ gallons. It is far better to underestimate the amount of water, and then add a little more at a time until you get a workable mixture, than it is to overestimate. If the mixture is soupy, it contains too much water. It will set, and might even hold up well enough, but certainly not as well as it would if mixed with the proper amount of water. Too much water dilutes the cement paste and weakens its bonding qualities.

In the interests of precise measuring, you will do well to make advance preparations. A sack of cement is exactly 1 cubic foot. Construct a bottomless box with a capacity of 1 cubic foot, and use it for measuring the sand and gravel. Mark a bucket so you can measure gallons, half gallons, and quarts in it.

Mixing the Concrete

Concrete can be mixed on any cemented surface, such as a garage floor or driveway, but must be hosed off before it has a chance to set. If such a surface is not available, you will have to construct a wooden platform of boards with edges straight enough to form a fairly watertight surface. The Portland Cement Association recommends a platform 7 feet wide and 12 feet long as being large enough for two men to work

FLOAT

LEVEL

BURLAP

SQUARE-TIP SHOVEL

WHEELBARROW

REINFORCING MESH
OR STEEL SCRAP

BUCKET FOR
MEASURING WATER

CEMENT HOE

LUMBER FOR FORMS

1 CU. FOOT MEASURING
BOX --- BOTTOMLESS

PLATFORM FOR MIXING

DRAWING 11.   *Needed Tools in Making a Concrete Pool.*

on simultaneously. Run a railing 4 or 5 inches high around three sides of the platform so materials won't be lost while they are being mixed.

Start early on the day that you mix and pour the concrete, for to be watertight a pool shell should be completed in one continuous operation. To do the job well and to enjoy it as you go, you should have at least one husky helper. While one of you shovels concrete into the forms, the other can be mixing a new batch.

Measure out 2 cubic feet of sand on the platform, make a nest of it, and pour in one bag of cement. With a square-ended shovel, turn the mixture over and over until it is well blended, showing no streaks of discoloration. Flatten the pile, cover it with 3 cubic feet of gravel, and continue mixing until gravel, sand, and cement are all distributed evenly.

Pour water into the mixture slowly while your helper continues to mix. The mixing is finished when the full measure of water is combined evenly with the solid ingredients. A good mixture is one soft enough to tamp easily into place in the forms, yet stiff enough to hold the marks when you scratch it with a trowel or shovel.

Pouring the Floor

The floor of the pool goes in first. Start at one end and *place* the concrete to the full thickness of the floor—tamping it in with special care at the corners—and back under the overhanging wall forms to the outer reaches of the excavation. A straightened-out garden hoe is an excellent tool for this job. The weight of the concrete will probably dislodge the reinforcing steel. Reach down through the wet concrete, lift the steel back into position, and tamp the concrete snugly around it as you go.

I want to stress the word *place,* for that is exactly how the wet concrete should be put into the form. If you scoop it up in your shovel and throw it in an arc into the form, you will completely undo your tedious job of mixing. The concrete will separate in mid-air. The gravel or crushed stone will land first, and the mixture of sand and cement will follow. The result will be a weak, and probably leaky, concrete shell.

Fill in the floor to the full length and width of the excavation. When it is 6 inches thick, it should just touch the bottom edges of the wall forms. If the pool outlet is set slightly below floor level, work the concrete into a gentle grade that slopes down to meet it. Tamp the finished pool floor to a depth of half an inch or so to submerge the larger pieces of aggregate and allow the concrete to present a smooth surface.

SMOOTHING

The natural finish of the pool floor is smooth enough for most pool builders. However, if you want an even smoother finish, work the floor over with a wooden float as soon as the concrete begins to set.

Few pool builders bother to finish any of the concrete except what will show above the water line after the pool is filled. Below the water line, in a healthy pool, the sides, whether rough or smooth-finished, will soon be hidden under a layer of algae.

FORMING THE WALLS

When the pool floor is placed, fill the wall forms, tamping the concrete with special care at the point where the wall joins the floor. Pools that leak usually do so at this point. A good, solid bonding of the concrete there will prevent it.

Work around the perimeter of the pool, adding only 6 or 8 inches of height to the walls each time around. As each layer is placed, jab the tamping hoe vigorously between the inside form and the concrete to work the aggregate back into the mass and give the walls a smooth face.

When the side forms are filled, finish off the top surfaces with a wooden float as soon as the concrete has begun to set. The top edging need not be finished, of course, if you plan to decorate it with brick, flagstone, or cast concrete coping.

SETTING

Let the concrete set 48 hours before taking off the forms. Use a brick to rub smooth any scars from the forms or any other irregularities in the concrete. *Concrete does not harden by drying, but by setting.* Protect it from the drying action of sun and wind by keeping all exposed surfaces covered with wet burlap sacks or straw, and keep them wet with occasional sprinklings for ten days.

Wait until the concrete of the pool has set completely before you attempt to lay brick or other decorative material around the rim.

Copings for the Pool

You can hardly choose a poor finish for the rim of your pool. It is really a matter of personal preference. I would remind you only that a formal pool calls for a formal finish—brick, tile, cut stone, or cast concrete coping, as illustrated. A natural pool calls for a natural finish— which means natural flagstone. The random shapes of field stones do

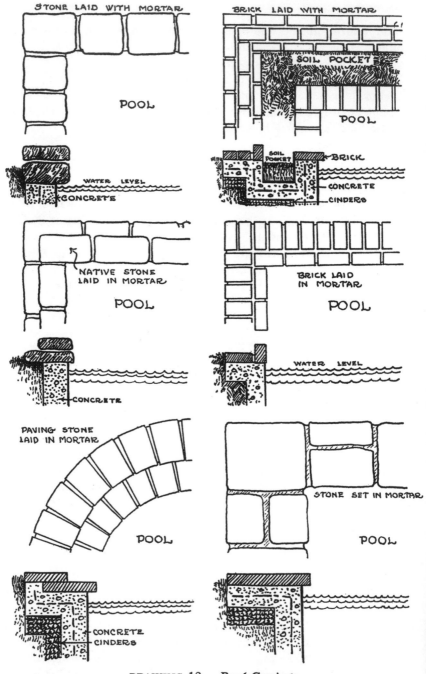

DRAWING 12. *Pool Copings.*

not lend themselves to the construction of a pool rim, and I have never seen a rim so constructed that looked right.

There is one all-purpose finish for the rim. You can smooth-finish it with a wooden float when the concrete has begun to set, or smooth it with a brick after the wooden forms have been taken off. The plain concrete rim thus achieved looks well on either a formal or an informal pool.

Securing an Ornamental Rim

Decorative tiles or similar ceramic materials chosen as capping for the rim of the pool will require special cements, which the tile dealer will be able to supply.

For securing bricks, cast concrete coping, or stone to the pool rim, use a mixture of three parts of sand and one part Portland cement, adding water to the dry mixture until a workable mortar is obtained.

If the rim is to be of flagstone, make a series of trial arrangements before you cement the stones in place. Natural-looking stone arrangements are tricky to achieve, and few people hit upon one they really like the first time. When you cement the stones in place, keep the mortar well hidden, for the sight of it will destroy the natural illusion you want to create. If you do slip, cover any exposed mortar with a handful of earth.

Special Effects

Although only flat, stratified rock, such as flagstone, can be used attractively to cap the pool rim, there are many artistic possibilities for rock work in the area surrounding the pool. Well weathered field stones in a variety of sizes, shapes, and colorings can be piled here and there along the border for interesting effect. The rocks are not only attractive in themselves, but provide a natural setting for border plants.

Moss

Here is a simple trick a friend of mine recommends when you want a mossy edging for your pool. Gather a quantity of moss in the woods. Shred enough to fill half a quart jar; fill the rest of the jar with buttermilk. Give it a thorough stirring, and then with a paint brush apply the mixture heavily to the rock or concrete surfaces. Adjust your garden hose to the finest spray it will throw, and keep the moss damp with frequent sprayings for a few days until it takes root.

47

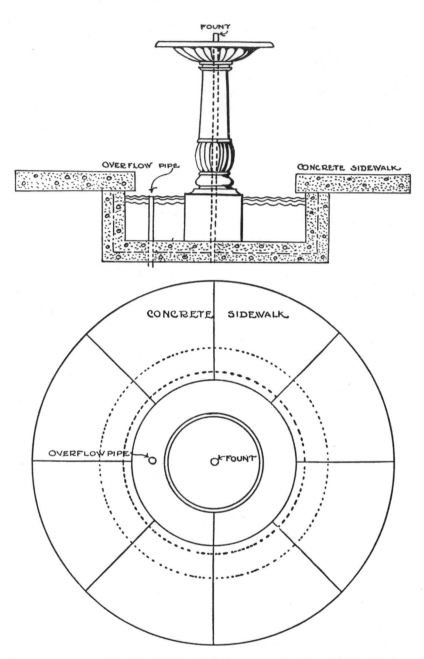

DRAWING 13. *Fountain with Concrete Pool and Sidewalk.*

FOUNTAINS AND SPOUTS

Everybody who builds a water garden, it seems, has trouble deciding whether or not to put in a fountain. A few years ago, the question would have been decided for you. I would have had to tell you then that, unless you had a very large basin or healthy water-lilies and goldfish were of secondary importance, the fountain would have to be ruled out.

A constant stream of clear water gushing into a pool from an outside source keeps the temperature far below that necessary for water-lily growth. It also keeps the water too clear, too free of that microscopic plant life which thrives in a healthy pool and which fish need in addition to the prepared foods they get.

In recent years, however, fountains have been developed which draw their supply of water from the pool itself, and such fountains may be used with no ill effects at all. Powered by electrically operated pumps, they are efficient and dependable, and can be bought for about thirty dollars. The whole assembly—base, motor, pump, and fountainhead—is scarcely as large as a loaf of bread, and can be set down and put into operation in a matter of minutes.

But be sure you want a fountain before you order one. A fountain provides a beautiful sight indeed, but it looks well only in a formal or semiformal setting. It looks terribly out of place in a natural or rustic pool.

DRIPSTONES

If your pool is of rustic or natural design, you need not be deprived of the musical sound of falling water. In fact, such pools can have something which, in my opinion, is even more pleasing than a fountain. The device is called a dripstone. The water supply for a dripstone is provided from the pool itself, by means of the fountain pump just described.

A dripstone should overhang, as shown, so as to provide a sound chamber behind the spot where the dripping water hits the pool surface. I can think of no more pleasant and cooling sound on a hot summer evening than that offered by a dripstone.

A number of other interesting effects—miniature water wheels, cascades, and even windmills—can be operated by that same type of fountain pump.

DRAWING 14. *Two Types of Dripstones.*

LIGHTING THE POOL

Among the newest and certainly the most spectacular of pool arrangements are the safe, inexpensive, and practical devices with which the water garden can be illuminated at night.

There was a time when illuminated pools were few and far between. Some of the more energetic gardeners provided for underwater illumination by installing watertight glass panels and the necessary electrical connections in the walls while the pool was under construction. The effects thus achieved were beautiful indeed, but the added touches, which had to be installed by professional craftsmen, considerably increased the cost of the pool.

Some beautiful surface effects could be obtained, it was learned in subsequent experimentation, by placing bulbs here and there about the rim of the pool, situating them inconspicuously in clumps of border plants, and by beaming spotlights upon the pool from strategic locations well away from the immediate vicinity. These surface techniques, being both practical and inexpensive, are becoming more popular with every passing day.

An even wider variety of lighting arrangements is now available since some of the leading electrical laboratories have developed special lights for pools. Underwater lights, equipped with waterproof cord and fixtures, can be easily anchored beneath the surface of the water wherever desired. Floating lights, set into floating holders in the shape of lily pads, blend well with the pool's natural growths.

A stern word of caution on illuminating the pool: those companies now manufacturing floating and submerged lights have developed safe, shockproof fixtures and proper wiring and connections for them. These devices are the only ones that can be used safely. If you install pool lights, use the proper fixtures, *as directed by the manufacturer.*

This pool in the Owens garden, Deland, Florida, shows how lights can be used to illuminate a fountain for dramatic nighttime effects.

CHAPTER THREE *More Pool Designs*

Clay puddling, I am pleased to report, is an art in pool construction that went out with handlebar mustaches and high-wheeled bicycles. It never was much of an art, in my opinion, but I don't think any discussion of pool building would be complete without some mention of it, for it was one of the pioneer techniques of water gardening.

Puddling with Clay

The builder of a clay-puddled pool first made a concave excavation, sloping the sides carefully at an angle of not more than 40 to 45 degrees. He then lined the concavity with a 6- to 8-inch layer of the coarsest straw he could find. On top of the straw he put a 6-inch layer of clay, which he moistened and tamped down into the straw as tightly as possible.

All the clay-puddled pools I have seen required a constant trickle of water into them to make up for that lost by seepage. Spring or stream water, always 15 to 20 degrees colder than still water warmed by the sun, maintained a pool temperature too cold for good—frequently too cold for *any*—water-lily growth. A trickle piped into the pool from a household water system would be even colder, and expensive to boot.

The clay linings of these pools attracted crawfish as spilled molasses attracts flies. After a couple of them had burrowed through the pool's lining, many a pool enthusiast in the old days discovered that overnight his beautiful water garden had become just a mud hole, so to remain until he patched the holes and refilled the pool.

Clay-puddled pools are now blessedly of the past, and good riddance. Any structure that will enable a couple of crawfish to ruin a man's whole summer just isn't practical enough to bother building.

Natural dew ponds, also known as cloud ponds and mist ponds, are near-miraculous works of nature. They just happen, sometimes, in shady places that remain constantly damp, even in hot, dry weather. The mystery of them is their principal fascination. They have no apparent source of water, and yet they thrive, their cold, clear waters never seeming to diminish.

A few English water gardeners with plenty of time and even more patience have been able to construct them and make them work. An artificial dew pond is built, much as a puddled-clay pond, although on a much smaller scale. The layer of straw that goes into the excavation is much thicker, perhaps a foot or more of it. The clay lining is tamped in upon the straw in the conventional way.

Nature does the rest, sometimes with a little help in the beginning. In time, the pond fills with rain water. The nest of straw serves as insulation, so that the clay shell and the water in it remain somewhat cooler at all times than the surrounding air. Dew condenses nightly on the cool clay banks, runs down into the little pond, and replaces moisture lost by seepage and evaporation.

An amateur should not attempt to build a dew pond, because few of them work out. As only the very hardiest of aquatic growths can be coaxed to live in one, even if it does turn out satisfactorily, the water gardener receives little reward for his labors.

Puddling with Concrete

The one good word I have for the technique called puddling is that it is as good with concrete as it is bad with clay. It works out so well, in fact, that nearly half the pools being built in the country today are being puddled with concrete.

The one possible disadvantage of a puddled pool is that it may not have the permanent, indestructible strength of a sunken, straight-sided, reinforced concrete structure which has been poured into wooden forms. Handled correctly, nevertheless, puddled concrete will be strong enough to serve for many years with little or no repair work.

In other comparisons, the puddled pool comes out way ahead. It is cheaper because it takes less concrete. It is less work because it requires only a narrow, extremely simple form for the concrete. Most important of all, it enable a water gardener to dig his pool in exactly the shape he wants it, whether geometrical or in free form.

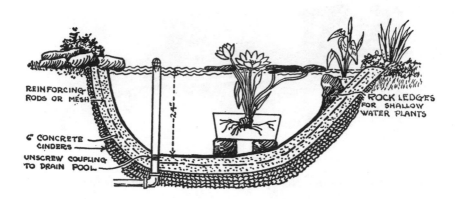

REINFORCING
RODS OR MESH

6" CONCRETE
CINDERS

UNSCREW COUPLING
TO DRAIN POOL

ROCK LEDGES
FOR SHALLOW
WATER PLANTS

24"

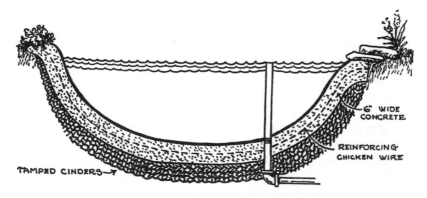

6" WIDE
CONCRETE

REINFORCING
CHICKEN WIRE

TAMPED CINDERS

DRAWING 15. *Puddled Concrete Pools.*

Puddling a Concrete Pool

You can make a puddled concrete pool in much the same way as a
pool poured into forms. There are just fewer steps to the job.

Use the same guides (given in Chapter 1) as to how big to make your
pool and where to put it. The shape, particularly if it is irregular, will
take a bit of pondering. Outline some trial shapes with the garden hose
or a clothesline and think about them a few days before you start
to work.

DRAWING 16. *Garden Hose Used to Produce Outline for Informal Pool.*

Once you have decided on the shape, move around the outside of the outline you have formed, driving stout stakes into the ground every 30 inches. Space them a bit closer along the sharper curves of the outline.

With a string level, determine which stake has been driven into the highest bit of ground, and plan for the rim of the pool to extend an inch or so above ground level at that point. From a mark on the high stake, use the string level to transfer the level point to all the other stakes, and mark them accordingly.

Strips of quarter-inch plywood, cut cross-grain, make the best forms. With shingle nails, fasten the strips lightly to the stakes along the level points. Apply the string level again (and again and again) and when you are sure the form for the pool rim is level, go around and nail the strips securely to the stakes.

If the site is uneven but the form for the rim is perfectly level, the form will now be touching the ground in some places, standing above it in other places. When you start excavating, use the dirt to bank in the low spots.

Here, as with other types of pools, the ideal water depth is 2 feet, and the ideal thickness for the pool shell is 6 inches. However, the pool walls can safely be tapered to a 4-inch thickness at the top if you prefer. The pool shell should set upon a 3- to 4-inch layer of tamped cinders or crushed stone. Therefore, the depth of the excavation will be 2 feet, plus 6 inches for the floor, plus 3 or 4 inches for the foundation layer of cinders or stone.

The end of the pool in which you will locate the outlet—if an outlet is planned—should be dug an inch or two deeper, with the rest of the floor sloping toward it.

DRAWING 17. *Stakes Driven Every 30 Inches Along Hose Outline.*
Nail ¼-Inch Plywood Strips to Stakes to Make Form for Concrete.

While excavating, do not make the slope of the walls any steeper than 40 to 45 degrees. Wet concrete won't stay in place on a steeper grade.

When the excavation is finished, and when whatever drainage and overflow facilities you desire are in place, spread the cinders or stone and tamp them into a 3- to 4-inch layer, upon both floor and sloping walls.

Reinforcing steel is even more important in a puddled pool than it is in a poured concrete shell. Spread the steel upon the tamped cinders. Short lengths of wire can be fashioned into huge hairpins which are quite effective in pinning the steel into place and holding it in position so the concrete will envelop it evenly.

DRAWING 18. *Reinforcing Walls and Floor with Wire.*

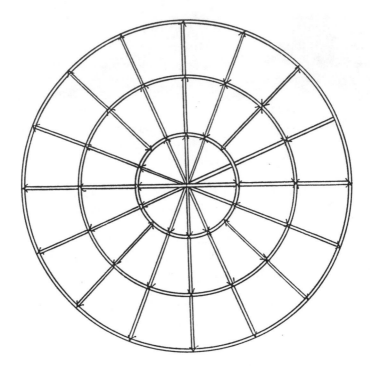

DRAWING 19.   *Reinforcing with Steel in Puddled-Pool Excavation.*

Unless you remember a great deal more solid geometry than I do, you will probably have trouble working out the volume of concrete required for any pool of irregular shape. The easiest thing to do is have a dealer in mixed concrete take a look at your ready-to-pour excavation, and then order according to his specification.

If you plan to mix your own concrete, estimate your needed volume as best you can, and keep the estimate on the high side.

Pour the floor first, working the concrete in well around the reinforcing steel and lifting the steel back into position from time to time as the concrete pushes it down. Tamp the wet mass in with special care at all corners.

Move around the perimeter of the pool as you build up the walls, depositing 6 to 8 inches of concrete each time around.

Here again, the natural finish of the pool floor will be smooth enough for all practical purposes. If you want a smoother finish for walls and rim, finish them off with a wooden float when the concrete has begun to set.

The concrete should set well enough overnight for you to spread a few planks over it the next day. Walk out on the planks, spread burlap, straw, or canvas over all the concrete surface, and keep it wet with the garden hose for ten days.

Safe Pools for Children

A number of water gardeners have written me to ask if there is any way of constructing an attractive pool around which toddling children can play in safety. Happily, there are a couple of types which I can recommend.

THE RAISED POOL

One of them is the raised pool. This pool is constructed like the sunken reinforced concrete pool, with two modifications. A complete set of inside and outside wall forms are required to shape the concrete shell, and the foundation of cinders or stone for it is made a few inches thicker and tamped with special vigor to give the pool a solid footing. Such pools can rest entirely on top of the ground, or they may be sunk part way.

You may recall that I told you that water-lilies planted in a tub or similar container and left above ground will not bloom. This does not apply to raised pools larger than a card table. The water mass in pools this big or bigger is enough to insure a constant temperature. Fish and water-lilies do as well in large raised pools as they do anywhere else.

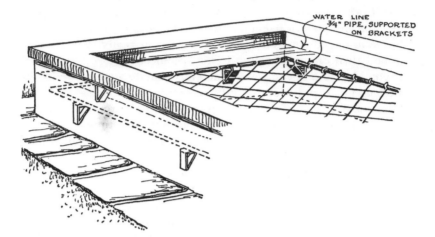

PIPE SUPPORTED ON BRACKETS 3" OR 4" BELOW WATER LINE
COVER WITH 4" OR 5" WIRE MESH

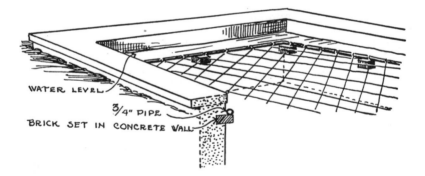

DRAWING 20. *Framework to Fit Pool for the Protection of Children.*

THE HIDDEN SCREEN

A device which can be quickly fashioned and made to fit into any pool of regular shape provides even more safety. With three-quarter-inch pipe, construct a frame which will fit as a snug rim around the inside of the pool. Cover this framework with strong wire fencing, 4-

or 5-inch mesh. Screw hooks or brackets into the pool walls to hold the framework in place 3 to 4 inches below the water line. If you have not built your pool yet, it is easy to provide a holding ledge for a safety frame by embedding bricks in the walls so that they extend an inch or two.

Water-lilies and aquatics grow freely through the fencing. Goldfish do not seem to notice it at all. The fencing cannot be seen from any point except directly above the pool. And, best of all, a child tumbling into the pool tumbles into only a few inches of water.

If your toddlers are particularly rambunctious and you want to play doubly safe, build the raised pool *with* the protective framework in it. Many water gardeners do this.

The Summer Pool

The quickest and cheapest pool that can be made of concrete is one called the summer pool. The earth into which it is built must be firm enough to hold the shape of a deep trench cut into it.

Stake out the dimensions of the pool, and then dig a narrow trench around the perimeter. The walls of this trench will serve as forms for the concrete. A 30-inch excavation for the walls is best. Eight inches is about as narrow as you can dig the trench, so the pool walls will be 8 inches thick.

Fill the trench to a depth of 6 to 8 inches with whatever stones, broken bricks, old iron, and other rubble you can find, reinforcing with the iron as efficiently as possible. Fill the voids of this rubble with a 1-2-3 mixture of concrete, tamping it vigorously to work out any air pockets. Add another layer of rubble and fill again with concrete, and repeat the process until the wall forms are filled.

After the walls have set three or four days, remove the earth from the center of the shell, going down to a depth of 30 inches. Cover the bottom of the excavation with a 6-inch layer of rubble, and work into it the same mixture of concrete you used in the walls.

Keep the pool covered and damp for ten days. Then coat the inside of it either with a waterproofing layer of pure cement mixed with water or with asphalt. Cure the pool to neutralize the alkalinity of the new concrete, if the concrete is exposed, and plant your water garden. (See Chapter 14 for other waterproofing methods.)

If you live where winter does not cause much frost upheaval in the ground, you may be able to maintain a pool of this sort without much trouble. Chances are, though, that the pool will require at least a new coat of waterproofing cement or asphalt every spring. Even if the pool is drained for the winter, a few cracks are almost certain to develop.

CHAPTER FOUR   *Curing the Pool*

A newly formed concrete pool, even after the prescribed period of ten to fourteen days to set, releases a tremendous amount of free calcium into the water the first few times it is filled. This water, like the strongly alkaline water in various streams in the West, is too bitter for man or livestock to drink. The most vigorous of water plants may be able to exist, but will do poorly, in water such as this. The gentler plant species will not progress at all.

Water too bitter for humans to drink is also too poisonous for gold-fish to "breathe." In fact, a green, or uncured pool will kill goldfish immediately. An improperly cured pool, one in which the water contains persistent traces of alkalinity, will kill them somewhat more slowly but just as surely. Their fins and tails will split and fray. Gills will become inflamed. Eventually, the fish will give up the ghost and rise to the surface, belly up, the weaker ones first, the hardier ones soon afterward.

It is needless, though unintentional, cruelty which can be avoided by curing the pool. There are various techniques for curing, and none of them involves much trouble.

Exploding Some Myths

"Natural Mellowing"

First off, let's explode some myths. There is one bit of advice that many casual water gardeners persist in passing on to novices, and it lets the novices in for headaches they would not ordinarily have. Build the pool, the self-appointed experts advise, fill it, plant it, sit back, and wait. They go on to say that everyone knows water-lilies won't grow well in a brand new pool, but a "natural mellowing" takes place after the first season, and the lilies will then begin to reach out a bit. After the flowers have become well established, goldfish, too, will find the pool livable.

One of the difficult things about beating down this misinformation is that it is partially true. Fill an uncured pool and plant it with strong-growing water-lilies and, sure enough, they'll grow. They won't grow well. Probably they won't even bloom. But they will grow. Also it is true that after the first season, if the pool is well situated in the sunlight, the lilies will begin to bloom.

But this so-called natural mellowing procedure is merely attrition on the part of Mother Nature. In a year of rainfall, and subsequent run-off through the pool's drainage system, the entire water capacity of the pool is replaced many times, resulting at last in a fill that is no longer alkaline.

So I can't say that the natural mellowing story is an out-and-out misrepresentation. I can say only that it is a very slow and disappointing way of doing business. Why put up with a green pool for a whole, wasted season when you can cure it quickly, plant it, and within a few weeks see growth in your pool that is really worth watching!

A Workable Natural Cure

Perhaps a great many water gardeners have confused so-called natural mellowing with a procedure we used to recommend to our customers. We told them to build their pools in the fall, finishing them up at a time when the pool couldn't be planted for several months. The natural washing action of rain, sleet, and snow through the winter did a fine job of scouring the free lime off the surfaces of the new concrete. This is still good, efficient practice if the time element happens to fit in with your own construction plans.

If you cure the pool in this way, I suggest you help nature a bit and fill and empty the pool a couple of times during the winter—early and late in the season, when there is no danger of freezing—letting the water stay in the pool two to three weeks each time. As a final test, fill the pool and dip a piece of pink litmus paper in the water. The litmus will turn blue if appreciable alkalinity remains in the water. In this unlikely event, fill and empty the pool a few more times.

Curing With a Coat of Paint

Sealing off the free lime in a new concrete pool with paint is another technique I cannot recommend, although many new water gardeners try it. This, I must say, is much more effective than natural mellowing. For a while water-lilies and goldfish do well enough in a pool so treated.

The bad thing about curing by painting is that the paint does not hold up well. Although I do not paint the inside of my own pools, I do not urge you against it. If you feel a coat of paint will make the pool look better, then apply it by all means. But apply it only as a beautification, *after the pool has been cured*. Paint sticks better and holds up far longer on chemically neutral concrete.

Many pool enthusiasts feel that it is an aesthetic necessity to paint the floor of a pool a dark color for the illusion of depth. A dark floor does give this illusion, and it will also make the pool surface reflect surroundings much more clearly, but painting the floor is not necessary. In the course of a week or so, fine siftings of soil from the planting boxes will have covered the floor and colored it up to suit the most exacting water gardener.

Best Curing Treatment We Know

If you will excuse a fellow a certain pride of craftsmanship, I'll describe this particular curing treatment as the best one I know. It is a treatment we developed at the Fisheries, and apparently it has worked perfectly for the hundreds of customers to whom we have recommended it.

1. Fill the pool to the brim and let it set for five days.

2. Drain the pool, refill it, and let it set another five days.

3. Drain the pool again.

4. Mix up a solution of 1 quart of ordinary kitchen vinegar and 10 quarts of water.

5. With a stiff brush (an old broom does splendidly) and generous sloshings of the solution, scrub vigorously over every square inch of the pool's inside surface. Mix more solution if you need it. The surfaces may bubble up a bit as the vinegar works on the free lime, but don't worry, it will not weaken the concrete.

6. Rinse out the pool with a brisk stream from the garden hose, and it is ready for goldfish and water-lilies.

SUBSEQUENT CURING TREATMENTS

Ordinarily, a sturdy, well-constructed pool needs curing only once, and that is when it is new. However, an extensive job of crack filling, an addition to the pool—anything which brings pool water into contact with an appreciable amount of new concrete—will necessitate another curing.

CHAPTER FIVE *Water-Lilies—Past and Present*

The flowering aquatic plants to which most of us refer collectively as water-lilies were among the first splashes of beauty that man noticed on this earth. Earlier plant forms there were in profusion, but the process of evolution seems to have favored water-lilies with quick development to their ultimate form. Remains of tropical water-lilies have been found in pre-Ice Age stratas in Europe, and these remains show the early types to have been of the same basic form that persists among tropical species today.

The dimmest beginnings of art and writing include the water-lily as well as closely related members of the botanical family. To the furled sepals of the lotus bud, historians trace the design of the Ionic capital and the basic pattern of the Greek fret or meander. Doubled, the meander forms the swastika, certainly one of man's earliest written symbols, representing good and evil in one part of the world, darkness and light in another, life and death, male and female, peace and conflict the peoples of the world. The cornucopia, that universal and ancient symbol of fertility and abundance, is thought by some scholars to have been derived from the filled-to-bursting seed pods of the lotus, which it resembles.

The Family Tree

The family tree of the water-lilies is confusing, made so principally by a score of early plant anatomists, horticulturists, and botanists, each of whom bent it this way and that to satisfy his personal bias in classification.

DIVISION, CLASS, AND ORDER

The basic lineage of water-lilies is fairly obvious, however. In the

One of the most popular of the hardy water-lilies is the white Gladstone.

Water-lilies blooming in a semi-wild state at the Three Spring Fisheries.

four great divisions of the vegetable kingdom, they fall under the largest of all—*Spermatophyta,* the flowering plants, and then into one of the two subdivisions—the *Angiospermae,* plants that reproduce through seeds fertilized within a closed ovary.

Under one of two classes encompassed by the subdivision, water-lilies are listed with the *Dicotyledoneae,* plants whose sprouting seeds are fed by food stored in two fleshy, leaflike appendages or cotyledons. Further, in a subclass of the *Dicotyledoneae,* they are listed with the *Archichlamydeae*—flowering plants which bear their petals separately.

Then they fall into the order of Ranales, a classification based on the manner of placement of the petals on the stem. Other plant families in this order are buttercups and magnolias, whose blooms to the imaginative observer show a certain structural resemblance to those of water-lilies.

FAMILY, GENUS, AND SECTIONS

Under Ranales, the family in which we are interested principally, is the *Nymphaeaceae*—the Water-Lily Family. The varied genera which spring from *Nymphaeaceae* include almost all the flowering aquatic plants which have ever been called water-lily or lotus. From this point on in the classification system, we no longer speak of all water flowers as water-lilies.

One inferior genus of the family is called *Nuphar,* plants commonly known as cow lilies, spatter docks, and yellow pond lilies. Another genus is *Victoria,* the most regal and spectacular of all flowering aquatics. Another is *Nelumbo,* from which springs the lotus species.

We shall discuss all of the genera later. At the moment, let us consider the most colorful and varied of all genera in the Water-Lily Family, the genus called *Nymphaea.* To it belong all of the true water-lilies.

Nymphaea are divided into two general sections, under which five important subgenera are listed. The groupings are based largely on structural differences in the blossoms and on habits of growth and bloom. In this book we are not concerned with minute botanical differences, but blooming habits are important to us.

The first section, the *Apocarpiae,* includes the subgenera *Anecphya* and *Brachyceras.* These are the tender or tropical water-lilies that bloom in the daytime.

The second section, *Syncarpiae,* includes the other three subgenera —*Castalia, Lotos,* and *Hydrocallis.* The *Castalia* are the hardy water-lilies. The other two are the tropical water-lilies that bloom at night. Water-lilies that spring from the subgenus *Lotos* are not to be confused with flowers of the genus *Nelumbo,* the basic form of which is the

Hindu or Sacred Lotus of India, the true lotus. The situation becomes even more complex when a water-lily species called lotus (from which many varieties have been obtained) is attributed to the subgenus *Lotos*. It may help to think of the water-lily species called lotus, and of the varieties obtained from it, as lotuslike water-lilies.

SPECIES AND VARIETIES

From now on, when we speak of hardy water-lilies, we are referring to the several species which branch out from the subgenus *Castalia*, and of the varieties obtained by crossbreeding those species.

The tropical day-blooming water-lilies we discuss will be species and varieties branching from the *Anecphya* and *Brachyceras* subgenera.

The tropical night-blooming water-lilies will be the species and varieties branching from the *Lotos* and *Hydrocallis* subgenera.

Guesswork, Oversight, and Confusion

Now that I have traced the family tree of the water-lilies, let me tell you that practically every limb and branch and twig of it has been attacked at one time or another by plant anatomists and horticulturists who would seek to rearrange it. One anatomist's genus is relegated to the rank of species by another, and a grouping that one man calls a species is considered merely a variety by others. The family tree that I have traced for you is the one that seems the most botanically practical to me.

For many, many years the quarter million known plant species in the world (with a few hundred new discoveries every year) were listed dozens of different ways and in considerable confusion. Then, from 1887 to 1909, two German botanists—Heinrich Gustav Adolf Engler and Karl Anton Prantl—published a thirty-two volume botanical work, *Die Natürlichen Pflanzenfamilien,* which is generally considered the clearest and most efficient in the field. It is widely followed in plant classification today. The simplest of the systems, it recognizes thirteen primary divisions in the vegetable kingdom, thirty-eight classes, about one hundred orders, and some six hundred families.

In this book, I follow the classification system of the two botanists, as it appears in L. H. Bailey's *The Standard Cyclopedia of Horticulture.*

In their dealings with water-lilies, early plant anatomists seem to have moved along one of three unfortunate paths: They alluded to water-lilies in the vaguest manner possible; they based whatever precepts they set down on guesses—frequently bad ones; or they overlooked water-lilies entirely. So it has been only in recent years that a

Marliac Rosea.

Marliac Albida.

Mrs. C. W. Thomas.

serious study of water-lilies has been attempted, perhaps because as "civilized," cultivated flowers, water-lilies are not much older than the War Between the States.

Sparse though the very early writings have been, they have sufficed to confuse the student today. The term *lotus* has been so consistently misapplied that it will probably continue to be for all time. As a case in point, *Nelumbo nucifera* has been acknowledged through the years as the Sacred Lotus of the Nile, purportedly the flower that appears so frequently in early Egyptian art. However, photographs of paintings, sculpture, jewelry, and other art forms plainly indicate that the flower looks like a water-lily, not a lotus.

It is highly probable that the so-called Sacred Lotus of the Nile was *Nymphaea lotus,* a fragrant, night-blooming tropical water-lily with great white blossoms, as large as those of a lotus. Three-thousand-year-old dried specimens of this have been found in the tomb of Rameses. Indigenous to Egypt, it still thrives there. *Nelumbo nucifera,* erroneously called the Sacred Lotus of the Nile, is a native of India and was not introduced into Egypt until around the time of the Persian invasion, five or six centuries before Christ.

Modern History

The latter-day history of water-lilies—the last hundred years or so—is somewhat clearer. It begins early in the last century with a white man's discovery of a strange and wondrous flower in the deep, wide lagoons of the South American jungles. The natives gave the strange plant many names—*Yrupe* or *Irupe, Dachocho, Marura, Morinqua. Yrupe,* literally *water platter,* seemed the most suitable. The rich purplish-green leaves, deeply veined on the underside, floated on the surface of the water in a magnificent expanse, often covering an area 7 to 8 feet wide. The edges of the leaves, upturned to form a 2- to 8-inch watertight rim, made the "platters" quite buoyant.

The flowers, up to 15 inches wide, opened at dusk, remained open all night, and closed again after sunrise. They released a delicious, powerful, and far-reaching fragrance somewhat like that of crushed pineapple.

The flowers changed color, almost perceptibly, as the amazed white man watched. The bud, when it first spread itself, was creamy white, which gradually gave way to a pink blush, then to a definite pink, and on through the shades of deeper pink until, on the second night of its life, the bloom appeared a deep purplish-red hue.

The large leaves of the Victoria regia *can support a child's weight.*
Photo by A. M. Friedrich in Paraguay.

The podlike fruit, as large as a baby's head, as well as the stems and bloom, was protected by strong, sharp spines which the natives believed to be venomous. A few of the hardier bushmen, however, dared to collect the fruit and break it open for the cluster of hard, shiny seeds, soft and mealy within. They called the seeds, which were considered a great delicacy, water corn or water maize.

DISCOVERY OF *Victoria regia*

The plant had many "discoverers." Haenke, who found it in Bolivia in 1801, was probably the first; then Bonpland in Argentina in 1819; Poeppig on the Amazon River in 1832; and D'Orbigny in Bolivia a year later. Robert H. Schomburgk, who discovered it in the Berbice River in British Guiana in 1836, sent specimens back to England, and two years later a description of the plant was given to the world. Dr. Lindley, who drew up the first account, named it *Victoria regia* in honor of the then reigning queen.

Practically every time *Victoria regia* was found in a new locality after that, travelers brought seeds back to England, where horticulturists made every attempt to grow them. Only a few were able to make the seeds germinate, and none of the plants survived. It was not until 1849 that *Victoria regia* was nursed to blooming maturity in England.

Rose Areys are collected by a local girl in a
typical wooden planting tub.

The Pekinese rubrum plenum *is a classic form of this Far Eastern flower. This lotus is only one of many lotus varieties available.*

Seeds were then distributed through England and Europe. They grew, and their descendants are growing today.

In fact, the cultivation of this exotic flower named for the Queen of England soon became a fad. And the fad became a part of contemporary culture. Is there a portfolio of Victorian illustration anywhere in the world that does not include a picture of a child standing or sitting in the middle of a formal water garden, supported by a giant leaf of *Victoria regia?*

But this was a hobby for the wealthy only. Seeds were expensive, and the tremendous spread of the plant required extensive pool space. Furthermore, a pool had to be heated artificially through much of the growing season because the plant was tropical.

So Victorias were grown and enjoyed by the wealthy. Other flower lovers adopted a less expensive version of the hobby—the culture of hardy and tropical water-lilies. Soon side and back yards were adorned with pools much like those that water gardeners are building and enjoying today.

Early Water Gardens

It is fortunate that in England, and later in Europe, the fad reached craze proportions, for it must have taken great enthusiasm to assemble a colorful collection in the early 1900's. *Nymphaea alba,* Europe's most widely distributed hardy native species, has a delightful, cup-shaped blossom which floats gracefully upon the water, as delicate in appearance as it is robust in habit. Undoubtedly it brought much pleasure to all who grew it. Few other flowers of the world surpass the beauty of its spotless, white, dewy freshness, but it probably fell somewhat short of perfection for those with a taste for rich color. However, it was fragrant, especially on the first day of blooming, the receptive period when the stigma is filled with nectar to attract insects for pollination.

AMERICAN SPECIES—*Nymphaea odorata*

The native American species, which Europeans soon began to import, were, to a large extent, merely more of the same. One of them, *Nymphaea odorata,* generally known as the New England Pond Lily, thrives in both northern and southern states, and as far west as the Mississippi River. *Nymphaea odorata* has a most heavenly scent, which made it a real asset in a European water garden. The pure species, however, is also white, though the chance varieties and hybrid forms which sprang up here and there tended toward blush pink. One of these, *N. odorata rosea,* endearingly known as the Cape Cod Pink

Water-Lily, became popular, although it hardly added a blaze of color to the water garden.

Another prominent American species, *Nymphaea tuberosa,* is a native of the West, particularly the Northwest. It is a vigorous, healthy grower and has a sweet fragrance, but it, too, bears only white blooms.

COLORFUL VARIETIES

Colorful varieties were to be found in the world, however, and enthusiasts discovered them and brought them home. One of the first and most beautiful was *Nymphaea alba rubra,* a Swedish variety of a widespread European species having pale-pink buds opening in the course of a few days to deep-red flowers, the spectacular orange stamens in lovely contrast to all the changing hues of the bloom. This *N. alba rubra,* however, proved to be very temperamental. It could live only in cold water, and it shocked easily in transplanting. But the splash of color it made among the white blooms in the European gardens must have been worth the great effort required.

Nymphaea mexicana, the native Mexican species, was far easier to transplant and propagate. Its blooms are bright yellow and are carried several inches above the water.

Nymphaea tetragona, another early English import, is white, but with big, bright-yellow stamens that give it color. The flower is one of the smallest of all the hardy water-lilies, actually miniature, prefectly formed and no larger than the face of a pocket watch. Although well distributed in India, Japan, Siberia, and Australia, it is generally regarded as "the native Chinese species," probably because it offers a pleasant tealike fragrance.

Nymphaea pygmaea is another miniature species that found its way into English gardens more than a century ago. Many horticulturists today insist that this one and *N. tetragona* are the same; others insist that they are distinct species, the *pygmaea* flowers being the larger and the plant the stronger of the two. I shall list them separately, since the *pygmaea* and *tetragona* varieties that I have handled show very different characteristics.

These were the first species assembled, and from them descended most of the hardy varieties we enjoy today. Other species made brief appearances—*Nymphaea fennica,* the Finnish species, which produces its white blooms only in extremely cold water; *N. candida,* the white Bohemian species; *N. flava,* the yellow Florida water-lily; *N. Wenzelii,* the white, star-shaped Russian water-lily, and various others. Few of these species are worth collecting. Either they are too temperamental to grow or their inferior blooms are not worth the work involved.

Left: Midnight. Below: A beautiful arrangement is possible by mixing different water-lilies. This bouquet is composed of Pink Opals and Gladstones.

Right: Persian Lilac. Below: Colonel Lindbergh (blue), Sunrise (yellow), and Golden West.

Latour-Marliac Varieties

A botanical genius, Latour-Marliac, who lived at Temple-sur-Lot in the south of France, did for hardy water-lilies what Technicolor did for motion pictures: he gave them color. Marliac, the son of one world-renowned botanist and descended, on his mother's side, from another, began hybridizing with a few species of hardies in the latter part of the last century.

No one knows just what species he used or how they and their varieties were crossed. However, excellent culture, combined with careful selection, soon began to produce startling results. From the late 1880's until the turn of the century, Marliac amazed the horticultural world with a seemingly endless presentation of superb new varieties. Although many of them lacked fragrance, practically all were robust and free flowering under a wide range of conditions. Best of all, they pre-

One of the most popular of plastic pools is the Aqualite. It can be used outdoors during the summer months and makes an interesting fish pond indoors when the weather is cold. Photos by Paul Stetson.

sented a gamut of hues vivid and varied enough to satisfy the most color-hungry water-lily fancier.

It is a safe presumption that this hybridizer obtained many of his initial results by crossing the European species with the prolific American *Nymphaea odorata* and *N. tuberosa,* or at least varieties of them.

Most of the Marliac varieties which are listed in this book fall into two major groups. The *Marliacea* are thought to have originated in an initial cross between the Cape Cod Water-Lily (a pink variety of *Nymphaea odorata*) and the white European water-lily *N. alba.* Marliac's hardy varieties of the *Laydekeri* group are thought to have started with *N. alba rubra* and varieties of the *N. tetragona* species as the parent plants. No one will ever know, for while the wizard crossed, recrossed, selected, and then recrossed again and again, he kept his records to himself.

Latour-Marliac died in 1911, and his secrets died with him. However, he left behind him scores of colorful water-lily varieties which reproduce easily enough to supply the world. The frequency with which the Marliac varieties appear in water-lily listings in this book will give you an idea of the tremendous impact the man made in his field.

Director Moore.

Louise.

C. E. Hutchings.

The famous Dorothy Lamour.

George H. Pring Varieties

Many sections of Europe, particularly the southern countries, would seem ideal for the cultivation of tropical day- and night-blooming water-lilies. However, the tropicals have never enjoyed great popularity there, probably because they were overshadowed in the beginning by Marliac's work with the hardies. It was Dr. George H. Pring, an Englishman by birth and an American by adoption, who brought tropicals to such perfection. As an attaché, and later as superintendent of the Missouri Botanical Gardens at St. Louis, Dr. Pring did for tropicals what Latour-Marliac had achieved with hardies. The hardy water-lilies, once mostly white, needed color. Marliac was able to develop every color in them except blue. (There still is no blue hardy water-lily species or variety.)

Tropical lilies once occurred in a nice range of shades in all the hues except yellow. Where Marliac sought color, Dr. Pring sought the absence of it. And he found it. Among the many new species he brought to the Gardens and the many new varieties he developed there were the St. Louis and the Mrs. George H. Pring, the world's first really worthwhile and dependable yellow and white (respectively) tropicals. Other varieties, both yellow and white, have since been developed, so that these hues in a wide range of shades now form a definite part of the tropical water-lily scale of colors.

Dr. Pring, who is also a world authority on orchids, continues his work today at the Gardens.

Multitude of Tropical Species and Varieties

At this moment we cannot say how many different kinds of tropical water-lilies there are because the number of species and varieties is nearly countless now, and new ones are being classified every year. The basic species which I list in this book, however, tend to overlap so as to be more than representative of the entire range of tropicals —in color, shape, foliage, growing, and blooming habits. As you will see, the difference between many of the listed species and varieties is barely discernible.

So don't hold it against me when you see two or more water-lilies with identical, or nearly identical, qualities. I merely want to be thorough.

CHAPTER SIX *The Hardy Water-Lilies*

Only seven major species of hardy water-lilies are recognized in *The Waterlilies,* the excellent 1905 monograph of the genus *Nymphaea* by Henry S. Conrad. But some present-day botanists claim there are many times that many species, probably because the plants of a single species grown in different parts of the country tend to develop regional characteristics. In time these characteristics assert themselves more and more plainly, until finally a botanist or plant anatomist decides the water-lily has developed such an individuality that it deserves a species name of its own.

I have set down many species in the list which follows, but certainly not because I want to take issue with accepted classifications. Many varieties have been included in some of the doubtful species. If I refuse to recognize the species in question, I would have to rename the variety. Therefore, in the interests of simplicity, I have left plants in the species originally claimed for them.

All of the hardy water-lilies bloom in the daytime, and most of them for three consecutive days. As a rule, the flowers float, although some varieties thrust them above the surface of the water, especially if the plants are crowded. The hardies grow throughout the North Temperate Zone, except on the Pacific slope of North America, and there are some growing in Alaska.

CHANGEABLE WATER-LILIES

Of all water-lilies, a group of hardies called Changeables is one of the most fascinating. A Changeable water-lily is just that. Its bud unfolds with a bloom of one color. Before the end of the first day, the hue of the flower begins to change to some other color. So, in three successive days of blooming, the flower presents three distinct hues. I have indicated which of the hardies are changeable. Catalogs frequently list these as Sunset Shades.

Sunrise.

Gladstone.

Gladstone.

Missouri.

Juno.

When I speak of an *extensive* grower in these lists I refer to water-lilies with blooms and leaves that cover 10 to 12 square feet of pool or lake space. *Medium grower* indicates a plant that covers 8 to 10 square feet. A *small grower* confines the leaf spread to 4 square feet or less.

Hardy Water-Lilies

Nymphaea alba—The native European species. Pure white, cup-shaped flower, 4 to 5 inches in diameter. Especially full of fragrance on its first day of opening. Round-ovate leaves, reddish or dark red when young, becoming a glossy dark green as they mature. Vigorous, extensive grower in pool or pond, and has been known to thrive in 11 feet of water.

> *candidissima*—A healthy, pure-white variety thought to be a cross of *N. alba* and *N. candida* species. Bloom larger than that of *N. alba* and with broader petals. Extensive grower.
>
> *plenissima*—A larger flowering form of *N. alba*.
>
> *rubra*—One of the oldest of the colored hardy varieties. A native of Sweden, it develops properly only in cold water. Blooms are pale pink upon opening, become deep, vivid red with age. Extensive grower when properly placed.

ALBATROSS—Marliac. Huge, snow-white flowers with rich yellow anthers. Unfolding leaves are purple, becoming deep green with age. Despite large blooms, plant confines itself to small area.

N. amabilis—Marliac. Also known as Pink Marvel. Large, tulip-shaped water-lily, salmon-white at first, becoming rose, then a glowing, silvery pink with a deeper pink center. Canary-yellow stamens. Fragrant. Remains open in the evenings for two or three hours after other hardies have closed. Difficult to catalog due to its changing colors. Is listed as a pink, a red, and a Changeable. Extensive or medium grower, depending upon space provided.

N. Andreana—Marliac. One of the largest hardy water-lilies, with 8- to 10-inch blooms of garnet-red shaded with yellow. Almost white sepals; mahogany stamens tipped with yellow. Glossy green leaves, blotched with red. Small grower.

ARC-EN-CIEL—Marliac. Salmon-white blooms with rose-splashed sepals. Fragrant. Extremely interesting foliage, green, oddly spotted with bronze, white, rose, and purple markings. Medium grower.

ARETHUSA—One of the *Laydekeri,* Marliac's fine group of red hybrids. Large, globular bloom with deep-crimson center and wide, deep-rose outer petals, all with a velvety sheen. A gardener's favorite.

N. atropurpurea—Marliac. Full-blown, wide, brilliant, deep-crimson flowers, probably the darkest of all hardy hybrids. Foliage purple, becoming green with age.

ATTRACTION—Marliac. A most satisfactory water-lily for those who love color, probably the reddest of the reds. Tremendous bloom, 7 to 8 inches in diameter. Changes from day to day. Predominantly garnet in early stages with white, rose-streaked sepals; darkens to a rich, deep red a few days later. Deep-mahogany stamens tipped with yellow. Extensive grower.

N. aurora—Marliac. Semidwarf blooms open creamy yellow, become orange next day, and finally deepen to dark red. Foliage, also miniature, prettily mottled with maroon. Excellent tub flower.

BARONESS ORCZY—Marliac. A pretty, rose-pink, cup-shaped variety, not too long in cultivation. Medium spreading habits make it good for the average pool.

BORY DE SAINT VINCENT—Marliac. Another of the newer reds, not yet under cultivation on a popular scale in the United States.

N. Brakleyii rosea—Fragrant blooms of dusky rose-pink, held just above the water surface. Medium grower.

N. candida—The native Bohemian species. Small, odorless, white flowers, with sepals tinged with green. The uniformity of color is attractively broken by a bright-red stigma. Solid-green foliage. Requires little pool space.

> *biradiate*—Similar to above, with the blood-red star at end of stigma more pronounced.
>
> *neglecta*—Very like species type. (Both *N. neglecta* and *biradiate* are inferior varieties, not recommended.)

N. Carisbrookii—Small, fragrant blooms of a delicate shade of rose, hardy enough for a pool, but more often grown in tubs.

N. caroliniana—Probably an accidental hybrid of *N. odorata rosea* (the Cape Cod Pond Lily) and *N. tuberosa.* Has the sweet fragrance, delicate rosy-pink color, and yellow stamens of the former; the robust habit of the latter.

> *nivea*—Marliac. Large, white, quite fragrant flowers and pale-green foliage. An enlarged version of *N. odorata,* although foliage is concentrated enough for small pools.
>
> *perfecta*—Marliac. Similar to above, including scent, but plant spreads more and blooms are salmon-pink.
>
> *rosea*—Marliac. Similar to above in scent and growth, but bloom is more perfectly formed and of deeper color.

CHARLES DE MEURVILLE—Marliac. A robust variety, capable of taking over its end of the pool. Flowers the color of good Burgundy wine.

Blue Beauty.

Newton.

Sumptuosa.

Comanche.

N. chrysantha—Marliac. Small, reddish-yellow blooms which deepen with age to cinnabar-red. Flowers freely within a small space. Generally considered one of Marliac's lesser efforts and not widely cultivated.

N. colossea—Marliac. Huge flesh-colored blooms, among the first to show in spring and continuing bountifully until frost. Extensive grower.

COMANCHE—Marliac. The largest and, many gardeners think, the finest of the Changeables. Bloom opens a warm shade of rose overlaid with apricot, becomes darker and more vivid day by day, and finally turns to a glowing amber color with a heart of fire. Foliage is purple, passing to olive-green flecked with yellow as flower ages. Plant thrives lustily in any reasonable location. One of the first to bloom in spring, it continues until frost. Listed as a yellow, a Changeable, and as a Sunset Shade.

COMTE DE BOUCHARD—Similar to Attraction, but smaller and of lighter hue. Purplish-rose blooms with apricot stamens. Sepals are white inside, providing beautiful contrast. Produces lots of flowers. Medium grower.

CONQUEROR—Marliac. Blooms range from showy pink to cherry-red, flecked with white. Sepals are white inside, and stamens are bright yellow. Long and prolific bloom, medium grower.

DARWIN—Marliac. Medium-sized blooms of red, boldly striped with white. Sweet scent.

DAWN—Excellent *odorata* variety, and one of the largest. Huge, globular, snow-white bloom, surrounded by white sepals barely touched with pink. Very fragrant.

N. delicata—White, tulip-shaped, a hybrid of *candida*. Attractive flower, but not a strong grower.

DOROTHY LAMOUR—A new miniature hardy developed by Three Springs Fisheries. The pale yellow bloom resembles a half-opened rose, in both form and size, and has a fresh, delicate fragrance. The 4-inch pads are bright green, prettily marked with chestnut brush strokes. Produces a lot of foliage and bloom, and lives on about half a pint of earth.

One of the most versatile of water-lilies. Its tiny size makes it ideal for aquarium culture. It does well under the artificial sunlight of a "Gro-Lux" or similar bulb, or in a sunny window location. In the outdoor pool—don't plant it outside until warm weather is here to stay —it thrives in either deep water or in shallow water at the pool edge.

N. eburnea—Marliac. Prettily shaped lily, on the small side, white, overlaid with interesting traceries of green and pink. Fragrant. Foliage exceptional shade of bright green.

N. Ellisiana—Marliac. One of the most brilliant reds. Small blossoms of intense vermilion, offset by orange-red stamens.

N. erecta—Small, slender, white bloom, held well above the water. Flourishes in shallow pools.

ESCARBOUCLE—Marliac. One of the finest water-lilies I could recommend. Blooms as large as soup plates, seeming to attain perfect form for everybody. Free blooming. Flowers are uniform vermilion, with garnet, yellow-tipped stamens. Escarboucle contrasts beautifully with practically every other water-lily. Or, given an end of the pool or a whole pool to itself, it turns the water surface into a fiery mass. Blooms deepen in a few days to dark wine-crimson. Extensive or medium grower, depending on how much space you give it.

ESMERALDA—Marliac. Small, star-shaped blooms of red streaked with white. A variety without much popularity.

EUCHARIST—Marliac. Small, full-blown, with rose-colored blossoms splashed heavily with white.

EUGENIA DE LAND—Another of the very good *odorata* varieties. Iridescent, rose-pink blooms, 7 to 8 inches in diameter, which ride prettily upon the water when there is room. Crowded, the flowers attain only medium size, and stand well out of the water. Blossoms are semi-double and star-shaped, with long, pointed, incurved petals. Golden stamens. A vigorous grower, and very fragrant.

FABIOLA—Marliac. A fine variety, with big, rich-pink blooms which open wide. Mahogany stamens. Flowers appear in early summer and continue until frost.

N. fennica—The native Finnish species, seldom cultivated because it thrives only in very cold, spring-fed pools—conditions under which few other water-lilies can survive. It is small, pure white or rosy in the true species type, with strongly curved petals and yellow stamens.

FIRE CREST—Small but interesting, and aptly named. Bloom is deep pink, opens wide, as if to show off the unique stamens, fiery red at the tips. Becomes deep red with age. An *odorata* variety, with a fine fragrance.

N. flava—Small, star-shaped yellow with a cluster of deeper yellow stamens. Grows from Florida through the southern states to Texas and Mexico. The egg-shaped leaves are dark purple underneath, deep green splotched with brown above. Frequently referred to as "the yellow Florida water-lily" or "the Florida species." Some botanists do not consider *N. flava* a species, but an offshoot of *N. mexicana* which has developed regional characteristics in Florida. Leaves of the species growing in Mexico are rounder, much thicker, and have less purple. There is little difference in the blooms.

Attraction.

Margaret Mary.

Rose Arey.

Aviator Pring.

Plate 12

Plate 13

Plates 12-17. To prepare and plant a tub garden, scrub a new zinc tub with vinegar *(Plate 12)* to neutralize it chemically. A coat of rubber base paint on the interior surfaces adds to the appearance, but is not necessary. (No preparation at all is needed if a white cedar tub is used. Dig an excavation to fit the tub *(Plate 13)* and allow the rim of

Plate 14

Plate 15

the tub to extend far enough above ground level *(Plate 14)* to keep out surface water. Surround the tub with stone, sod, or brick *(Plate 15)* and then add a mixture of fertilized soil *(Plate 16)*. Place weighted burlap over the soil *(Plate 17)* so that the water will not be cloudy when it is added.

Plate 16

Plate 17

Joe Cutak.

Omarana.

Chromatella.

Emily Grant Hutchings.

Plate 18

Remove the burlap, plant water-lilies in the tub and border plants around the edge *(Plate 18)*. Finally put in a couple of goldfish to destroy mosquito larvae.   ROCHE PHOTO

N. formosa—Marliac. Big flowers of delicate, pastel pink with cerise overtones, offset by a huge cluster of yellow stamens. Becomes deeper pink with age. Bursts into bloom soon after planting and continues to blossom well over a long period. Foliage pale green.

N. Froebelii—Small flowers, and many of them, of a blood-red hue. Fine for tubs.

N. fulva—Marliac. Small, thin, copper-red blooms spotted with sulfur yellow. Becomes deeper red with age. Sepals are yellow with a purplish stain. Difficult to grow, and hardly worth the effort.

GALATEE—Marliac. Soft, rose-colored blooms spattered with white. Becomes fairly large. Foliage is deep green with bold purple markings.

N. Gladstoniana—One of the biggest hardy water-lilies we cultivate. Recommended as one of the best of all hardies for medium-to-large pools. Waxy, pure-white blooms 6 to 8 inches in diameter. With clusters of golden stamens, blooms contrast handsomely with the dark-green foliage. Both flowers and foliage stand above the water, and both are excellent for cutting.

GLOIRE DE TEMPLE-SUR-LOT—Marliac. Because this is the water-lily Marliac named for his home, you expect something special of it—and you will not be disappointed. This lily is remarkable for both form and coloring. Blossom is very double, sometimes with more than a hundred erect, narrow petals (many gardeners compare it to an immense dahlia). A delicate shade of pink on opening, it fades in the course of a week to a cream color, then pure white.

N. gloriosa—Marliac. A long-established water-lily deservedly popular; many dealers report it the biggest seller of all the hardies. Blooms, 6 and 7 inches in diameter, open carmine-rose and deepen within a few days to dark rose, always with the scent of apple blossoms. Produces an abundance of symmetrical, semidouble blooms, but adapts itself readily to medium or large pools because leaves are quite small. A good flower for neophyte water gardeners, because frequently it producers flowers three weeks after planting. One of the very few water-lilies that does well in partial shade.

GOLIATH—Marliac. Large, tulip-shaped blooms with long petals of white, barely touched with pink. The flower is conspicuous for remarkable white stamens and orange-red petaloids, which together give an exotic effect. Extensive grower.

GONNERE—Marliac. (Frequently listed as Crystal White or *Snowball*.) Large, very double bloom with such a tremendous number of dewy white petals that from a distance it looks like a glistening globe floating on the water. A fine cut flower, for it is fragrant, and the olive-green sepals contrast beautifully with the bloom. Plant has a comparatively small leaf spread and is a strong grower in either medium or large pools.

Gloriosa.

Escarboucle.

Mrs. Hitchcock.

August Koch.

N. gracillima alba—Marliac. Listed as either a red or a yellow, and it is both. Small blooms are orange-pink on opening, and shade to canary-yellow within a few days. Bright-orange stamens, which hold their color. Green foliage is mottled brown or purple. Small grower, excellent for tubs.

HASSELL—A yellow hybrid from a crossing of a Marliac variety with *N. mexicana*. Plant is vigorous, producing 5- to 7-inch blooms with extremely long and pointed petals. The deeper the water, the more freely it flowers.

HELEN FOWLER—Small flowers, produced in continuous profusion, borne above water; of deep, dusky pink, with the fragrance of crushed almonds. Excellent for cutting, and good tub culture.

HERMINE—Marliac. Medium-sized, star-shaped, white blooms which extend 3 to 4 inches above the water. Green sepals and bright-green foliage give a cool, refreshing look. Not a large grower, but blooms profusely in small pools and tubs.

INDIANA—Marliac. Changeable with a nice succession of color. Flowers open delicate orange-red, deepen to coppery shades, and finally become dark copper-red. Foliage heavily mottled purple. Medium grower.

J. C. N. FORESTIER—Marliac. Huge, rich-rose bloom overlaid with apricot, passing to dark, and then to very dark coppery bronze. Blooms held well above water. Medium grower.

JAMES BRYDON—Distinctive among the hardies. The only very fragrant red, with the scent of sweet apples. Succeeds with much less sun than most other hardies and grows quickly. Blooms are of average size, about 5 inches in diameter, and of an overall dark-red hue with a bluish cast, somewhat granular in appearance but not streaked or splotched. Stamens are dark orange, tipped with yellow. One of the freest flowering of the hardies, and the purple foliage restricts itself to a small pond area.

JAMES HUDSON—Marliac. Large, stellate flowers, purplish-crimson. Outer sepals are white stained with rose.

JESSIEANA—Large, of classic form, delicate, even shade of pink. Small grower.

JO ANNE PRING—Pring. A pygmy with deep-pink blooms shading to faint pink at the center. Stamens are unusual, the outer circles deep pink, the inner yellow-orange. Dark green leaves 2 to 3 inches in diameter.

N. lactea—Marliac. Medium-sized flowers of pale pink passing to milky white with age, contrasting prettily with bright-green outer sepals. Fragrant. Medium grower.

N. Laydekeri HYBRIDS—All the red and pink water-lilies which make up Marliac's *Laydekeri* group are on the small side, have small foliage of uniform green, and require very little pool space, making them ideal for tubs. Parentage of these hybrids, like that of Marliac's other issues, is a mystery. One parent of the hybrids which follow, however, is thought to have been *N. tetragona*.

> *fulgens*—A rich amaranth bloom with rosy-white sepals and fiery-red stamens. Becomes a deeper crimson-magenta as it gets older, and glows like a jewel in the sunshine. Stamens are bright red. Very free flowering.

> *lilacea*—Soft pink passing with age to rose-lilac. Yellow stamens. Exquisite fragrance, like that of a tea rose.

> *purpurata*—Somewhat larger than other hybrids of the group and by far the most profuse bloomer. As many as a dozen blooms may open at one time if planted with room to expand. Blooms are large, rose-crimson, often flecked white, and with brilliant orange-red stamens.

> *rosea*—Considered by many to be the loveliest of the group. Blossoms are deep rose-pink, cup shaped, and have a pretty way of bobbing about on the water. Good fragrance. Comparatively weak grower, however, so inexperienced water gardeners wisely omit it.

LEVIATHAN—Marliac. Strong, extensive grower with large, soft-pink blossoms.

LIVINGSTONE—Marliac. Long-petaled, tulip-shaped flowers, bright red, flecked white. Stamens are mahogany-red. Fragrant. Small grower.

LOOSE—Large American variety resembling a tropical in that it is star-shaped with a stout stem which holds it as much as a foot above water. Snow-white, with a nice fragrance.

LOUISE—Medium size, cup-shaped, double bloom in one of the deepest shades of clear, brilliant vermilion ever seen in a hardy. Petals sometimes brushed white at tips. Golden center adds to flamelike look of the blossom. Foliage clear green. Three Springs Fisheries developed this flower recently by crossing the Escarboucle, brilliant red, and the Mrs. C. W. Thomas, delicate shell-pink. Stock is still limited, but increasing.

LUCIANA—Small, star-shaped blooms of rich, glowing rose. Sweet scented. Small grower. Floats the first year, thrusts blooms above the water after it becomes established.

LUCIDA—Marliac. Large, free-growing plant with rose-vermilion blooms, shading darker toward the center. Foliage variegated green and purple.

Mrs. C. W. Ward.

Mrs. C. W. Thomas.

James Brydon.

Roseum Plenum.

LUSITANIA—Marliac. Flowers of deep rose, with bright, mahogany-colored stamens. New foliage purple, changing to green with age. Extensive grower.

LUSTROUS—American hybrid with shimmering, satiny-pink blooms. Sepals pink inside, brown outside. Cluster of thick yellow stamens. Strong grower, but short leaf stems hold it to a small area.

MME. BORY LATOUR MARLIAC—Marliac. Comparatively new variety, on the small side, with pale-pink blooms.

MME. DE BONSEIGNEUR—Marliac. Also new, not yet cultivated widely. Small pink blooms, streaked darker pink and red.

MME. JULIEN CHIFFLOT—Marliac. A friend describes this as a "veritable Betty Grable of a lily." And it is. Huge star-shaped, rich-pink blooms, sometimes up to 10 inches across. A thick cluster of rich-yellow stamens sets off the flower beautifully. Medium grower.

MME. MAURICE LAYDEKER—Marliac. Truly beautiful. Medium-sized, globe-shaped blooms of bright and even cherry-red.

MME. WILFRON GONNERE—Marliac. Double, outer petals of the cup-shaped bloom are white, spotted deep rose. Centers are flushed with warm pink.

MARGUERITE LAPLACE—Marliac. Soft, rose-colored blooms 7 inches or more in diameter, deepening around the edges. Becomes delicate lilac-rose with age. Broad, incurved sepals also rose, lightly stained with green. Flower opens wide, and blooms freely all summer. Foliage is purplish-green. Extensive grower if given room.

MARK HANNA—Marliac. Pink blooms of medium size. Once popular, but seldom cultivated now.

N. Marliacea HYBRIDS—The hardy varieties Marliac produced in this group now known as Marliacea are the world's best. They include a full range of color and size with blooms of classic form. Plants thrive in a variety of conditions, and all bloom freely. Some are fragrant. Year in and year out, they are best sellers.

albida—Often catalogued as Marliac White. Large, snow-white bloom with broad, waxy petals and a clump of rich-yellow stamens, held just above the water. Sepals tinted pink. Exceptionally fine fragrance. Foliage deep red on the underside, dark green above.

carnea—We list this, as do many other dealers, by the more popular trade name, Morning Glory. Bloom is star-shaped, the pale pink of apple blossoms, with a profusion of yellow stamens. Has a fine, sweet, vanilla scent. Very free bloomer. Has produced as many as five flowers at once the first year, three times that many the second. After plant has been established a year or two, sepals and outer petals develop a rosy tinge at base. Fine lasting quality as cut flowers.

chromatella—One of the prettiest of all water-lily color combinations. Four- to 6-inch blooms are rich, creamy yellow with bright-yellow stamens, contrasting strikingly with olive-green foliage, bronze marked. Healthy, extensive grower, plant soon fills the end of a pool. When crowded, leaves and blooms thrust themselves above the water. Should be divided every other year to keep it in check.

flammea—Blooms of glowing amaranth, flecked white. Olive-green leaves mottled chestnut-brown. Small grower.

ignea—Vivid carmine, on the small side, with conspicuous red anthers. Foliage similar to that of *flammea,* above.

rosea—One of the best of the hardies for cutting. Large, cup-shaped blooms are deep rose-pink, shading darker toward the center. Blooms have a waxy, dewy freshness unsurpassed by any other water-lily. Good fragrance. Leaves are purplish-red at first, becoming deep green with age.

rubra punctata—Medium size, globular flowers of a deep rose-carmine shade.

MARY EXQUISITA—Large, star-shaped, shell-pink blooms with delicious scent. Free and steady bloomer, medium grower.

MARY PATRICIA—Large, cup-shaped bloom, one of the daintiest peach-blossom pinks imaginable. Generous bloomer, plant spreads very little. Fine for tubs.

MASANIELLO—Marliac. Large, peony-shaped flower with blooms held well above the water. Cup-shaped, pink, spattered carmine. Conspicuous orange-yellow stamens. Fine scent. Free bloomer and grower.

MAURICE LAYDEKER—Marliac. Small, deep-rose blooms, flecked white. Few gardeners cultivate the plant, for it has a weak constitution.

METEOR—Marliac. Medium-sized blooms of red, streaked white. Not widely cultivated.

N. mexicana—(See *N. flava,* which many botanists consider the same species.) *N. mexicana* is somewhat less hardy than other species of the subgenus to which it belongs. Flowers are small and star-shaped, yellow, with deeper-yellow stamens. Leaves are small, round, deep green, blotched with brown above, purplish-green with black markings on the underside. Flowers are carried above water. Like many of the night-blooming tropicals, this extends itself by runners.

N. Moorei—An Australian variety with the deepest yellow among water-lilies. Stamens are a lighter, brighter yellow. Foliage is pale green, heavily spotted purple. Medium grower.

MRS. C. W. THOMAS—Fragrant, free blooming, shell-pink, developed

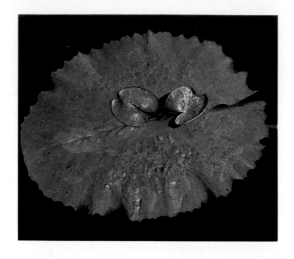

Above: A viviparous offshoot showing the new plant growing from a parent leaf. Below: A frog rests on the buoyant leaf of the N. gloriosa.

Escarboucle

Rose Arey

Gladstone

Marliac Rosea

Chromatella

111

at Three Springs Fisheries and named in honor of my grandmother. Flower is semidouble, and has been called the most delicate pink lily ever produced. Medium grower.

MRS. RICHMOND—Marliac. Immense globular bloom of deep pink, shading to bright strawberry-red in the center. Petals are broad and full, and stamens bright yellow. Free flowering.

MURILLO—Marliac. Large, star-shaped blooms with broad, pointed petals of bright rose, flushed white at edge. Sepals are white, stained rose. Flower floats low on the water. Medium grower.

NEPTUNE—Marliac. Star-shaped, of deep, velvety rose, heavily shaded crimson. Inner petals faintly spotted white, extreme outer petals almost white, touched rose. Garnet stamens. Foliage is maroon, becoming green with age. This is a favorite among water gardeners, and generally described as "aristocratic." Medium grower.

NEWTON—Marliac. This water-lily, for which we imported our growing stock from Japan in the 1930's, has an Oriental look in form and color. It thrusts large, star-shaped, cherry-red blooms well above the water. Long, narrow petals give it a distinctive form, and the white sepals and orange stamens contrast prettily with the petal hue. Medium grower.

N. nitida—Rare Siberian species, sought only by collectors. Flowers are small, white, and cup-shaped, with very blunt petals. A botanical oddity; the rootstock is perpendicular instead of horizontal. Small grower.

N. Nobilissima—Marliac. Much like Newton, but with shorter blunter petals of a more subdued rose shade.

N. odorata—The pond-lily species of North America. Its two principal virtues are fragrance and fertility. It crosses readily with other species and has produced a number of accidental hybrids of fine form and color in eastern North America. This is one of the parents Marliac used to produce many of his colorful varieties, which are often freer blooming than *N. odorata,* but, alas, not always with the odorata fragrance. In species form, *N. odorata* is medium-sized, pure white, and cup-shaped with a strong, pleasing fragrance. Foliage is pale green. Medium grower.

alba—An improved form of the above.

exquisita—Marliac. Small, rose-carmine, a very delicate hue. Small grower.

gigantea—Perhaps best known as "the Southern odorata." White blooms from 4 to 7 inches in diameter. Foliage deep green on the upper side, purplish on the underside. Very free grower, particularly in deep water. Blooms fragrant.

minor—An old and loved American variety, usually known as the Mill Pond Lily. Half to a quarter as large as the average lily, with blooms 2 to 3 inches across and leaves 3 to 5 inches. A rapid grower and prolific bloomer in shallow or deep water. Good for tub culture. Flowers are pure white, dainty and very fragrant. Leaves are soft green, with reddish undersurface.

> *floribus roseus*—Similar to above except that the outside of petals and sepals is tinged pink. Medium grower.

rosea—The Cape Cod Pond Lily, intense pink, deepening toward the center. Has one of the most pleasant scents of all water-lilies. Foliage purplish-green.

> *rosea prolifera*—Fragrant with delicate pink blooms, deepening to rich rose and later to carmine in the center. Medium grower.

sulphurea—Marliac. A pretty hybrid of *N. odorata* and *N. mexicana*. Blooms are sulfur-yellow and fragrant. As the plant ages, long, slender stems thrust the flowers higher and higher above the water. Foliage is green, with chocolate markings. Free blooming and prolific within a small pool space.

> *grandiflora*—Marliac. Quite similar to the above, but with larger blooms and foliage. Also confines itself to small pool space.

Turicensis—Soft-rose, medium-sized blooms with a sweet scent. Medium grower.

OPALISQUE—Marliac. Medium-sized blooms of soft rose, changing to shell-pink with age. Golden stamens. Thrusts blooms above water.

PAUL HARIOT—Marliac. A small plant with large, interesting blooms that open about the color of a Talisman rose, turn orange-pink the next day, and finally darken to deep red. Shows more color range than any other Changeable water-lily. Blooms are held erect. Foliage dark green, spotted maroon. Fine for tubs. Almost all dealers carry it.

PHOEBUS—Marliac. Another good Changeable, somewhat larger, but still good for tubs. Blooms open yellow, striped red, with fiery-orange stamens. Within a few days the hue deepens to coppery red. Foliage rich green, mottled brown.

PHOENIX—Marliac. Small, bright-red blooms streaked white. Compact grower.

PICCIOLA—Marliac. Tremendous blooms, often 9 to 10 inches in diameter, of vivid amaranth-crimson. Strong and extensive grower.

PINK OPAL—One of the most popular pinks. Blooms are star-shaped, a delicate shade of pink, and excellent for cutting. The fragrance of a single bloom will perfume a room. Flowers are borne erect above the

A closeup of water-lilies adapted to crowded conditions. Photo by Dr. Herbert R. Axelrod.

Castaliflora, a day-blooming tropical. Photo by Paul Stetson.

water. Foliage is green with a bronzy overcast. Excellent for small pools and tubs.

PRESIDENT VIGOR—Marliac. Large blooms of glowing rose. Medium grower. Seldom cultivated in recent years.

N. punctata—Small, rose-lilac, flecked carmine. Requires shallow water.

N. pygmaea—In the pure species form, a small white flower with a heavy cluster of yellow stamens. Blooms, which measure only 1½ to 2 inches across, have a delightful tea scent. The plant is slightly larger and hardier than *N. tetragona,* although many botanists consider the two species the same. In a strict botanical sense, they are. One of the best for tubs and small pools.

> *alba*—Although this hybrid is a cross between *N. pygmaea* and *N. alba,* there is no difference to be seen between its blooms and foliage and that of the true *N. pygmea* species.

> *helvola*—Marliac. Also listed as Yellow Pygmy. A dainty little plant with sulfur-yellow, star-shaped blooms 2 inches or less in diameter. The tiniest, and probably the prettiest, of the *N. pygmaea* varieties. Very free flowering. The many blooms ride gaily upon the water, even in a tub garden. Olive-green mottled maroon foliage leaves seldom more than 4 to 5 inches across.

> HYPERION—A new red pygmy, of increasing popularity in England, somewhat larger than the usual run of pygmaea varieties. Free flowering, and fine for tubs.

> *rubis*—Marliac. A nicely formed miniature, carmine streaked white.

> *rubra*—Slightly larger than most pygmaea forms, rose-colored changing to rich garnet-red.

RADIANCE—Iridescent, shell-pink flowers often 7 to 8 inches in diameter. Petals pointed and incurved. Fragrant.

RENE GERARD—Marliac. Large and free growing with rich rose-colored blooms flecked and streaked crimson. Star-shaped, and held erect.

N. Robinsonii—Marliac. An old time favorite. Floating blooms are a glorious orange-red, usually 4 to 5 inches in diameter, with vivid orange-red stamens. Green foliage is spotted maroon. Grown by many for its beauty of form. Broad petals are rolled near the tip.

ROSE AREY—Huge, rose-pink with pointed petals curling at ends. Profusion of yellow stamens giving a heart of molten gold. Rich, fruity fragrance, probably the most sweetly scented of all hardies. Dependable strong grower. Foliage is green with a reddish cast.

ROSE MAGNOLIA—American variety with flesh-pink blooms held well above the water. Medium grower.

Rosita—Marliac. Small, purple-pink, star-shaped flowers. Medium sized when it thrives, but very difficult to grow.

N. sanguinea—Marliac. A friend describes this as "a true lady of great beauty." Huge red blooms, streaked white, with a handsome cluster of orange-red stamens. Foliage olive-green, blotched brown. Small grower.

N. seignouretii—Marliac. Small bloom with sulfur-yellow petals, buff-colored at base. Flower stands well above the water. Gorgeous color combination, but the variety propagates so slowly and grows so poorly that few dealers stock it.

Sioux—Marliac. Another Changeable, and a good one. Rich chrome-yellow on opening, with inner petals suffused bronze. Passes to deep orange, and then to copper-red. Blooms are held erect. Foliage mottled brown and purple. Small grower.

Sirius—Marliac. There is no neutral reaction to this flower. Gardeners like it a lot or they cannot stand the sight of it. Large bloom of delicate fawn color, the petals lined with red. Outer sepals white, spotted red. Fiery-red stamens. Foliage green, spotted brown and purple. (Gardeners who don't care for it describe it as "dirty, light tan, splattered red.") Medium grower.

Solfatare—Marliac. A Changeable lily, small to medium sized, opening creamy yellow, becoming orange, and then red. Has been described as a small brother of Paul Hariot. Flowers are star-shaped. Foliage green, heavily mottled maroon. Small grower, good for tub culture.

N. somptuosa—Marliac. A strange variety with enormous blooms, yet confines its growth to a small area. Globular blooms, very double, of rich strawberry-pink. Stamens are clear orange, an interesting contrast. One of the first to bloom in early summer.

Souvenir de Jules Jacquier—Marliac. Vigorous, free growing, with globular blooms of mauve-pink. Extensive grower.

N. speciosa—Marliac. Medium sized with flesh-pink blooms.

Splendida—Marliac. Medium-sized blooms of clear ruby-red.

N. suavissima—Marliac. Small, fragrant blooms that stand well above the water. Rose-pink, a delicate shade.

Sultan—Marliac. Large, cherry-red shading to a deeper color at the base, and prettily streaked creamy white. Does very well in a small place.

Sunrise—Often listed as Giant Yellow. The largest of the hardy water-lilies, with blooms often nearly a foot across, bright yellow, fragrant, and carried well above the water. One of the first to open in the morning. Leaves are egg-shaped, with crinkled sides, dark green above,

H. C. Haarstick, a very popular night blooming tropical. Photo by Paul Stetson.

A star lily, one of the blooming tropical varieties, it has large flowers. Photo by Paul Stetson.

and red-flecked, dark brown below. Strong grower requiring a comparatively small space.

N. tetragona—The baby of the water-lily species. In pure species form, the flower is small, white, very dainty, no larger than half a dollar. Quite prolific, and grows rapidly, sometimes producing blooms the same season that seed is planted. Frequently called "the Chinese species" because of its pleasing tea fragrance. First imported from China by English and American gardeners. Miniature foliage is olive-green.

> *angusta*—The scattered varieties of *N. tetragona* differ little from the true species type. There are two forms of the *N. t. angusta: indica,* from India, has petals of average length, leaves long and tapering and spattered dark brown; *orientalis,* from China, has short petals, and foliage of uniform olive-green.

> *grandiflora*—Produces somewhat larger flowers.

> *himalayense*—Indian variety, same as species type.

> *lata*—Northeast Asian variety, same as species type.

> *leibergi*—North American variety, same as species type.

N. tuberosa—Native North American species which thrives west of the Mississippi River and in the north-central part of the country. Extremely strong grower, will take possession of pool or pond if allowed. Pure species type bloom is white, without scent, except for a faint odor of apples.

PAESTLINGBERG—Austrian variety, similar to species type, but with much larger flowers.

> *Richardsonii*—Large, globular, white blooms with pretty pea-green outer sepals. Slightly fragrant. At one time one of the most popular whites in the United States, but not under wide cultivation now, probably because it is not a heavy bloomer.

> *rosea*—Medium-size, cup-shaped blooms of soft pink, very fragrant. Foliage is light green. Strong and extensive grower and must be kept in check.

> *rubra*—Large blooms of rosy red with clusters of ruby-red stamens, pleasant fragrance. Not too popular, for the plant produces a lot of foliage and comparatively little bloom.

> *Tulipformis*—Marliac. Huge, tulip-shaped blooms, deep rose-pink.
Medium grower.

VESUVE—Marliac. Small flowers of classic form, glowing shade of red with bluish overtones. Small grower.

VIRGINIA—A new variety from Three Springs Fisheries obtained in a cross of the Sunrise, a robust yellow, and the Gladstone, a large hardy white. The Virginia is a glamorous, star-shaped bloom 6 to 7 inches in diameter. Dewy white petals surround an innermost row of petals which are touched with a delicate blush of yellow gold, rather like a warm ray of sunshine. Stamens warm, sunlit yellow. Slightly fragrant. Pads huge, light green, darkening with age on top side.

N. virginalis—Marliac. Considered the purest white and one of the largest of all hardy water-lilies. Blooms, sometimes a foot wide, consist of broad, shell-shaped petals, slightly incurved. Very fragrant. Pale-green foliage contrast prettily with the bloom. Good grower.

WILLIAM DOOGUE—Huge, cup-shaped blooms with broad petals, delicate shade of pink, passing to white with age. Free grower and bloomer.

WILLIAM FALCONER—An old-timer not cultivated widely today, more's the pity. Large blooms of dark, velvety red, shading almost to black at the base, with a cluster of yellow stamens for a beautiful contrast. Foliage red in the beginning, becoming green, shot with a network of red veins. Shy bloomer, compared to many of the newer varieties, but worth pampering.

W. B. SHAW—A charming shell-pink with narrow, pointed petals, deliciously fragrant. In hot weather the young flowers become flushed with apricot. An early bloomer, and a medium grower.

YELLOW PIGMY— The same as *N. pygmaea helvola.*

Above: This Nymphaea was found wild in the Brazilian jungles by Harald Schultz who photographed it for Tropical Fish Hobbyist magazine. Below: Afterglow, a tropical day blooming lily. Photo by Paul Stetson.

This beautiful lotus, Nelumbium, and some pods. Photo by Paul Stetson.

CHAPTER SEVEN *The Tropical
Water-Lilies*

Tropical water-lilies do everything on a grander scale than the hardies. They grow wider and taller and in a greater range of color. Their blooming habits are more versatile, half of them blooming in daytime, the rest opening at night. Almost all of the day bloomers and a few night bloomers have fragrance. Many carry their blooms aloft, well above the surface of the water; and long, strong stems make most of them excellent for cutting.

There are more species of tropicals than of hardies, and they hybridize more readily, which has resulted in a tremendous number of varieties. (Incidentally, I use the terms hybrid and variety interchangeably.)

The foliage of most tropicals is spreading and luxurious, and that of many of the species and varieties is toothed and crimped or fluted at the edge. Most of them require more pool or pond space, half again to twice as much as the hardies.

Tropicals are not as versatile as the hardies, however, when it comes to growing, for they must have comparatively shallow water at the start. They do well in pools, large and small. They thrive in ponds when planted around the shallow edges or propped up in the deep water to a level from which blooms can break the surface.

In Hawaii, and in those fortunate areas of the United States which are never troubled by frosts, the night-blooming tropicals are not limited to seasonal life spans. They live continually year after year, and bloom the year around with only brief rest periods.

As with the hardies, I include several species and varieties which may seem identical. That is intentional, for I want to present a complete range of colors and shapes, even if I have to overlap a little to do it.

124

Several species and varieties of day-blooming tropical water-lilies have an interesting characteristic that few other flowers have. They are viviparous, that is, they bear their young alive, in the form of miniature plants and blooms which sprout from an umbilicus at the center of mature leaves. (Viviparousness is discussed in detail in Chapter 9.)

Day-Blooming Tropicals

AFRICAN GOLD—Pring. A new yellow of fine, clear hue and good form.

AMERICAN BEAUTY—Flowers reddish, lemon-chrome at the center and 6 to 10 inches across. Large, orbicular leaves, bright green on top, brilliant red with green veins beneath, with a wavy margin.

N. ampla—Tropical American species with white, star-shaped blooms, golden stamens.

speciosa—The same, but not quite so small.

ANTOINETTE CHAIZE—Distinct coloring. Lavender-blue blooms brushed at petal tips with deep gentian-blue.

AUGUST KOCH—Pring. An old favorite, and a very good' one with 7- to 8-inch blooms of pale violet, quite fragrant. Stamens are reddish-yellow; sepals lilac. A profusion of blooms the year around if plants are taken indoors in winter. One of the few water-lilies that do very well with a minimum of sunlight. Viviparous. Leaves are dark green and only 12 to 14 inches in diameter. Excellent for small pools. Very good for cutting.

AVIATOR PRING—Pring. Hybrid vigor appears in this big new prim-rose yellow. The first yellow variety that meets all the requirements of the grower. A good propagator and occasionally viviparous.

BAGDAD—Pring. Blooms of pale purplish-blue on short stems, just above the floating leaves. Viviparous.

BLUE BEAUTY—Often listed as Pennsylvania or *N. pulcherrima*. A cross from *N. coerulea* by *N. capensis* var. *zanzibariensis*. Blooms 10 to 12 inches across and are deep blue. A striking yellow disk in the center is surrounded by golden stamens with violet anthers. Dark-green leaves, with long, tapering lobes, and often more than 2 feet in diameter.

BLUE BIRD—Well-shaped blooms of deep blue. Viviparous.

BLUE STAR—Pale, clear blue bloom. See Star Lilies.

BLUE TRIUMPH—Blue flowers up to a foot across, borne in great profusion. Green foliage flecked bronze.

BOB TRICKETT—Large flowers, 10 to 14 inches across, of Campanula-blue with yellow center, similar to Mrs. Edwards Whitaker but fuller

Comanche Hara is a large lily which changes colors as it ages. Photo by Paul Stetson.

Isabelle Pring, a pure white tropical day blooming lily. Photo by Paul Stetson.

and more cup-shaped. Buds green, leaves large and orbicular, green above, red with green veins beneath.

N. Burttii—An interesting species first introduced into cultivation and identified at the Missouri Botanical Gardens in 1929 by Dr. Pring. Seeds, thought to be those of another species, were sent to the gardens from the Tanganyika Territory of East Africa by B. D. Burtt, a botanist engaged in research there. Of the several seeds planted, only one germinated, and in time produced spectacular 8-inch blooms, primrose-yellow, and very sweetly scented. An important find, because for many years. *N. stuhlmannii* and *N. sulfurea* were thought to be the only yellow tropicals. The plant is still an enigma. Difficult to propagate and grow, but hybrids reproduce readily from tubers. The plant proved to be a new species when studied at the botanical gardens, and so was named for the discoverer.

N. calliantha—African species with light-blue or purple star-shaped flowers. Sepals are deep yellow.

> *tenuis*—A variety just as unstable in hue. The flowers open either white or pale blue.

N. capensis—Commonly called the Cape Blue Water-Lily. Blooms are 8 to 9 inches, a little deeper than sky-blue, with blue-tipped yellow stamens. Sepals are green outside, white flushed pale blue inside. Foliage is green, sometimes tinted purple. Fragrant. Grows freely throughout southern and eastern Africa, and in Madagascar.

> *forma rubra*—A miniature with brilliant rose-colored blooms and a sweet scent. Excellent for tub culture.

> *madagascariensis*—Madagascar variety similar to species type, but with much smaller blooms.

> *zanzibariensis*—Often listed as Royal Purple Lily. Similar to species type with rich purple-blue blooms and yellow stamens tipped navy blue. Fragrant. Free flowering. This variety has produced two garden hybrids which have become quite popular.

>> *azurea*—Like parent, but with delicate blue flowers.

>> *rosea*—Similar, but with deep rose-colored blooms.

N. castaliflora—Pring. Striking hybrid in both size and coloration, obtained by Dr. Pring by crossing two forms of *N. zanzibariensis rosea*. Delicate pink blooms 8 to 10 inches across. Heart of the bloom is a breathtaking cluster of bright-pink anthers, held erect by yellow stamens. Fragrant. Large leaves, green mottled red and deeply notched.

CELESTE—Pring. Viviparous with violet-colored blooms.

N. citrina—An African species with star-shaped yellow blooms. Poor propagator and grower, cultivated only by hybridists and collectors.

CLEVELAND—Rose-pink blossoms.

N. coerulea—The so-called Blue Lotus of the Nile. Not a lotus, but a tropical water-lily of classic species form. Blooms are 6 to 7 inches in diameter, sky-blue, and very fragrant, opening shortly after sunrise and closing about midnight for some growers; they keep usual day-blooming hours with others. Sepals are green spotted black. Grows in northern and central Africa.

> *albiflora*—A rare Egyptian variety with white flowers and the same blooming habits.

COLONEL LINDBERGH—Big sky-blue flower, with wide petals, on long, slender stems. Fragrant. Leaves are large and oval, green marbled brown. A very strong grower.

N. colorata—African species, introduced in 1938. Flowers comparatively small with broad purple-to-lilac petals. Leaves very abundant. rather small and forming a pleasing pattern. Adaptable to limited space.

DAISY—Pring. A comparatively new variety with large white blooms. Viviparous.

N. Daubeniana—Small variety that does best in shallow water. Tremendously popular with fragrant, light-blue flowers. Produces the most beautiful children in the water-lily family. Best viviparous form. Practically all the floating leaves bear tiny, perfect miniature plants, complete with miniature blooms. Compact grower, excellent for tubs and small pools. An ancestor of many of today's best viviparous forms.

DIRECTOR GEORGE T. MOORE—Pring. Rare among flowering plants, blooms of true navy blue, 8 to 10 inches, in great profusion. Glowing, rich-purple leaves, small but numerous.

N. Eastonensis—Another unique shade, a grayish, almost metallic, blue. Attractive, deeply toothed foliage.

EDWARD C. ELLIOT—Pring. Delicate pink 8- to 10-inch blossoms. Yellow stamens tipped pink.

N. elegans—A species that grows freely in Texas and Mexico. Small flowers, delicate lavender-blue with sturdy golden stamens tipped blue. Sepals are green, streaked and spattered black. Free flowering.

N. flavovirens—Commonly called the Frog Water-Lily. Robust little Mexican species with star-shaped blooms, pure white in the center, touched green on the outside, borne well above the water. Delightful lily-of-the-valley scent.

GENERAL PERSHING—Pring. A cross of Mrs. Whitaker and *N. castaliflora,* considered the most successful hybrid and thought by many to be the most beautiful water-lily of all, with 10-inch blooms shaped like a chalice. Very double, fragrant, and of clear, warm pink with a fresh crisp texture. Stamens are yellow, tipped rose.

N. gigantea—A big-flowering species which originated in the lakes and marshes of Australia and New Guinea, sky-blue flowers a foot in diameter.

> *alba*—Large, peony-shaped, white flowers held well above the water with cadmium-yellow, club-shaped stamens. Fragrant. Leaves pale green above and below, with indented margin.

> ALBERT-DE-LESTANG—Flowers and foliage similar to the above except that they are flushed blue the first day and the stamens have a purplish ring at the base.

> *forma media*—Like the species type but considerably smaller.

> *violacea*—Still smaller, with much darker-blue flowers.

GOLDEN WEST—As pretty a lily as I have ever seen, salmon-pink when it opens, changing within a day or two to warm apricot with a heart of golden stamens. Free blooming and fragrant. Foliage is green, speckled maroon.

N. gracilis—A long-stemmed Mexican species with lily-of-the-valley fragrance. Small blooms are white with yellow stamens. Profuse bloomer and exceptionally fine for experiment, for it hybridizes readily. Crossed with *N. capensis zanzibariensis,* it has produced some of the finest tropical hybrids. Another of the questioned species, perhaps not a species but only a rough, uncultivated form of *N. flavovirens.*

> *azurea*—Same as parent species with very pale-blue flowers.

> *purpurea*—Rich-purple flowers.

> *rosea*—A pink form.

> *rubra*—Rich, deep red.

N. Henkeliana—A novelty among tropicals, medium-sized, flat, medium-blue flowers with a delicious violet fragrance.

HENRY SHAW—Pring. An old and ever-popular variety with huge, saucer-shaped blooms the color of bluebells, sweet scented, open from sunup to sundown. Stamens are chrome-yellow. Adapts growth to large or small pool, blooming quite freely in either.

N. heudelotii—Grows in shallow, slow-flowing streams of central Africa and is the baby of all tropicals, with leaves only 2 inches in diameter and bluish-white flowers only half an inch across. Interesting to collectors, but not a rewarding garden plant. Dr. Pring is currently using the species to breed tropical pygmy varieties.

> *nana*—Miniature white blooms on an even smaller plant.

INDEPENDENCE—Unusual, one of the few pinks that is viviparous. (See also Peach Blow, Pink Platter, Talisman, and Wild Rose.) Large and plentiful blooms, opening early, closing late, and of an even shade of rich pink. Begins to bloom when very small, and flowers and foliage grow up together. Very adaptable, good in tub or large pool. Foliage is green shaded brownish-red.

INDEPENDENCE BLUE—The same, except that blossoms are light blue.

ISABELLA PRING—Pring. Developed by the famous hybridizer, who named his first two pure-white lilies for the ladies of his family, this one for his daughter. Bloom is huge, up to 10 inches in diameter, full petaled, and very fragrant, with crisp texture. Viviparous. Stamens are golden yellow, foliage light green.

JANICE—One of the few viviparous whites. The blooms, as they age, sometimes develop a light-blue blush.

JUDGE HITCHCOCK—Flowers cuplike, up to 8 inches across, violet, merging to paler violet toward the center, golden stamens tipped blue. Leaves on the small side, dark green flecked reddish-brown, purplish beneath. Propagates well from tubers, but not viviparous.

JUPITER—You often smell this one before you see it, for it is very fragrant. Blooms are large, deep purple, and of fine texture.

KING OF THE BLUES—A free-blooming variety with deep, navy-blue flowers, yellow stamens tipped blue. Sepals are blue with purple overtones. Develops 7- to 8-inch blooms.

N. Listerii—Medium-sized blooms, rich blue.

DITTMANN—Strong grower with rose-colored blooms.

MARGARET MARY—One of our new developments, the first water-lily practical for aquarium culture both summer and winter. Blooms are star-shaped, about the size of a silver dollar, baby blue petals and a golden center. Floating pads are about 4 inches diameter. Grows in half a pint of earth. Viviparous. Does very well under artificial sunlight of a "Gro-Lux" or similar bulb if a sunny window position cannot be found for it. Also does well in the outdoor pool if set out after continuous warm weather arrives.

MIDNIGHT—Flowers abundant, small, with few large petals and many smaller stamenlike petals toward the center. Rich deep purple with only a small golden center. Buds dark green. Leaves small, dark green, sparsely flecked reddish-brown, purple beneath.

N. Maynardii—Huge blooms, up to 9 inches, of a pale shade of heliotrope.

N. Micheliana—Free growing with pink-lilac flowers.

N. micrantha—A strange species discovered on the West Coast of Africa, viviparous, but not until the third season after planting. Small bloom., almost perfectly white the first season, with a bluish tinge the second, and definitely blue-white the third. Foliage is quite small, in proportion to the bloom. Does well in shallow water.

MRS. C. W. WARD—Rich rose-pink, star-shaped bloom often 10 to 12 inches in diameter with a big cluster of rich yellow stamens. Might be called a pink twin of Blue Beauty, often planted with it.

Mrs. Edwards Whitaker—Pring. A tremendous bloom, up to 12 inches, lavender-blue on opening, finally almost white with pale-yellow stamens tipped lavender. Not free flowering due to tremendous size of bloom. Adjusts well to large or small areas.

> marmorata—Same as above, but blooms only up to 8 inches in diameter and consists of numerous thin, lavender-blue petals. Leaves green, streaked and mottled chestnut-brown.

Mrs. George H. Pring—Pring. A cross of Mrs. Whitaker and N. ovalifolia. Resembles Mrs. Whitaker in form and growing habit but is pure white with yellow, white-tipped stamens and quite fragrant. The first white tropical widely cultivated by water gardeners.

Mrs. Woodrow Wilson—Easy viviparous variety with huge lavender-blue blooms of fine texture. Extensive grower.

> gigantea—Pring. Similar but with even larger blooms of light blue. Very fragrant.

N. ovalifolia—East African species, with small deep-blue flowers that stay closed in dull weather.

Pamela—Broad-petaled, saucer-shaped blooms, somewhat deeper than sky-blue, frequently a foot wide and borne on long stems. Leaves are green, marbled brown.

Panama Pacific—Medium-sized flowers opening deep blue and changing to a deep red-purple within a few days, bright-yellow stamens, very fragrant. Blooms every month of the year if taken indoors before frost. Viviparous.

Patricia—Small with a profusion of crimson blooms. Viviparous. Does well in tubs and small pools.

Peach Blow—Large, full, rounded flowers with many petals and stamens, deep pink, lighter toward the center. Leaves light green, sparsely flecked, fading in age; light green flushed red beneath. Freely viviparous.

Persian Lilac—Flowers moderately large and pink, full and rounded with broad petals, the golden stamens tipped pink. Leaves smallish, light green sparsely flecked brownish, red beneath.

Pink Delight—One of the newer varieties with carmine-pink blooms.

Pink Pearl—Medium-sized, silvery pink blooms with yellow stamens surrounded by a ring of pink anthers. Produces a continuous display.

Pink Platter—Flowers large, wide, flat, moderately full, petals long and narrow, stamens golden below, pink above. Leaves light green prominently flecked reddish-brown. Viviparous.

Pink Star—Pale pink bloom with a touch of lavender. See Star Lilies.

N. polychroma—African species with large, bright-blue flowers touched with mauve.

N. primulina—African species with large, primrose-yellow blooms and purplish foliage.

N. pulcherrima—See Blue Beauty.

RED STAR—Clear red bloom, less prolific bloomer than other star lilies. See Star Lilies.

RIO RITA—Flowers moderately large, deep brilliant pink, almost red, opening wide, the petals broader than Pink Platter, base of stamens bright golden. Leaves smallish, dark green sparsely flecked reddish-brown, red beneath. Weakly viviparous.

ROYAL PURPLE—Vigorous, viviparous form with 6- to 8-inch blooms of deep red-purple.

ST. LOUIS—Pring. One of Dr. Pring's most famous hybrids and the first yellow tropical of importance. Star-shaped, 10-inch blooms of light yellow with deeper yellow stamens. Foliage green, mottled bronze.

ST. LOUIS GOLD—Pring. Medium-sized plant producing citron-yellow flowers 7 to 8 inches across. Leaves 10 to 12 inches in diameter, dark green flushed chocolate-brown, fading green with age. Suitable for small pools.

N. scutifolia—Species similar to *N. capensis,* considered an offshoot by many botanists. Star-shaped blooms, sky-blue and fragrant.

SHELL PINK—Flowers clearer pink than General Pershing, large and firm, bowl-shaped. Leaves dark green flecked reddish-brown, reddish on underside. Sparingly viviparous.

STAR LILIES—Beloved, old-fashioned, day-blooming tropicals, for their blooms are crisply star-shaped and held well above the water on stiff stems. They are among the hardiest of the tropical water-lilies, and prolific bloomers. Water gardeners have reported close to a hundred blooms from one plant in a single season.

STELLA GURNEY—Gurney. Star-shaped flowers of an even, light-pink hue.

N. stellata—Medium-sized flowering species, wild in southern Asia, Java, Borneo, and the Philippine Islands. Star-shaped, light-blue flowers in the species type with little or no fragrance.

rosea—Good variety. Slightly larger, soft-pink flowers.

N. Stuhlmanii—African species, small sulfur-yellow flowers, stamens orange-yellow, sepals a yellowish-green. Sweet scented.

N. sulfurea—Smaller African species, deep-sulfur shade, sweet odor. Seldom cultivated.

SUNBEAM—Pring. New viviparous variety with large, brilliant yellow flowers. Considered the most brilliant yellow among water-lilies.

TALISMAN—Pring. Viviparous hybrid named for the red and yellow rose of the same name. Fine form. Highly viviparous.

N. vivipara—Generally accepted as same species as *N. micrantha.*

WHITE STAR—Waxen white petals. See Star Lilies.

WILD ROSE—Bright, solid, large-petaled, pink flowers with large golden center, stamens pink tipped. Leaves dark green flecked reddish-brown, light green flushed red below. Viviparous.

WILLIAM STONE—Violet-blue flowers shaded amaranth.

YELLOW STAR—Large, shallow, starlike yellow flowers borne well above the water, with relatively few, long, tapered petals. Leaves large and green. Excellent lily for mass display.

ZANZIBAR PURPLE—See *N. capensis zanzibariensis.*

Night-Blooming Tropicals

N. amazonum—Central and South American species, poor for horticulture but interesting. Flowers are large, dirty-yellow white with a strong, pleasant odor of sliced peaches. Blooms open only twice, spreading their petals in early evening and not attaining full size until shortly before sunrise. Blooms submerge when closed.

> *goudotiana*—A sort of bearded variety of the species with long hairs at the top of the stalk.

N. Arnoldiana—Medium-sized blooms of rose-carmine.

B. C. BERRY—Hybrid similar to James Gurney. Flowers shallow and 8 to 9 inches across, amaranth-purple, lighter toward base of petals. Leaves dark green, scarcely mottled, indented at margin.

N. Bissetii—An old favorite. Huge, cup-shaped, 8- to 10-inch blooms with very wide petals of delicate pink. Foliage green, with orange-bronze overcast. Very free flowering.

N. blanda—Small-blooming species, wild in Central and South America and Jamaica. Blooms are thin and yellowish-white, hardly worth cultivating.

> *fenzliana*—As unattractive as the species type, slightly larger.

N. columbiana—Good for contrast with lighter shades. Blooms are dark red.

N. Deaniana—Pretty, old-fashioned water-lily with cup-shaped blooms of clear pink with yellow stamens.

N. delicatissima—Pale-pink blooms and dark metallic foliage.

N. dentata—Central and west African species, may be a variety of *N. lotus.* Large, white, narrow-petaled flowers, sometimes 15 inches wide, with golden stamens red at base. Foliage green and quite toothed.

> *grandiflora*—Even larger blooms, white, with stamens brown at base.
>
> *superba*—Known commercially as Juno, one of the world's best. Huge, pure-white blooms with very wide petals that give a chalice shape.

Sepals green with faint greenish-white streaks. Stamens pure saffron-yellow. The only *N. dentata* hybrid of glistening white, which sets the flower apart, the others having some discoloration at the base of the stamens. Leaves are large, deep green, and finely toothed.

DEVONSHIRE—One of the oldest and choicest night bloomers, bearing as many as ten huge, bright-red flowers at one time. Beautiful under artificial light. Fine for lakes and ponds, for a single plant will easily cover 200 square feet or more in one season.

EMILY GRANT HUTCHINS—Gurney. Striking new variety, large, amaranth-red with curving petals and classic cup-shape. Foliage smaller than that of most tropicals, bronzy green, different enough to be quite noticeable.

FRANK TRELEASE—Gurney. One of the most popular night bloomers, " a man's water-lily," with huge deep-crimson blooms that seem to glow. Red-brown stamens. Easy to propagate, but shy on bloom.

N. Gardneriana—Small-flowering South American species with blooms of an unattractive red and red-brown stamens.

GEORGE HUSTER—Beautiful brilliant red, 12 inches across in ideal conditions. Velvety texture shows up well under artificial light, Thought to be a seedling of *N. Omarana* with *N. rubra rosea* as the pollen parent. Reddish-bronze foliage with crimped edges.

N. Gibertii—Small-flowering species which grows wild in Paraguay, 2 to 3-inch white blooms faintly marked with purple lines.

H. C. HAARSTICK—Pring. A national favorite. Blooms are large, with long, graceful petals of clear, rich red with red-gold stamens. Requires a lot of space and produces a profusion of bloom.

N. indica—The so-called White Lotus of the Nile, Egypt, and Africa. The white, sweet-scented blooms range from 5 to 10 inches in diameter. Species is quite similar to, in fact is the African counterpart of, *N. pubescens*.

BRAHMA—Fiery-rose flowers, not much cultivated in the United States.

GRAEBNER—Similar but of deeper color.

ISIS—Wide, concave-petaled bloom, delicate pink.

SPIRA—Similar but slightly deeper pink.

JAMES GURNEY—Pring. Crimson passing to deep purple-red in maturity.

JUNO—See *N. dentata superba*.

N. kewensis—Very old variety in England and America. Delicate pink, green and brown mottled foliage.

Can you see Johns Hopkins campus reflected in this lily pond in Baltimore, Md.?

LA REINE DE LOS ANGELES—Ten-inch blooms glistening white with exceptionally broad petals.

N. Lotus—Native to west and central Africa, especially Egypt. The species type (which also is frequently listed as White Lotus of the Nile —see *N. indica*) is of average size. White blooms tinged pink on the outside. Stamens are yellow. Only faintly fragrant.

pubescens—Grows freely in India, Java, Australia, and the Philippine Islands. Small white flowers have green stamens and are sweet scented.

MISSOURI—Pring. "Made for the moonlight," huge bloom, up to 14 inches wide, of pure, gleaming white with far more petals than most tropicals. Foliage is green, splotched maroon. For full development, plant requires plenty of well-enriched soil, warm weather, and at least a 9-foot area.

MRS. GEORGE C. HITCHCOCK—Pring. Huge, rose-pink bloom held well above the water. Unusual mahogany stamens.

136

N. Omarana—American hybrid with an Oriental air. Blooms 10 to 12 inches of glowing red with a faint white line running down the center of each petal. Particularly beautiful when lighted by the rising or setting sun. Foliage large and bronzy red, deeply toothed. As the flower matures, sepals and outer petals droop, revealing the deep-orange stamens.

N. Ortgiesiana alba—Huge open flowers of creamy white with purple base. Sepals also creamy, striped green.

rubra—Clear pink shade and quite numerous blooms.

PRESIDENT GIRARD—Medium-sized blooms of rose-carmine.

PRIDE OF CALIFORNIA—Fine form and blood-red coloring.

N. pubescens—A species native to India, Australia, Java, and the Philippine Islands. Flowers are small and white. One of the early English imports.

N. rubra—Native of India and Brazil, one of the most beautiful night-flowering species. Medium sized, very bright-red flowers with red stamens turning to red-brown. Foliage is red-bronze, becoming dark green as plant matures. Parent of many fine hybrids, the Devonshire a notable example.

N. rudgeana—Free-growing South American species with small greenish-yellow blooms and a strong, pleasing lemon odor. Seeds gathered by natives for food.

RUFUS J. LACKLAND—Gurney. Blooms open crimson, shade with age to deep purple.

N. stenispidota—Brazilian species with large crimson flowers, small foliage.

N. Sturtevantii—Huge rosy-pink, cup-shaped blooms with orange-brown stamens. Strong, extensive grower that needs plenty of pool space and a larger than usual planting box. Foliage is bronze with crumpled edges. A group of these is a breathtaking sight on a sunny morning.

N. zenkeri—West African species with 2- to 3-inch white blooms.

CHAPTER EIGHT *Planting the Pool*

After the pool is completed, many a water gardener's first action is to cover the floor with a 5- to 6-inch layer of earth. Having thus "simulated" a natural environment, as he thinks he should, he then proceeds to plant—and to wonder thereafter why his water-lilies don't do as well as the ones next door.

Planting On the Pool Floor

I can't imagine why so many gardeners persist in planting directly on the floor of a deep pool, or even in permanent built-in boxes, for there isn't a dealer I know who recommends it. It makes for muddy, awkward maintenance work, and furthermore does not get the lilies off to a good start.

In either case, it is necessary to plant the pool while it is empty and then to add the water. This is risky business, since water-lilies are shipped after growth has started and plants can easily be rendered inactive again by a severe shock. Water fed into a pool from a household tap is cold enough to give many species just such a stunting shock. Plants will recover, but perhaps not until well along in the season.

The alternative is to add enough water to cover the crowns of the plants for only an inch or so. In the course of a day the sun will warm the shallow water, and the probability of shock be greatly reduced. In a few days, a few more inches of water can be added, and so on until the pool is full. This procedure is usually safe enough but awfully slow and tedious.

Of course, if the pool is shallow, say only 12 to 15 inches deep, there is no choice but to plant directly in soil spread on the bottom. Pools this shallow can be filled with water immediately and then allowed to warm up for several days before they are planted.

Planting in Movable Receptacles

Planting in one of the many kinds of movable receptacles has advantages which are obvious. Most important, it enables a gardener to clean out his pool as early as he likes in spring, fill it with fresh water, and let the water be warming under the sun until planting time.

Movable boxes also make the work far easier. With a box, wooden pail, or small tub, you can work where you choose, and in a comfortable position, setting the receptacles into place in the pool when you are finished. Then you can rearrange them in the pool as often as you like without damage to the plants. You will also find it a simple matter to take up a particular lily, should you want to fertilize it or cut a rootstock from it for a friend.

PROTECTING THE ROOTS

You will have a cleaner, healthier pool if you prop up all planting receptacles a few inches from the floor. It is easy, with a clear floor, to take a rake now and then and pull out leaves and twigs that fall in and otherwise might accumulate on the floor and decompose, eventually fouling the water. Propped-up boxes also give goldfish a lot more freedom, and provide them with shade, which they need in hot summer weather.

Cigarette lighters, rings, keys, and so on, *do* get dropped into pools from time to time, and you may have to get into your pool one day to retrieve something of the sort. You can kill a water-lily quite easily by stepping on the root, but you can wade among them safely enough if the roots are confined in containers.

Planting receptacles are an absolute necessity for water-lilies in farm ponds to which livestock have access. Horses and cattle will walk *around* the boxes, buckets, or tubs of lilies, but will walk right on a plant if it is not protected.

CONTROLLED GROWTH

Movable receptacles also have the advantage of controlling growth. Water-lilies, in their many varieties, are much like people. Some are shy and retiring; some bold, ambitious, and ruthless, and the strong crowd out the weak in short order if they are not restrained. The most practical way of keeping a strong, prolific water-lily in check is by planting it in a container where you can limit the food supply and thus prevent over-zealous spreading. For a weaker species, you can keep soil and fertilizer in one spot where roots will have exclusive access to it. Boxes are a great help also when you set out the tropical water-lily seedlings you have developed indoors during the winter. Turned loose in a pool with an assortment of adult plants, the seedlings can be quickly overwhelmed.

REGULATING DEPTH

The ideal water depth for lilies in a pool ranges from 2 to 3 inches for some varieties to 2 to 3 feet for others. A single species—particularly a tropical seedling—will do far better if, in early stages of growth, it passes through increasing depths by progressive stages. Placing a planting box in the water at the exact depth you want is quite easy. Simply prop it up at the desired height with bricks. As the season moves on and growth progresses, you can increase the depth gradually by pulling out one layer of bricks at a time.

Planting Boxes, Buckets, Tubs

Water-lilies can be planted in much the same kind of container you use for your porch flowers—with one exception. Because of the tremendous growth they make in a season, water-lilies require quite a bit more soil and fertilizer. Even the shy ones are voracious, and the more luxuriant the foliage and bloom, it seems, the healthier the appetite.

At this point, I think it would be a good thing to mention that the tremendous blooms pictured in water-lily catalogs are not exaggerations. Flowers *will* attain the near unbelievable size the dealers claim they will, provided plants are set out and fed according to directions. So give them plenty of sunlight, plenty of soil, and plenty of fertilizer. Don't cheat water-lilies on their food allowance and they won't cheat you on bloom.

The ideal container is about 18 inches square and 10 inches deep, although, if you must, you can get by with something a little smaller— say a cubic foot of earth. Anything larger then 2 by 2 feet by 10 inches deep is a waste of space. As for strength, any container will do that will hold together well enough for you to move it about and take it out of the pool occasionally.

A stroll through your basement, garage, or outbuilding will probably reveal a number of receptacles that will be very satisfactory for planting. Orange crates and bushel baskets are too flimsy. Wooden packing boxes, the kind once widely used to ship canned goods, are excellent. Cardboard cartons are worse than useless; after a week under water they disintegrate and drop the lily root, soil, and fertilizer onto the pool floor.

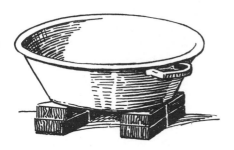

DISHPAN

CEDAR PLANTING PAIL

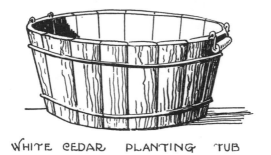

WHITE CEDAR PLANTING TUB

PLANTING BOX

SHALLOW PLANTING BOX

DRAWING 21.   *Planting Receptacles to Use in the Pool.*

Such flimsy cartons work out well enough on the soft dirt bottom of a pond, where mess is not a problem, and give the plant a slight advantage.

Wooden tubs, buckets, and half-barrels are fine, so long as they are clean and have never held any substance containing oil.

Metal tubs, buckets, and similar containers also do well, but don't use any such container made of copper. An old-fashioned dishpan, the kind which turns up at every country auction, is excellent.

Any water-lily dealer will sell you, or tell you where to buy, planting boxes, tubs, and buckets. It is also a simple matter to nail together your own. Make planting boxes of used lumber, if possible; otherwise buy cypress or white cedar. Other new woods exude a "flavor" that is harmful to goldfish.

Avoid redwood. It discolors the water with an exudation which stunts water-lilies. If boxes have wide cracks, line with wrapping or newspaper to prevent soil from washing out.

Soil

It is important to start with proper soil, since the basic food for both hardy and tropical water-lilies is good, firm garden loam which you should enrich in ways which we will discuss later. Starting with a poor soil, and trying to build it up with fertilizer, does not work out well. In light or weak soil, regardless of how well it is fertilized, water-lily growth will go into foliage.

Swamp muck, although it may look black and rich enough to grow hair on an egg, will not do. Actually, there is very little nutritive material in muck. What there is will very likely be in the form of only partially decomposed vegetation. As decomposition is completed in the pool, gases are produced and the muck turns sour, fouling the water and creating an unhealthy environment for goldfish.

River mud cannot be used for the same reason. Leafmold, although it contains plant food, will foul a pool as it decomposes. Heavy clays are very good for water-lilies since they contain potash. However, they cannot be used unless well mixed with lighter soil, for it is difficult for lily roots to penetrate solid clay and absorb food from it.

I would emphasize again the importance of starting with the best possible soil, which an experienced water gardener will tell you is either a good fibrous loam or garden soil fertilized as I suggest below. If the soil is too light, the growth will go into leaves instead of blooms. Lotus plants do well in soil with up to a 25 per cent mixture of clay in it, but the roots of most water-lilies have trouble penetrating and utilizing soils with heavy clay content.

The soil should be free of peat moss, sand and rotted wood.

142

Fertilizers

If you live on a dairy farm or have a friend who does, your best bet is natural fertilizer. That means well-rotted cow manure, one part to three parts of garden soil. Use commercial dried cow manure much more sparingly, at a ratio of one part to eight or ten parts of soil, or 4 quarts to 1 bushel of soil.

Never use fresh manure of any kind. It will sour whatever soil it is put into, color pool water to a point of unsightliness, and probably promote a quick and heavy growth of green slime.

Next best—and I place them second on the list only because you can't get them free—are the various commercial fertilizers offered by most water-lily dealers. The one we recommend to our customers is a 10-10-10 mixture—that is, 10 units of nitrogen, 10 of superphosphate, and 10 of potash. Such fertilizers come with explicit mixing instructions, most of them prescribing about a pound or a "double handful" to each container of soil. All-purpose commercial mixtures also are satisfactory applied at about the same ratio.

Many water gardeners prefer bone meal, a good-sized double handful of it to each plant container. It is a good fertilizer, but I don't recommend it too strongly, since water-lilies can't seem to do as well on its phosphates as they can on manure, prepared fertilizers, and other richer nitrogenous compounds.

Blood meal is probably as good as any other available water-lily fertilizer, but it requires a certain amount of forethought. Add about a quart of it to each bushel of soil and, for best results, do this mixing two or three weeks ahead of planting.

I get letters now and then from water gardeners who report they are producing healthy lilies with a one-to-ten mixture of dried sheep manure and garden soil. I also hear from gardeners who claim wondrous results from horse manure mixed with soil. I would just have to see good results from these fertilizers with lilies before I'd believe them. I have seen too many plantings killed by sheep and horse manure.

I advise against experimenting with other manures, for most of them decompose so rapidly they produce enough heat to burn roots. Poultry guano makes a particularly hot fertilizer.

One good additive for any fertilized soil (but never used *instead* of fertilizer) is sod. Small chunks of rotted sod are especially beneficial.

Most gardeners look upon tropical water-lilies as annuals, let them die when winter comes, and order new plants in spring. A few take some of their tropicals indoors at the end of the season and propagate them during the winter. In either case, tropical water-lilies must be set out anew in the pool each summer. And they must be set out, of course, in a fresh supply of soil and fertilizer.

Hardy water-lilies may be left in the pool from one year to the next, but the gardener must remember to repot them occasionally. A hardy lily planted in barely a cubic foot of soil and fertilizer may have to have its food supply replenished even after one season. If planted in something more capacious, say a container holding a cubic foot and a half or more of soil, then a hardy lily probably will do well for two or three seasons—even longer—without a change of soil. It is good to lift the hardies up every three or four years, whether they seem to need it or not, to prune them down a bit, and to trim a few of the growing points from the rootstocks.

Occasionally there are signs of "hunger"—leaves much smaller than they should be and of a sickly yellow color, small blooms and not many of them, or general apathy and lack of healthy growth and expansion.

It is dangerous to uproot a lily and replant it in a box of fresh soil and fertilizer in the middle of its growing season, but it is easy enough to give hungry plants additional food without disturbing them. Make "vitamin pills" for them as large as grapefruit by mixing bone meal with just enough clay to bind it. Without lifting the lily container from position, thrust one of the pills next to the roots. Very large plants should get two such pills. Or make an even quicker pill by putting a good handful of blood meal into a paper bag, and thrust the bag into the soil beneath a root. The good results of either treatment will show in a few days.

COMPOST

Thus far we have been speaking of planting soil and fertilizer as materials to be brought together on the day of planting. If you can prepare the soil ahead of time, you will not only make planting a more leisurely job, but you will also provide better plant food for your lilies.

The best compost is started in the fall. Use the same good heavy garden soil, six parts to one part of fresh cow manure, and place the compost bed under a shed roof, where rain and sun won't hit it directly; or, if it must be outside, cover with boards, linoleum, or other watershedding cover. Layer the materials, an inch of manure to six of earth, and turn the mixture with a spade about every six weeks. Turn it again just before you use it.

Bone meal, a double handful to each cubic foot of soil, makes another good compost. Turn it the same way.

Planting Methods

Hardy water-lilies come from the dealer in one of two forms—a piece of rootstock with growing stems, leaves, and probably a bud or two, or just a piece of rootstock.

ROOTSTOCKS

Rootstocks are of three kinds. Those of the *odorata* species are long, fleshy rhizomes, earth colored, with the size and shape of a 6- to 8-inch section of broom handle. Eyes, like potato sprouts, occur every few inches along the root. The eyes develop into new plants.

Rootstocks of the *tuberosa* species are of similar size and shape, but are covered with spines like those on an alligator pear, and the stems are hairy. Both species propagate by sending up new plants from eyes along the roots. If left alone for many years, roots grow to 3 feet or so. In your pool, roots will lengthen enough in a year or two for you to cut off section which will soon make nice new plants for your friends.

The rootstocks of the Marliac Hybrids, most of them crosses with *odorata or tuberosa* varieties, or both, form a tight perpendicular tangle, crowned by a single growing point. As the mass grows larger and larger it produces additional growing points, and thus the Marliacs propagate themselves. A water-lily of this type may be about the size of a small pineapple when first set out. Two or three years later, if undisturbed, the plant may have a dozen growing points with a root area of bushel-basket proportions.

WHEN TO PLANT

If you plan to plant a number of water-lilies, it is a good idea to have soils and fertilizers mixed and containers collected, and perhaps even filled. The nurseryman will not send plants to you until the weather in your particular area is safe for setting them out. As I have said, growth will already have started. Plant as soon as possible after arrival as a safeguard against drying out, which might check new growth. Avoid exposure to sun. Even half an hour of it is harmful. If you cannot plant, open the box or package anyway, put the plants in a shady place, cover with a piece of wet burlap, and keep it wet.

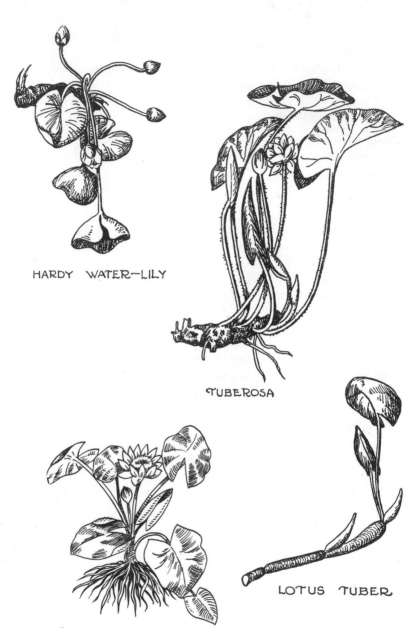

HARDY WATER—LILY

TUBEROSA

TROPICAL LILY

LOTUS TUBER

DRAWING 22. *Hardy and Tropical Water-Lilies as They Come from the Dealer.*

MARLIAC

TUBEROSA

ODORATA

DRAWING 23.   *Hardy Water-Lily Rootstocks*

The time you receive your order of hardy water-lilies will depend on where you live. If in Horticultural Zone 3, a broad band extending from New York to Chicago and points west, safe planting time will be about mid-April. If you live south of Zone 3, you can plant somewhat earlier; if you live north of it, you will plant later.

Time of shipment for hardy water-lilies will also depend on the judgment of your dealer. If there has been a late spring and summer is slow in getting underway, your dealer may not ship until well into May—comfortably beyond any possibility of a late killing frost.

The dealer will ship tropical water-lilies with the same safety factors in mind. If you live in Zone 3, you probably will get your tropicals around the first week of June. Your hardies, by that time, ought to be well started, but the tropicals make up for late arrival with a long season. In mild winters, I have seen the tropicals blooming as late as the first week of December, long after the hardies have given up for the year.

PLANTING THE HARDIES

Planting is simplicity itself. Dry soil does not bind well, so wet the soil in the container so that you can press it snugly in and around the root. Lay *odorata* and *tuberosa* type roots horizontally, an inch below the surface of the soil, with the growing tip extending above the surface. This tip may be only a sprout. It may be developing flower and leaf stems a few inches long, or even up to 2 feet.

Place a flat stone, as large as your hand, over part of the root to keep it submerged, but be careful not to touch the growing point. Cover the soil surface in the container with sand, finely crushed stone, or gravel, but keep this also away from the growing point. This top layer will keep goldfish from disturbing the soil and thus clouding the pool.

If the stems of the lily you are planting are fairly well developed, set the container in the pool so that 16 to 18 inches of water covers the crown. If the leaves lack an inch or so of reaching the water surface, don't worry about them. They will adjust themselves to their water depth within a few days.

However, if growth has just begun to develop, prop up the container so that only a few inches of water cover the point. There the warmth of the sun will easily penetrate the water to stimulate growth. After a week or so, as stems and leaves develop rapidly, the plant can be dropped down to full depth.

Plant the pineapple-shaped Marliac roots perpendicular, with just the crown extending above the surface of the soil. Set them in the pool, near the surface if necessary, as you would *odorata* and *tuberosa* plants.

Watch the level of the water after planting either hardies or tropicals. If thè water lowers appreciably the stems will curl in order to keep the buds under water until they are ready to open. You will get quicker blooms if the plants are placed in their proper, comfortable level.

First-day blooms come out an hour later and close an hour earlier. Both opening and closing take about an hour.

Planting the Tropicals

Planting of the tropicals differs only a little from that of the hardies, but the differences are important. As I have indicated, they are set out about six weeks later, when water in the pool attains and holds to a temperature of about 70 degrees. Tropicals are planted shallower. At Lilypons, they do best with about a foot of water above the crowns.

Tropicals produce more foliage and more flowers than hardies, and therefore need more food. Use the same mixtures of soil and fertilizer for both, but plant the tropicals in containers half again as large as those for the hardies.

Tropical water-lilies are also sent from the dealer as growing plants. Their roots will be encased in a moist packing material. Remove this, prepare a hole for the root in the planting receptacle, and place it in carefully, packing the earth around it snugly but not tightly. Cover the planting soil with sand or gravel, as you did with the hardies.

Although hardies extend their long-stemmed leaves easily to the surface from a submerged position, the tropicals do best if at least a few of their leaves float comfortably on the surface when they are first planted. The container can be lowered in the water as the plant grows.

Be especially careful to protect leaves and roots of tropicals from wind and sun before they are planted. Their leaves are extremely thin, and wither easily. Untangle the stems so the leaves can float easily, and make sure all leaves float right side up.

Deep Planting

Any of the containers I have suggested for pools can also be used in a natural pond. In deep water, where there is no danger of trampling by livestock and where the gardener has no intention of ever disturbing the plants, lilies can be set out in flimsy containers, or without containers at all. In fact, if they are used, the flimsiest of containers are preferred, for they disintegrate quickly and allow the roots to spread and seek nourishment where they will.

Bushel and half-bushel baskets serve the purpose nicely here. Fill each one with soil, plant the root, cover with a layer of stones to hold the root in place (being careful not to touch the growing point). Slip a rope through the basket handles, lower the basket into place, and then pull up the rope.

There is also the traditional method of planting lilies in deep water. I am giving it last because I like it least. This method consists of tying a water-lily root firmly to half a brick, rowing out to the desired planting spot, and heaving root and brick overboard. If the root happens to land topside up, this is a good system. However, if it lands the other way, you may break off the growing point or the stem, or bury the root in such a position that it cannot grow.

A better deep planting approach is the "hot dog" method. Take a piece of sod as large as a table place mat, 5 or 6 inches thick. Spread out the sod, grass side down, and work some fertilizer into the dirt. Place the water-lily root in the center, roll the sod up like a hot dog, and tie into shape with cloth tape. (Cord or wire quickly cuts through the turf.) Drop into pond.

When planting in deep water, be sure to mark all the selected areas ahead of time with long poles. This enables you to hold to the planting pattern you wish. Once a plant has been lowered, even if the water is only 3 or 4 feet deep, it is practically impossible to find it until leaves and blooms reach the surface, unless the planting place is so marked.

PLANTING IN SHALLOW WATER

Most professional growers, who can raise and lower the level of their natural-type ponds at will, prefer to plant directly on the bottom through 3 or 4 inches of water. You can plant this way in any pond shallow enough for you to touch bottom with your hands. Sink the head of your shovel at an angle into the mud floor and pry up a wedge of soil. Place the lily root in position beneath the wedge, pull out the shovel, and press the wedge firmly over the root with your foot.

An excellent shallow water planting technique is the "hot dog" method, applied more carefully. Plant a water-lily root in this one with the growing point barely exposed at the top.

Wade to the planting site with the bundles of sod and roots, hold the bundles under water until they are water soaked, then set them in place and leave.

For such free and natural planting as this, use only the Marliac type water-lilies if you want to keep strict control of them, for Marliacs do not spread widely. Forms of the *odorata* and *tuberosa* turned loose on

Plate 19. Ordinarily, a fountain looks out of place in an informal water garden. This simple spout of water, however, fits in charmingly. The sight of falling water is always pleasant, and the sound of it has a psychologically cooling effect on a hot day.

their own would soon take over a whole pond, the *tuberosa* being the more prolific.

Tropicals can be planted freely anywhere, since they will not live over the winter in most places. If they do survive, their growth will not get out of hand. (Except, of course, in the tropics. It happens now and then in the Canal Zone and the West Indies.)

151

CHAPTER NINE

Propagation, Culture, and Winter Care

Do not waste your time and effort trying to cross a hardy water-lily with a tropical water-lily. They do not cross. Nor do day-blooming and night-blooming tropicals.

The most widely used method of propagating hardy water-lilies is by root division. Plants have to be brought up from the bottom of the pool every second or third spring anyway, removed from the containers, and replanted in fresh supplies of soil and fertilizer. The roots are divided at this time.

Hardies can be divided successfully at any time in their normal growing season, from the latter part of April to the first or second week in October. The only disadvantage of disturbing the plants in their heavy growing season is that it will rob you of some blooms. We feel we do better by dividing ours in April or May. If you would rather divide the hardies later, do so in the Fall. Plant these Fall divisions and set them low in the pool to sleep for the winter. Each will come to life in the Spring as a new plant.

Propagation of the Hardies

Whether or not you want to start new plants, root division is still necessary every two or three years. Rootstocks of some of the stronger-growing forms, if left alone four or five years, become quite cumbersome. At this stage many of them become torpid, their vitality seriously impaired. Keep this in mind if the blooms and foliage of your plants begin to look sickly and listless after years of faithful, vigorous production. Division usually restores health quickly.

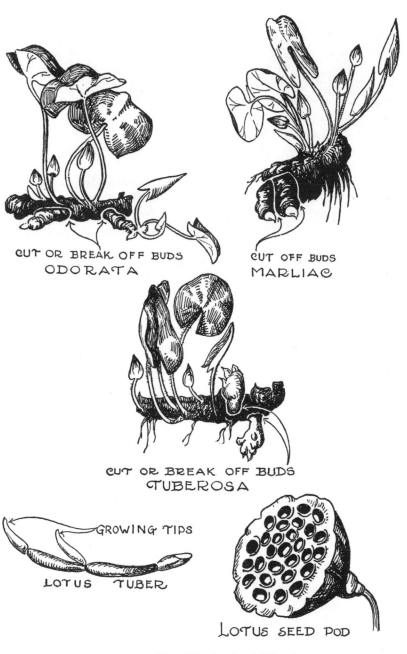

CUT OR BREAK OFF BUDS
ODORATA

CUT OFF BUDS
MARLIAC

CUT OR BREAK OFF BUDS
TUBEROSA

GROWING TIPS

LOTUS TUBER

LOTUS SEED POD

DRAWING 24. *Methods of Division.*

By Root Division

Root division is a quick and simple operation. First, wash off the roots so that you can see what you are doing. You will notice growing points, which look like the eyes of sprouted potatoes, springing from the long, cylindrical *odorata* and *tuberosa roots*. With a sharp knife, cut each root into 6- to 8-inch sections, making sure that each section has a growing point or two. Plant the sections as you would rootstocks from a dealer, and each "eye" or growing point will produce a new water-lily.

The Marliac-type root, a thick, tight, shapeless tangle, seems more difficult to divide at first glance. Wash it off and then examine it carefully. You won't have much trouble recognizing the clean and tender growing points with bits of last season's stems clinging to them. With a long, sharp knife or a hacksaw, cut the root clump into three, four, five, or more pieces, leaving one or two growing points on each piece. Then set out the divisions as you would new water-lilies.

Every time you divide roots you will have more left than you can give away. It seems a shame to throw away all that potential beauty, but it is far better to get rid of your extra stock than to overcrowd your pool by keeping it.

By Seed—Hybridization

Hardy water-lilies can be propagated by seed, but it is a slow, painstaking process, with not much assurance to the amateur hybridist of enough new plants to pay him for his time and effort. The hardies, as a group, are notoriously reluctant to set seed. However, working with seeds is extremely interesting. So, to those water gardeners who play the game for the game's sake, and not alone for the prize, here is the procedure:

Make up your mind at the beginning whether you want to reproduce plants like the parent species or variety form, or try for a new hybrid. If you want true reproduction, you need only keep matching parent plants to themselves, and protecting them from stray pollen. You can help out with the pollination if you like, but most of the hardies that set seed at all are self-seeding. If you want to try for a new hybrid, you will combine—or *try* to combine—the colors and characteristics of two different species or varieties.

The Best Time. To propagate next summer's water-lilies by seed, we begin, of course, with this summer's blooms. Save your experiment for late summer, since flowers are more fertile and receptive then. Select

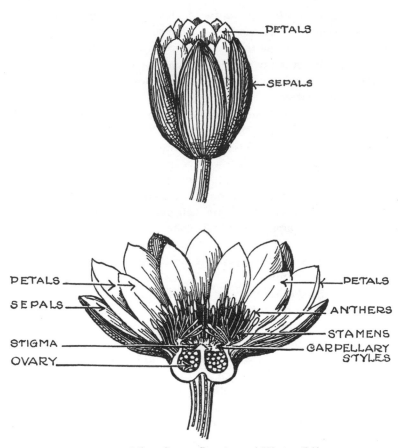

PETALS

SEPALS

PETALS

SEPALS

STIGMA

OVARY

PETALS

ANTHERS

STAMENS

CARPELLARY
STYLES

DRAWING 25. *Cross Section of Water-Lily.*

the pollen and the seed parents carefully, keeping in mind just what colors and characteristics you want to combine, and making doubly sure that the seed parent you have selected is a fertile one. Many water-lily forms, especially among the varieties, are quite sterile.

Nymphaea odorata and practically all of its varieties—particularly *caroliniana, gigantea, minor, rosea,* and *luciana*—set enough seed to make your experiment worthwhile. This is also true of the species types of *N. alba, candida, flava, mexicana, pygmaea,* and *tetragona,* and *N. tuberosa* is a good bet in its species type and in the *rosea* and *richard-sonii* varieties. You may also have fair luck with *N. gladstoniana.*

155

Once you have selected the two forms, you may want to conduct a double experiment. Use one form as the seed parent in the first experiment, the other form as the pollen parent. In the second experiment, reverse the roles of the two parents. The progeny should be the same in all such cases of reciprocal crosses, but the double effort will give a better chance for success.

Selecting the Seed Plant. Now you must wait for nature to produce for you a set of circumstances favorable for hybridization. First, the bloom which is to be the seed parent must be freshly opened. You can watch a particular bud for a few days and get a pretty good idea when it is going to break into bloom. The day before it does, open the bud, trim off its anthers, and keep the bud covered with cheesecloth to protect it from insects. As the bloom will open naturally in the forenoon, it will be easy to catch. When the bloom opens, you will see a drop of sticky nectar resting precisely in the middle of the stigma. Cover the bloom with cheesecloth to keep out insects and wind-borne pollen, and go get the pollen parent.

Selecting the Pollen Parent and Making the Cross. The pollen parent you select must be a flower in its *second* day of blooming. This is absolutely necessary, for the pollen on the flower's anthers is not ripe and cannot be liberated from the anthers until the second day. This flower, too, should have been spotted and protected from stray pollen by a covering of cheesecloth. With tweezers and a pair of manicure scissors, snip off a couple of pollen-laden anthers and place them carefully, pollen-side down, upon the drop of nectar in the chosen seed parent. The cross has now been made, but this is only the first of several intricate steps in hybridization. If you are making a reciprocal cross, use other flowers of the same species, in the same process, with the parental roles reversed.

Protecting the Cross. Take a square of cheesecloth somewhat larger than a man's handkerchief and cover the fertilized bloom to protect it from further fertilization by insects or wind-borne pollen—and wait. And wait and wait and wait. While you are waiting, it might be a good idea to repeat the performance with other blooms as often as you can. As I mentioned before, hardy water-lilies are reluctant to set seed, and your chances of getting seed you can plant are, frankly, fairly poor.

Development of Seeds. In about a week, if the cross has been unsuccessful, seed pod and stem will begin to rot. If the hybridization "took," the seed pod will begin to swell after a couple of weeks, dropping beneath the water as it enlarges. Tie a string around the stem of the seed parent, if you like, so you can pull it up and look at it occasionally. The enlarging seed pod becomes the "fruit" of the water-lily. Two or three

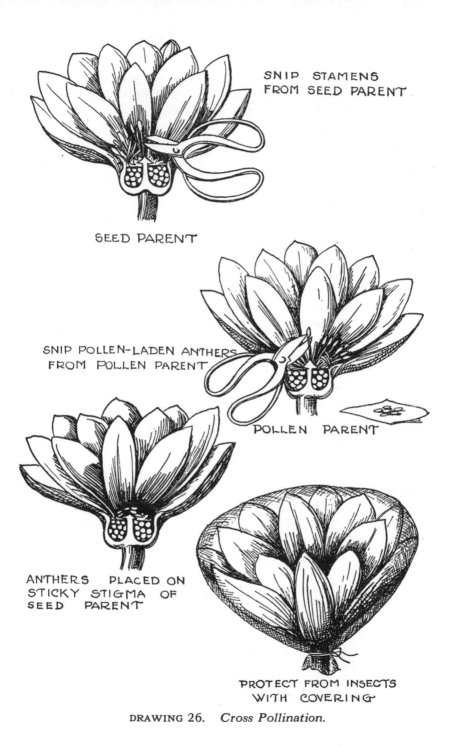

SNIP STAMENS
FROM SEED PARENT

SEED PARENT

SNIP POLLEN-LADEN ANTHERS
FROM POLLEN PARENT

POLLEN PARENT

ANTHERS PLACED ON
STICKY STIGMA OF
SEED PARENT

PROTECT FROM INSECTS
WITH COVERING

DRAWING 26. *Cross Pollination.*

157

days before it is completely ripe, it will rise to the surface again. Finally it will burst, scattering the seeds.

Water-lily seeds are greenish-black or brown, some like tiny apple seeds, others as large as peas and almost globular. Some species and varieties produce only six or seven seeds; others, particularly among the tropical species, produce ten times that many.

If the seeds had not been caught by the cheesecloth you fastened around the pod, they would have been kept afloat by a coating of colorless mucilaginous matter. This is nature's way of allowing the seed to float away from the mother plant and establish itself in a new, less crowded place where it will have a better chance of survival. The buoyant matter dissolves in a few days and the seed drops to the bottom.

Remove the seeds from the cheesecloth and put them in a jar of water. Plant as soon as possible, after coatings have dissolved, but keep seeds in water until you do.

Sowing the Seeds. Fill a shallow pan with finely screened soil, and sift a thin layer of fine sand over it. Sow the seeds and cover with a quarter-inch or less of soil. Saturate the soil with water. Let the pan remain in this condition for a day or two to give the seeds a chance to become thoroughly soaked. Then lower the pan into water, with the seeds $\frac{1}{4}$ to $\frac{1}{2}$ inch below the surface.

Both the germinating seeds and the seedlings which will develop from them must be kept in water at a temperature of 70 to 80 degrees. Finally, the seedlings appear, looking very much like tender new shoots of grass. Transplant them to 2-inch pots as soon as they have formed their first floating leaves, and keep them submerged a few inches.

Care of Seedlings. From this point on seedlings require not only warm temperature, but also full sun. As they grow, move them to 3-inch pots, then to 4's. Mix a small amount of well-rotted cow manure or other acceptable fertilizer with the potting soil in the 3-inch pots. Fill the 4-inch pots with the regular mixture of soil and fertilizer recommended for adult lilies.

Maintain the plants in this way, moving them into ever larger pots as growth warrants, until time for planting outdoors in midsummer. The frequent transplantings are necessary. You must supply pots only as large as the plants need, because inactive submerged soil in a larger container will turn sour. Your seedlings will die if it does.

After you plant outside, wait as patiently as you can for your new hybrid to bloom. Who knows? Perhaps you will have developed a hardy blue water-lily, which does not exist at the present time. If you do, incidentally, please get in touch with me. I will trade you my hat and dog and practically any amount of money I can raise for it.

Plate 20. *A large pool assortment of tropical water-lilies, at the home of E. K. Van Swearingen, Alexandria, Virginia.*

PROPAGATION BY RUNNER

There is only one species of hardy water-lily, to my knowledge, that reproduces in any way other than by root division or seed. This is *Nymphaea mexicana,* which sends long, slender runners out through the mud from its rootstock. The runners terminate in new plants, which take root, develop, and then send out runners of their own. If this species is not watched, it can make a spreading nuisance of itself.

FASCIATION

You have undoubtedly heard of people "going to pieces" under nervous strain, and there may have been times when you felt like it yourself. But you will never see any living thing go to pieces in a more complete and literal fashion than various species and varieties of hardy water-lilies when afflicted by a strange malformation called fasciation.

The sight is most alarming. If it occurs while you have been away for a weekend, you will come back to plants that look as if a giant had taken a club and smashed the leaves into a thousand pieces, but each piece will be a perfect miniature leaf an inch or two wide. One water-lily plant will cover the whole end of a pool with these tiny leaves. There will be no blooms, large or small.

Nobody seems to know what causes fasciation. We know only that it happens to some water-lilies when they get old, after they have bloomed normally and well for a number of years. And we know that some species and varieties are more prone to it than others, as *Nymphaea Ellisiana, Marliacea carnea* and *chromatella, gloriosa,* and *N. pygmaea alba, alba rubra,* and *helvola.*

The main root of an affected plant will be useless thereafter, so there is nothing to do but pull it out. It will be difficult to examine the root closely, for it will be covered with a tight and twisted mass of small leaves and stems. By removing some of the leaves, however, you probably will be able to find a few normal growing points. These can be cut off and planted as rootstocks. They will grow normally and not revert to fasciation, at least not for several years.

Don't worry about other water-lilies in the pool. We do not know much about fasciation, but we do know that it is not catching.

Propagating the Tropicals

BY SEED—HYBRIDIZATION

Most water gardeners treat tropical water-lilies as annuals, allowing them to die off in the winter, ordering new stock in the spring. And yet they can be propagated in many more ways than the hardies can, although, it is true, not as easily.

All you have to do to carry the hardies through the winter is to lower them to the pool bottom, where they will be safely below the frost line. To carry the tropicals over, a certain amount of winter work indoors is necessary. Because they are inexpensive, most water gardeners prefer to order new stock every year and avoid the winter care.

As with the hardies, propagation of tropical water-lilies by hybridization is a fascinating pursuit for those who want to take the trouble. The procedure is the same, but infinitely more rewarding if you are working with the tropical species. These seed quite freely and produce successfully from seed. Many tropical hybrids do not seed freely.

The better seed-bearing day-blooming tropicals for hybridization include *Nymphaea capensis, coerulea, gracilis, flavovirens,* and *elegans; N. capensis zanzibariensis, rosea, azurea,* and Blue Beauty.

160

Plate 20

Plates 20-23. Four steps in the construction of a puddled concrete pool, a technique recommended for irregular shapes. *Plate 20* shows excavation, with bed of tamped stone forming the foundation. *Plate 21* shows floor and walls formed of concrete, without use of forms. *Plate 22* shows emplacement of stones around edge to make a natural setting. *Plate 23* shows the completed pool, with bog plants covering the awkward place where the earth meets the edge of the pool.

GENEREUX PHOTOS

Plate 21

161

Plate 22

Plate 23

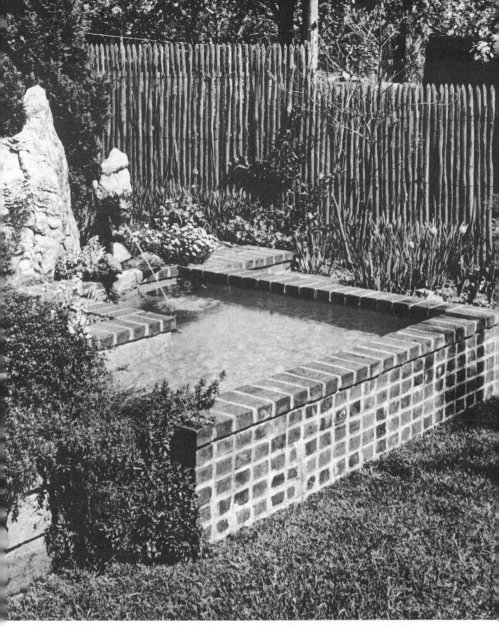

Plate 24. Pools situated partially or completely above ground level are attractive and have two special advantages—toddling children are safe around them, and the pool walls make a comfortable place for the water gardener to sit and enjoy his flowers and fish.

Plate 25. The *Victoria regia* is the most spectacular plant of the water-lily family with huge, cup-shaped bloom, having a strong fragrance of crushed pineapple, and tremendous floating leaves. The flower, about to emerge from the four-inch bud shown near the center of the photograph, opens creamy white and changes, through deepening shades of pink, to deep purple-red.

A. AUBREY BODINE PHOTO

The better night bloomers for hybridizing include *Nymphaea lotus* and *dentata, N. dentata superba* and *magnifica, Bissettii, Omarana,* George Huster, Jubilee, *N. rubra, N. Deaniana,* Missouri, Mrs. George Hitchcock, and B. C. Berry.

Selecting the Seed Parent. Like the hardies, the tropicals are most fertile late in the blooming season. Select the seed parent, and two or three days before it opens naturally, carefully force it open. Snip off the stamens and remove them with tweezers. Slip a rubber band over the tip of the bud to keep it from opening again, or cover with cheese-cloth to keep out insects and foreign pollen.

Selecting the Pollen Parent. Two days later select the pollen parent, a bloom in its second day (or night) of flowering. Snip off the pollen-laden anthers (as you did when you hybridized the hardy water-lily) and place them upon the sticky stigma of the chosen seed parent. Take extra care in this procedure. While you transfer them, cover the anthers by putting them into an envelope or bottle. The tropicals are exceedingly fertile and readily pick up unwanted pollen from the air.

Collect the resulting seeds, plant them, rear the seedlings, and finally, as with the hardies, plant them outdoors, but somewhat later in the season.

BY ROOT DIVISION

Hybridizing and propagating the tropicals by seed can be interesting, but there are surer, less troublesome ways, the simplest being root division. Before freezing weather, dig up tubers of the tropicals. They look like nuts or miniature sweet potatoes. Store them in a jar of cool, moist sand for the winter. Cover the jar, for mice love the roots. Keep this winter bedding material moist to preclude dry rot. Some of the tubers, even if they are kept moist, will undoubtedly rot anyway, for it takes professional knowledge to winter them with confidence. However, a few of them will probably get through in good enough condition to plant again when established warm weather arrives.

Give yourself every chance. Save only what healthy planting stock you need. Examine the larger tubers, the ones which rot most readily, and you will notice that many have developed tubers resembling small walnuts. These are new tubers. Cut them off and store them in the clean, cool, damp sand, and most of them will keep.

Don't throw away the old tubers which produced the last season. These can be easily identified, for leaf stems converge on them at the point where they emerge from the tuber. Packed into winter bedding as the new tubers were, many of them will come healthily through the winter and produce the following season.

A month before you plan to plant the tubers outdoors, take them from the sand and plant them in soil in shallow water indoors. If kept at 70 to 80 degrees they will produce leaves in two weeks. At this point transfer the plants to pots, keep them submerged at an ever increasing depth as the plants grow, and maintain them this way until it is warm enough to move them to the pool outside. Temperature is important. Cooled to a temperature below 70 degrees, the tubers might "go to sleep" and remain dormant for some time.

VIVIPAROUS REPRODUCTION

Several day-blooming tropical water-lilies have the mysterious faculty called *viviparity,* the ability to bear their young alive. A new baby waterlily brought forth by viviparous reproduction is a sight that no flower-lover will forget, and every water gardener should have at least one "vivip," as we in the trade call it.

As the leaf of a viviparous water-lily becomes mature, a discolored bump forms at the umbilicus, the point where leaf and stem join. The bump breaks after a few days, and tiny, perfectly proportioned leaves begin to form and develop, sometimes growing to the size of silver dollars. Then on some varieties, a perfectly formed miniature of the parent bloom unfolds.

In the meantime, the tiny plant develops a small tuber and root system, out of sight, on the underside of the leaf.

It is easy to nurse these miniatures to maturity. Simply pluck off a plant-bearing leaf and spread it flat on a pot of saturated earth, pinning the leaf in place with pieces of twig. By the time the big leaf has decomposed, the little plant will have established itself as a healthy, growing tropical, ready for planting in the pool.

Often development at the leaf umbilicus will contain several growing points and several root systems, the whole making up a multiple-headed plant. This can be easily divided. Nurse a multiple plant along as you would a single plant. When the individual growths become discernible—with a single growing crown to each—remove from the pot and divide with a sharp knife. An unaltered multiple plant will produce foliage and blooms, but not as big nor as perfect as those of a plant divided off and allowed to grow alone.

Those tropical species which are viviparous are somewhat smaller in growth than the others. However, they have been crossed with a number of the larger hybrids, so that now we have several viviparous hybrids of tremendous size.

The viviparous forms are a problem. The dozens of small plants born in your pool in a single blooming season will be far too numerous for

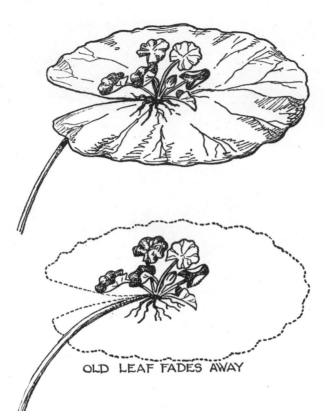

OLD LEAF FADES AWAY

YOUNG VIVIPAROUS PLANT
REMOVED AND POTTED

DRAWING 27.   *Reproduction of Young Viviparous Plant
from Center of Leaf.*

Plate 26. Dr. George H. Pring, of the Missouri Botanical Gardens, the world's leading authority on tropical water-lilies, gathers pollen for crossbreeding. His experiments have produced the first worthwhile tropical yellows and whites. These were once comparatively rare.

A. AUBREY BODINE PHOTO

the space. And they will be far too pretty to throw away. The only consolation I can offer is that nobody else knows what to do with them either.

Only the day-blooming tropicals are viviparous. The Isabelle Pring (white), Peach Blow (pink), and Talisman (tea rose pink) are especially viviparous. Normally viviparous are the Daisy (white), Bagdad, Blue Bird, Dauben (blues), Celeste (violet), Independence, Patricia, Pink Platter, Panama Pacific and Wild Rose (pinks). The Shell Pink and Rio Rita both pinks, are weakly viviparous.

Viviparity varies with the location. It shows up at its best in the South. The farther north, the less spectacular its growth.

CHAIN PROPAGATION FROM TUBERS

With so many viviparous plantlets, you will hardly have need of a system of chain production of plants. But there is one, and you might like to try it out of curiosity.

Plant a healthy tropical tuber deeply in a 3- or 4-inch pot of the conventional soil-and-fertilizer mixture. Place it in the pool with the rim of the pot 2 inches below the surface of the water. The tuber will send up a shoot, and the shoot will quickly become a small, floating plant. At the point where it rises from the soil in the pot, a spreading root system will have begun to develop.

To obtain your plant, push your fingers into the soil below the root system and pinch in two the shoot which still connects tuber and new plant. The separated plant can then be potted. In due time the pinched-off shoot will develop a new plant, and it can be pinched off, too, as soon as it becomes big enough to pot.

With this treatment, an active tuber can produce three, four, or even more plants in the early part of a summer. All of these plants will grow true to type.

Winter Care

Storing the roots of hardies and tropicals in winter is a simple and uncomplicated business, but some precaution is necessary. Find a place for them in a storeroom or cellar corner that is cool and dry. Remember that rats and mice love the roots, so either keep your premises free of the pests or store the roots in metal containers. If you store them dry, remember to perforate the containers to allow some air circulation.

There are several ways of carrying hardies through the winter.

Most gardeners simply remove whatever stones and bricks they have

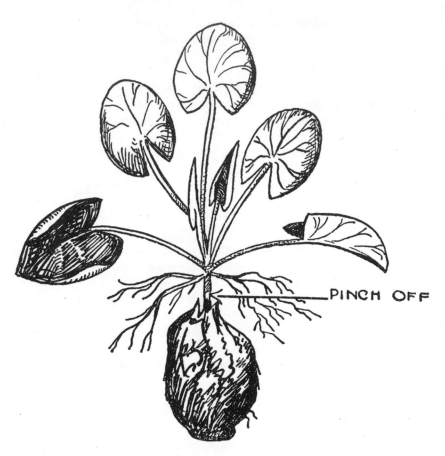

PINCH OFF

DRAWING 28.   *Chain Propagation from a Tuber.*

placed underneath the planting receptacles so as to let the boxes rest on the pool floor. Here they will be well below the frost line in most parts of the country and will safely survive the winter. Roots of the hardies are not harmed unless actually frozen solidly in ice.

If the frost line goes dangerously low in your part of the country, play safe by covering the pool with boards. Then cover the boards with leaves, evergreen boughs, straw, or any other convenient insulation.

You can also winter the roots of hardies inside. Take them out of the planting boxes, wash them, trim off excess root and stems, and store in clean sand, kept damp. I know gardeners who store hardy tubers in all these ways, and each thinks his way is best.

WINTERING THE TROPICALS

In areas which do not have killing frosts, tropical water-lilies can be left outdoors in pond or pool the year around, and cultivated much the same as hardies. The tropicals are not seasonal, and they will continue to bloom until their foliage is killed by frost. Being such heavy feeders, they must be given a new supply of soil-fertilizer mixture each summer if they are planted in containers. On their own in a natural mud bottom, they probably will not need this attention.

In most sections, however, the tubers of tropicals must be taken inside if they are to be kept alive. Their winter storage methods—burying in clean, damp sand—have been discussed earlier in this chapter under Root Division.

Some of those rare hobbyists who maintain indoor pools have had good luck with winter culture of the Daubeniana, the August Koch and other tropicals which bloom with comparatively little sunlight. Sunny window positions for such growth are, of course, necessary. Submersible heaters, controlled by thermostat, are available to maintain summer water temperature—about 70 degrees—in the indoor pool.

Day to Day Care

Beyond coping with plant and animal pests, all the day-to-day culture of waterlilies amounts to is casual grooming from time to time. Keep an eye on your more expansive lilies and accessory aquatics. If they produce more foliage than you want, cut and discard some of the excess leaves. Cut, or pinch off down near the rootstock, leaving no stems to decompose and foul the pool water. Remove the stems of expired blooms in the same way and for the same reason.

171

CHAPTER TEN *First Cousins of the Water-Lilies*

Other genera of *Nymphaeaceae* might be considered as first cousins of the hardy and tropical water-lilies. Like cousins, these various showy flowering plants bear the same family name and have a certain family resemblance. Unlike cousins, they do not spring from a common ancestor, but are grouped under one family name merely because they have developed along the same lines and have in common various structural characteristics and habits. (The family also has its plainer genera, including the Fanworts or Water-Shields, *Cabomba,* which have not yet developed into recognizable water-lily forms.)

All of the genera we now describe can correctly be called water-lilies —and often are. Each group, however, has special characteristics, and these differentiate it from the others.

Genus Victoria—Grandest of All

I include this magnificent plant with academic rather than practical intent, since few nonprofessionals have time, space, or patience to cultivate it. Gardeners for estates and public parks, however, will find it worthwhile for it is the most spectacular of all the aquatics. And if you live near a park or garden in which a *Victoria* is growing you will find the sight of it well worth the effort of a Saturday or Sunday excursion. Certainly hundreds of people drive miles on late summer weekends to see the Victorias we cultivate at Lilypons.

The foliage is striking, for the leaves often measure 6 feet or more across with edges turning up to form a straight-sided rim. Leaves are rich green above and appear to be quilted in a geometric pattern. Underneath they are purplish-green and heavily marked with thick, barbed

172

Plate 27. Viviparous water-lilies produce offspring which are miniature in both blooms and foliage. A nodule forms at the junction of stem and leaf, breaks, and sends leaves and flower stem upward, roots downward. Transplanted, the miniatures become normal, full-sized plants.

veins radiating from the center. The compartments formed by the network of veins are filled with a gas generated by the leaf cells. It is this gas trapped in the leaf that makes it so buoyant.

The platter-shaped flower is also enormous, 10 or 12 inches in diameter, and with a very strong fragrance of crushed pineapple. It is night blooming, and it usually opens for three consecutive evenings, creamy white at first, passing to light pink, deeper pink, and finally to purplish-red.

The seed pod, which is as large as a grapefruit and covered with sharp spines, contains a cluster of hard, shiny, black seeds.

SEEDS TO POOL

Although it is perennial, the Victoria has to be treated as an annual and must be given more of practically everything—sun, space, heat, time, patience, and care—than any other aquatic. Seeds are gathered in fall and stored in bottles of water to keep them from drying out, which would be death. The hard-shells are punctured by filing or cutting and then planted in January or February, in shallow pans of fine, un-fertilized soil with 3 to 4 inches of water. At this stage they are kept at 80 to 85 degrees and exposed to full sunlight.

The more active seeds begin to germinate in two to three weeks. As soon as seedlings form the second tiny leaves, they are moved to sub-merged 3-inch pots filled with a mixture of two-thirds screened soil and one-third rotted cow manure. As plants grow, they are moved to larger and larger pots, finally reaching 10-inch sizes when they are ready to set outdoors in the pool.

Victorias have to have a basin at least 30 feet across and 3 feet deep in the center. They must have rich, nourishing food and plenty of it to produce their immense leaves and blooms. Therefore planting recep-tacles must have minimum dimensions of 2 by 2 feet and a depth of 1½ feet, and be filled with the same mixture of heavy loam and ferti-lizer required by the hardy and tropical water-lilies. (See Chapter 8.) Victorias are set into the soil, much as tropicals are, and buried up to their growing points. Planted outdoors in full sun as soon as the season has become consistently hot, Victorias begin producing foliage quickly, but the blooms usually do not develop until well into August.

Only three forms are in cultivation, and these are comparatively rarely grown.

SPECIES AND VARIETIES

Victoria regia is, of course, the most widely known species of the genus with flower and leaf of the classic form we have just discussed. A native of the tropics. *V. regia* does poorly north of the Mason-Dixon Line.

V. Cruziana—Somewhat hardier South American form from Para-guay. It requires a little less heat than *V. regia* and therefore can be planted somewhat farther north. Flowers are similar but appear earlier, and the foliage is lighter green.

V. Randii—Brazilian form of similar size and shape, has foliage of a reddish cast and marked by prominent red veins. White flowers pass to a deep crimson in their two or three nights of blooming.

Genus Nelumbo—the Lotus

The lotus is one of the oldest flowering plants in the world and has been admired—even revered—through the ages for its awe-inspiring

Plate 28. The parent plant of this Manchurian lotus lived some thousand years ago. The flower was brought into bloom at the Kennilworth Aquatic Gardens in Washington, D. C., from seeds unearthed in the bed of an ancient lake, where they had lain dormant in peat.

A. AUBREY BODINE PHOTO

beauty. The lotus has been featured in man's first crude drawings, and the Egyptians, it is said, made it the "parent of ornamentation." Certainly the lotus was a basic motif in early Assyrian and Persian art.

A native of India, the lotus was sacred to the ancient Hindus, the bloom representing their country, the leaves, the surrounding countries and cultures. To the Buddhists, it symbolized the most exalted representation of man—his head held high, pure and undefiled in the sun, his feet rooted in the world of experience.

In other times, to other peoples, the magnificent blooms of the lotus, fed by roots buried in the mud, have symbolized a king with a common touch, beauty coming from filth and squalor, hope arising from chaos. In very early civilizations, the flower was the emblem of female beauty and fertility—a symbol of life itself.

I have heard a dozen people, I suppose, describe the lotus as "a big water-lily." It is not. There is a world of difference which can be seen at a glance. Blooms and foliage are not formed the same way. Both are much larger than those of water-lilies.

How the Lotus Grows

The different species and varieties grow from 2 to 3 feet to 8 to 9 feet high. The leaves, usually bluish-green, are round, often 2½ feet across, and gently frilled at the edge. They are shaped like shallow bowls and without the customary notch at the junction of stem and leaf. Stout stems support the leaves from a central point and usually in a flat position, particularly in uncrowded areas, and the leaves hold rain water for hours after a shower. A leaf and stem look rather like a parasol, and are often so used by our young visitors.

In many species and varieties, leaf surfaces are covered with thin layers of wax, which causes drops of dew and rain to sparkle in the sun and roll around on the leaves like quicksilver—a beautiful sight. In some forms, leaves are covered with a fine, floury nap, which is also waterproof, and dew and rain water spell magic on these plants, too.

The huge and showy blooms, like tremendous, full-blown roses, are frequently 10 to 12 inches across and are borne high above the foliage on long, stout stems. Like those of the water-lilies, lotus blooms open over a period of three days, at first partially and only for a few hours, then for several hours on the second day, and finally, on the third, they unfold completely. After that petals begin to drop away.

Plate 29. Like other members of the water-lily family, the lotus lends itself to a variety of interesting forms. This one, *Nelumbo pekinensis rubrum flora plenum,* a popular double, with petals of bright rose-carmine surrounding a golden-yellow center.

A. AUBREY BODINE PHOTO

Plate 30. A cousin of the water-lily, the lotus, grows six to eight feet above the surface of the mud and shallow water, where the banana-shaped roots do best. The blooms, clustered around a sulfur-yellow seed pod, are often as large as a man's hat.

A. AUBREY BODINE PHOTO

Growing near the shore under trees or overhanging grasses, lotus leaves catch not only rainwater but also dropping seeds. Often these seeds sprout, and the lotus leaves become miniature roof gardens. I have seen such leaves bearing up to 30 2- and 3-inch seedlings.

Most of the lotus blooms are fragrant, some quite powerfully so. Scents are distinctive and comparable to no other flowers I know. I notice that the fragrance of the lotus is usually described as "mysterious" or "Oriental."

A most interesting feature is the big funnel-shaped pod. At first this is downy and yellow. When it dries, it becomes woody. It has a form much prized for winter bouquets, to which lotus pods give attractive variation.

REPRODUCTION

When you order a lotus from a dealer, you will receive it one of two ways.

If you order early, probably you will receive an adult tuber a year or two old. This is approximately 20 inches long, and consists of an elongated fleshy body (resembling a sweet potato) about as thick as a shovel handle. It will have a growing point and one or two joints. If planted when hardy water-lilies are planted—in established warm weather—the adult lotus tuber probably will produce profuse foliage and bloom the first year.

If you order later in the season, you may receive a runner. This resembles the adult tuber, with the exception that it is much thinner—about the thickness of the little finger. It is growth which has developed since the previous autumn. When set out early in June, many runners bloom well the first season. Many suppliers, however, do not guarantee full blooming until the second season.

The lotus reproduces most quickly through its long, slender rootstock, which forms a joint every 12 to 18 inches, with a tapered growing point at the end. Plants sprout and grow from both the growing point and the joints of this runner. Under ideal conditions, a planted section of rootstock will double its length within a few days, and in one season may develop a 20- to 30-foot root.

Usually the lotus sends out a single chainlike runner—composed of one elongated section growing from the tip of another—growing in a fairly straight line. Its direction is influenced by different factors. It will seek rich, watery earth in which to send up new plants. It will grow around areas of hard, rocky earth. A growing point may show itself briefly above the ground or water surface, then submerge again as the rootstock extends itself.

Thus a lotus planted in one spot may send its roots beneath a sidewalk or even a street and crop up in some totally unexpected place. In view of this vigorous spreading habit, coupled with a stubborn tendency to remain wherever it becomes established, you must confine the root of the lotus to a planting box when you set it out. Unless, of course, you plan to let it take over a vast area of pond. Many water gardeners decorate great sections of their estates beautifully—with a tropical appearance—by letting the lotus do just that.

Though sometimes slow to start, the lotus grows quickly and strongly when it becomes established. The rootstock is tender, and flees from frost. As the weather turns colder, it sends its root deeper and deeper into the mud, sometimes to a depth of five feet. By the time frost kills off the foliage, the plant will have established a goodly length of rootstock safely below the frost line. As the weather becomes warmer, the growing root heads for the surface again.

The lotus can also be propagated by its seeds, though it is a hit-or-miss proposition. Remove the brown seeds—each resembles the meaty part of an acorn—from their dried pods in autumn. Keep them covered in a jar of water. Score the tough seed shells with a file, and in February or early March plant them an inch deep in a 6-inch pot of earth. Keep the pot submerged until warm weather is established, then transfer each sprouting seedling to a planting box in the outdoor pool.

CULTIVATION

The lotus does best in a wooden tub, half-barrel or planting box. Veteran water gardeners who use boxes nail triangular blocks into the corners so as to turn the growing rootstock, for on occasion a root will grow into a corner, trap itself there, and fatally injure its own growing point.

The lotus grows in the same kind of soil with the same fertilizer prescribed for the hardies, but for very handsome results is also given an extra 2- to 3-inch layer of rotted cow manure in the bottom of the box.

To plant, scoop out a depression in a receptacle filled to within 6 inches of the rim with soil and fertilizer. Place the root in the depression and cover with an inch or so of earth, letting half an inch of the growing tip or tips stick out. THIS IS THE SECRET OF SUCCESS: GROWING TIP OR TIPS MUST ABSOLUTELY STICK OUT OF THE SOIL.

Lay a flat rock on the covered root (it may float if you don't), being careful not to touch the growing point. This waxen, brittle point is exceedingly tender, and can be killed by careless handling. Cover the soil with sand, again avoiding the growing point.

The planting receptacle can now be set down into the pool in such a position that the tip of the lotus is covered by 3 to 4 inches of water. Or, if the container is watertight, the receptacle can be placed on a sunny porch or terrace, or out on the lawn. If so placed, keep the receptacle filled to the brim with water. A couple of small goldfish swimming around at the base of the growing lotus will add interest, and the fish will eat any mosquito eggs that may be deposited in the water.

Plant the lotus rootstock in a natural pond the same way, in a box if it is to be controlled, under an inch of mud and 3 to 4 inches of water if the lotus is to be allowed to spread freely in the pond. Vigorous and stubborn though it is, the lotus is sometimes difficult to get established. Newly planted lotus, in some cases produces a wealth of foliage and blooms the first season. In other cases it may produce only some foliage the first summer. Nearly all produce heavily by the second year.

The quickest, most abundant growers are the yellow Luteum, the pink Speciosum, and the red Roseum Plenum.

WINTER CARE

Planted in a natural pond and given freedom, the lotus takes care of itself. Growing in a receptacle either in or out of the pool, it will also take care of itself provided water does not freeze down to the crown of the root. It will be killed if ice touches this crown. If there is such danger, take the plant indoors when the foliage dies down in fall. Keep the soil moist, but not saturated, and the plant cool, that is, 35 to 40 degrees, through the winter. Be sure rats or mice haven't access to it, for both love to eat the roots.

On rare occasions, a water gardener has been able to grow the lotus at a sunny window and even bring it into bloom during the winter. This is usually a disappointing project, however, for unless plants are kept cool and dormant, roots almost invariably rot.

Every other year, remove the roots from the planting receptacle. Fill it with a fresh supply of soil and fertilizer, and plant one healthy new section of rootstock, broken from the parent plant. You will have a number of root sections left over to increase your own plantings, if you wish, or to share with friends. Ordinarily a plant sprouts and grows from each joint, but it is good practice to allow two or more joints to each section off rootstock broken or cut off for planting elsewhere. In dividing a section of rootstock, divide mid-way between joints.

POTTED LOTUS

At Three Springs Fisheries there has been developed a new lotus strain which gives the flower lover exciting new possibilities in the decoration of patio, terrace and flower garden. Our strain is a somewhat smaller version of the Oriental lotus, and it can be grown above ground in a 20-inch pot.

The new strain is fragrant. The plant, if given plenty of sun, grows as high as a man and spreads huge, pale green, round leaves 18 to 24 inches in diameter. The flower buds, as they unfold, are of artistic shape, and they produce blossoms 5 inches in diameter.

The first variety of the new strain placed on the market is a rich pink which is called the Mikado.

Other varieties, of established shape and color but still in the final stages of development, are these soon-to-be-marketed forms: Goddess, white; Mandarin, yellow; Flame of India, red; Vesper, white tipped red.

AVAILABLE LOTUS VARIETIES

Only a few forms of lotus are listed botanically, and a comparatively small number of these are distributed commercially. Most dealers in this country carry only three or four forms, and only the largest have more than half a dozen.

N. album grandiflorum—Also known as Asiatic Lotus and sometimes listed as *N. album floribundum*. Generally considered to be the finest white lotus variety. Huge leaves of deep green. Blooms, a foot or more in diameter, have a strange, delicate fragrance. A popular commercial variety.

> *striatum*—Hybrid obtained from the *N. album grandiflorum,* and a very good one. Vigorous grower with fragrant white blooms, streaked at the tips with carmine. Excellent for cutting. Commercially available.

N. album plenum—Known commercially as Shiroman. Japanese variety with huge double flowers, creamy white lightly brushed with green on opening, becoming pure white a day or two later. Fragrant and profuse. Hold up well when cut. Plentiful.

GROSSHERZOG ERNST LUDWIG—Beautiful hybrid obtained by crossing *N. luteum* var. *flavescens* and Osiris. Bears huge blooms of rich, deep pink, with a striking contrast of bright-yellow stamens and light-green ovaries. Exudes a powerful and pleasant fragrance. Foliage of classic form, a powdery blue-green. Fairly easy to procure.

N. japonica rubra—Fast-growing form with tremendous, open, double flowers, sometimes 15 inches across. Blooms are white, with a heavy, rosy blush. Bluish-green foliage, covered with a fine nap and very handsome. A few dealers have it.

Kermesiana—Japanese variety with outstanding carmine-rose blooms which are of a unique satiny texture. Huge leaves and blooms produced in great profusion. A few dealers have it.

KINSHIREN—A profuse, free-flowering Japanese variety with huge white flowers lightly brushed with pink. Available.

N. luteum—Also called Water Chinquapin, Duck Acorn, American Lotus. North American species from southern Canada and eastern and central areas of the United States. Leaves, 1 to 2 feet wide, held 2 to 3 feet above the water. Fragrant sulfur-yellow blooms range from 4 to 10 inches in diameter. Requires 5 to 6 years to become well established in a wild setting, and it does not produce a full quota of blooms until that time. Quite plentiful.

> *flavescens*—Marliac. Differs from the parent species in two ways: Leaves are marked in the center with conspicuous spots of red; blooms are smaller and borne much more profusely. Fairly plentiful.

N. pekinense rubrum—Also known as Chinese Lotus. Darker than any other lotus, fairly large blooms, bright rose-carmine and very fragrant. The plant produces flowers and foliage in profusion. Available.

> *floraplenum*—A hybrid identical to parent except that it is double. Fairly rare in the United States.

POTTED LOTUS—A new strain of Three Springs Fisheries development, a smaller form of the Oriental lotus, which can be grown above ground in a 20-inch pot. Approximate height 6 feet; round, pale green leaves 18 to 24 inches diameter. Blooms 5 inches, fragrant.

Varieties include Mikado, rich pink, now on the market. Soon to be marketed, though stock will be limited: Goddess, white; Mandarin, yellow; Flame of India, red; Vesper, white tipped red.

N. roseum plenum—Also known as Double Dawn. Huge, globular flower of·rich pink, very double, and borne freely. A robust plant that often attracts more attention than any other blooming in our ponds. Plentiful.

N. speciosum—Probably the best-known species, and known variously as Egyptian Lotus, Sacred Egyptian Lotus, Sacred Lotus of the Nile (although not a native of Egypt, but of India), and Hindu Lotus. Distributed freely in a wild state in India, the Philippine Islands, Japan, and the northern section of Australia. Leaves, bluish-green on the surface and pale silvery green underneath, held well up from the water. Blooms, with a delicate, haunting scent, borne profusely, grow to 12-inch widths. Deep rose on opening, becoming paler with age. By the end of the third day the petals are creamy white, with a rosy-pink blush at edges. Plentiful.

OSIRIS—Strong-growing, free-flowering variety introduced by Marliac. Cup-shaped blooms, 8 to 10 inches across, of deep pink. Bluishgreen foliage. Plentiful.

Genus Nuphar—Spatterdock

Just as there is many a family which has an uncle it does not brag about, so *Nymphaeaceae,* the Water-Lily Family, has a genus called *Nuphar.* It is commonly known as Spatterdock. Cow Lily, and Yellow Pond-Lily. In form and habit, it is similar, but far inferior, to the hardy water-lilies.

The thick leaves, like those of the hardies except that they tend to heart shapes, sometimes float, sometimes are held above the water.

At the end of a thick, clumsy stem, the plant supports a 2- to 3-inch bloom with five or more golden-yellow, concave sepals. The bloom is cupshaped, almost spherical. Most casual observers mistake the sepals for petals. Actually, it has numerous petals, but they are so insignificant that they appear to be a cluster of short stamens.

Nuphars, native to the State of Missouri, thrive in either warm, stagnant pools or in cool running streams throughout the United States east of the Rocky Mountains.

This humble plant has uses. Cattle eat the blooms and foliage. There is an old wives' tale to the effect that the leaves, when dried and burned, produce a smoke which will drive cockroaches out of a house. The Spatterdock is very hardy and will survive in places where hardy and tropical water-lilies cannot grow.

It is widely claimed that the nuphar will thrive without sun, but I have yet to have the claim proved. I know it will produce a great deal of foliage in deep shade, but I have never seen a shaded nuphar produce blooms. It is not unattractive seen at a distance. It is not pretty enough to cultivate in a pool, but a cluster of nuphars in a far corner of a natural pond—where they are only a small, incidental part of the show—will add some color to the view.

Only a few of the larger dealers carry nuphars. They are planted and propagated the same as hardy water-lilies. There are a number of species which grow wild practically all over the world. These are the more common North American forms.

SPECIES AND VARIETIES

Nuphar advenum—One of the most common forms. Leaves about a foot wide, round to oblong, with a wide notch at the point where stem joins leaf. Blooms, 2 to 3 inches in diameter, have bright-yellow sepals touched with green or purple. Deep yellow or pale red stigma. Both blooms and foliage held above the water.

N. kalmianum—A much smaller species, with floating leaves no larger than saucers and a pale yellow bloom an inch or less in diameter. Spreads swiftly in the shallow water along the margin of a pool or river.

N. macrophyllum—Strong-growing southern species with bloom similar to that of *N. kalmianum*. Foliage, however, is large and ovate. One of the few members of the Water-Lily Family which will grow in running water.

N. minimum—Also known as Dwarf Pond-Lily. A very free-flowering species with tiny, pale yellow blooms and miniature floating leaves.

N. orbiculatum—A large and robust southern form with round, bright-green leaves somewhat fluted at the edges. Yellowish blooms about 2 inches wide. Stems and undersides of leaves covered with white down.

N. polysepalum—One of the largest of the North American species. Leaves are elongated, and the yellow bloom is 4 to 5 inches wide. Both blooms and leaves stand out of the water along shore, float in deeper water.

N. rubrodiscum—Also called Red Disk Pond-Lily. The elongated leaves range from 3 to 10 inches in length, float in deep water, stand erect in shallow. Yellow blooms, less than 2 inches in diameter, with conspicuous red centers.

EURALE FEROX

The *Eurale Ferox* falls into a little known genus of the water-lily family. Once, before the *Victorias* were discovered, it was the giant of the family.

It is indigenous to China and India. Its flat, floating leaves are 4 to 5 feet in diameter. Its purplish blooms are inferior to those of other water-lilies, and for this reason it has never become popular with water gardeners.

For size, however, it commands a certain respect. It grows hardily in outdoor ponds, and re-seeds itself from year to year, in climate comparable to that of St. Louis, Mo.

CHAPTER ELEVEN *Aquarium Water-Lilies and Other New Forms*

Never ending experimentation is bringing the refreshing hobby of water gardening more and more into the year-around pattern of family living.

In the last few years Three Springs Fisheries introduced two new and unique water-lily forms, one a hardy, the other a tropical, which are robust enough to thrive in an outdoor pool in hot weather, small and prolific enough to bloom indoors under natural and artificial light through the winter as well.

These are the first tiny water-lilies dependable enough to market for planting in an indoor aquarium.

The same experimental gardens have also developed a new, somewhat smaller strain of lotus which can be planted conventionally in pool or pond, or set out in a sunny corner of lawn or patio in 20-inch pots.

New shapes and colors are also emerging along traditional water-lily lines. See *Louise* and *Virginia* among the hardy water-lily listings.

Now we may be on the threshold of new and even more varied water-lily shapes, sizes, colors and color combinations by way of mutations produced by the radioactive treatment of seeds, bulbs and tubers.

AQUARIUM WATER-LILIES

The *Margaret Mary* is a tiny, star-shaped bloom, not much bigger than a quarter with pale blue petals and golden center flowers. The blossom is held above the water surface of the aquarium, surrounded by floating, clear-green leaves. The leaves are of proportionate size, about 4 inches in diameter.

185

Planted in a pint of earth with its crown at the soil line, the lily in its container should be placed into the aquarium so the soil is at least several inches below the water level. This water-lily grows especially well if given a sunny window position. If such is not available, it also grows quite well under the artificial light of a "Gro-Lux" or similar bulb. When winter skies are gray, it may be necessary to supplement natural light with a few hours of the artificial sunshine to give it a total of 5 or 6 hours of light a day.

In the summer, after hot weather has arrived to stay, the *Margaret Mary* also thrives in the outdoor pool or tub garden.

The new plant, the first to prove out as practical for aquarium culture the year around, is a day-blooming tropical. The blossom unfolds in the forenoon, closes its petals as dusk approaches. Blooms last three days, and as one retires another is taking shape.

It has the added interest of being viviparous. From the centers of some of its mature leaves it sprouts even tinier miniature forms of itself. These, if snipped off and given a pot of earth of their own, extend their root systems and grow into normal, mature plants.

The *Margaret Mary* is named for Margaret Mary Brosius Thomas, first great-granddaughter of the Three Springs Fisheries founder, G. Leicester Thomas.

The *Dorothy Lamour* is a miniature hardy yellow water-lily with a soft, lemon-yellow bloom an inch in diameter. The bloom, which has a fresh, delicate fragrance, is shaped rather like a half-opened rose.

It produces a luxurious growth of floating, 4-inch, bright green leaves prettily marked with chestnut brush strokes. It also produces blooms lavishly, and soon decorates the aquarium or corner of the outdoor pool in a distinctly tropical motif. This is why we named it the *Dorothy Lamour.*

This water-lily, planted in the aquarium indoors, has the same soil and light requirements as the *Margaret Mary.* It is more versatile, however. Planted outside, it does very well in deep water or in the shallow water of the pool edge or a tub garden.

POTTED LOTUS

At Three Springs Fisheries we call them "Potted Lotus" for want of a better name.

They are five color varieties of a new strain of Oriental lotus. They can be planted conventionally with their roots submerged in a pool or pond, or they can be grown in 20-inch pots in a sunny position on lawn or patio.

The plant shoots up to a height of about 6 feet. Its pale green leaves are round and close to 2 feet in diameter. The rainwater they catch and hold takes on the appearance of quicksilver.

The blooms are 5 inches in diameter, and headily fragrant.

Marketed at .present is a rich pink called the *Mikado*. Other set forms, of which the stock is now being built up, are the *Goddess,* white; *Mandarin,* yellow; *Flame of India,* red; *Vesper,* white tipped with red.

ATOMIC AGE FLOWERS

Down through the ages botanists have undergone hardships and risked their lives traveling into the unexplored corners of the world in search of new rareties. Now we may very well be on the verge of finding a wealth of additional new rareties by traveling into the most fascinating, and possibly the most rewarding, realm of all—the fourth dimension.

This fourth dimension is time. Specifically, it is the time of the future.

This spectacular botanical idea can be summed up under the heading of deliberate plant mutations induced by the effects of radioactivity on seeds, tubers, buds and bulbs. It is a new science, but already striking varieties have been produced by it in some fruits, vegetables and flowers, and indications now point strongly to a fast growing application of it in many horticultural fields.

Nature produces change in her living things, in the form of new plant and animal varieties, by evolution, an extremely slow process. New forms of plants and animals sometimes happen as "sports" by natural accident. More often they evolve in some changed form because they are shaped that way by environment, by certain organic chemicals taken in from the food which supports them, by the amount of space in which they have to grow, and by other factors. Man, by patient selective breeding and cross-breeding, has been able to speed up the evolution of many new forms, but it is a slow and gradual process.

The action of radiation upon plants or their seeds speeds up this gradual evolution. It takes giant steps. Through its violent effects it produces "sports" or mutations which Mother Nature might have taken centuries to develop, if they were ever to develop at all. Thus, the application of radioactive treatment for induced mutations may truly be said to be an exploration into the fourth dimension, a search in the future, for new plant rareties.

Here's how it works:

The cells of all plants and animals contain chromosomes which, in turn, contain dominant and recessive genes. It is the dominant genes which determine such characteristics as the inherited blue eyes or red hair of a baby, or the exclusively pink petals of a certain flower. But it is the recessive, frequently dormant, genes which are important to us in this botanical study.

Let us consider a yellow flower which, on occasion, shows a tinge of richer yellow approaching an orange hue. This would indicate that the dominant genes are yellow, and that the recessive genes are red.

Collect the seeds of one of the richer yellow flowers, and expose them to radioactivity. Dr. C. J. Speas, of Oak Ridge Atom Industries, Inc., at Oak Ridge, Tennessee, irradiates seeds of vegetables and flowers with radioactive Cobalt 60, giving them usually from 2,000 to 2,500 roentgens of exposure. Some seeds die. Usually 80 per cent of the seeds come through, still viable.

We have hoped in this exposure to kill off the dominant yellow genes in the seeds, thus allowing the red genes to become dominant. If we do so, the treated seeds will sprout, grow and produce something new—red blooms on a flower which never before has produced anything but yellow blossoms. Perhaps. Maybe. Possibly.

At this stage, irradiation is still pretty much a hit or miss proposition. From the atom-bombed seeds of our yellow flower we may sprout yellow blossoms, red blossoms, red and yellow blossoms, orange blossoms, blossoms with no color at all, or plants with no blossoms at all. We may get a dwarf plant or a giant, or a plant with an entirely new blossom shape. Or we may achieve a beautiful red bloom—which after a generation or two reverts to its original yellow color.

For many years experts have been trying to come up with a truly blue rose or a pure white marigold. Water gardeners have alway lamented the fact that among the hardy water-lilies there is not a single blue blossom. The day-blooming tropicals show a wide variety of beautiful blues. But there is no way for the tropicals to lend their blue to any of the hardies, for the two forms cannot be cross-bred.

Perhaps now, through the irradiation of seeds, we may one day find our blue hardy water-lily.

As a starter, if you have a water-lily pool and would like to join in the search for a blue hardy, let me give you a few pointers:

First, my definition of a marketable blue would be a hardy water-lily that would grow and bloom outdoors in the spring and summer. It would be a perennial. Pale shades of lavender or some hue with a blue cast wouldn't count. To be called a blue, a blossom would have a color immediately and definitely identifiable as blue.

I would suggest you perform your experiments with seeds. Exposure of tubers or other parts of a living plant might give you more immediate results, but this would require the handling of the radioactive material, a dangerous business for all but experts.

A number of professional laboratories (see list at end of chapter) are now irradiating seeds of flowers and vegetables. Some of them will work on a custom basis with materials sent to them. Some won't.

"We do not do custom irradiation as we thought in the beginning of our company we might be able to do," says Dr. Speas. "The custom irradiation of seeds, bulbs, etc., is not a matter of just putting in some of the seeds and shooting them with a helter-skelter dose of gamma rays. There is a lot more to it than that. The number of seeds, bulbs, etc., that would have to be irradiated and the number of various doses, etc., makes the cost of custom irradiation extremely high. People don't understand this, and it takes so much explaining that we have stopped doing it..."

Other laboratories, however, do accept custom work. It is wise to write to them before forwarding materials for irradiation.

Irradiation can effect some wondrous results, but it can not bring out the blue color in a plant that does not already contain blue genes. So look for a trace, a suggestion of the color you wish to attain in a flower.

One of the most likely hardy water-lilies for such an experiment would be the *William Falconer*. This hardy has a very deep red, velvety bloom, shading almost to black at the base of the petals. In this deep red hue an observer can see a tinge of blue. This is merely a suggestion. You may see traces of blue in some of the other hardy species.

Probably you will have to obtain your own seeds for experimentation. I do not know a dealer who sells clearly identified water-lily seed. Water-lily fanciers get all the new plants they want by root division, or by ordering new growing plants, and so avoid the bothersome business of growing their flowers from seeds. At Three Springs Fisheries we harvest only the seeds we need for our own use, due to the cost of labor in producing and harvesting them.

On a small scale, however, it is not difficult to grow your own seeds.

As soon as the bud of some selected plant shows above the water, cover it loosely with a piece of cheesecloth, tieing the cheesecloth on the stem. Use a piece large enough to give the bud ample room to flower. The flowering will occur the day after the bud emerges.

When the bud has flowered, loosen the cheesecloth, and with your finger wiggle the anthers to shake off the pollen to fertilize the seeds. Cover the bloom again, and leave it undisturbed for two weeks. In this time the bloom will have died, and presently the bud will swell.

Cut the cloth enclosed bud off the stem, remove the cloth, take out the seeds, and spread them to dry. When they have become hard they are ready to mail off to a laboratory to be irradiated.

When you get back your treated seeds, follow planting instructions set down in Chapter 9. The laboratory will provide instructions for additional planting details, for carefully calculated time lapses between the time of radiation and the time of sowing must be observed.

If your experimental bloom has become uncovered at any time during the early stages of this process, start all over again. Insects and wind borne pollen present the constant threat of cross-pollination, which will give you an impure seed. Several experimental blooms in process at one time will give you a far better chance of success.

Accredited laboratories which perform irradiation of seeds include the following:

Brookhaven National Laboratory, Associated Universities, Inc., Upton, Long Island, New York 11973.

Nuclear Science and Engineering Corporation, Box 10901, Pittsburgh, Pennsylvania 15236.

Oak Ridge Atom Industries Sales Corporation, Box 229, Evanston, Illinois.

Suggested reading: "Create New Flowers and Plants—Indoors and Out," by John James, published 1964, Doubleday & Company, Inc., Garden City, New York.

CHAPTER TWELVE

Lists of "Bests"

This is a chapter my customers have, to a large extent, helped me write, for it consists principally of my answers to the questions they most frequently ask. This summary must necessarily be generalized. If you have some out-of-the-ordinary problem on which I have not touched in this book, please feel free to write me about it. I will give you the best advice I can.

BEST KINDS TO CUT

One or two water-lilies floating in a large glass, silver or ceramic bowl, with a lily pad for background, make an effective arrangement. And, generally speaking, any water-lily that pleases you can be cut for a table centerpiece or other decoration. Those hardies which seem to hold up best indoors include *Nymphaea odorata* and *rosea*, *Marliacea rosea* and *chromatella*, W. B. Shaw, James Brydon, and *N. Robinsonii*. All of them are fragrant. Other good hardies for cutting include *N. Gladstoniana*, Gonnêre, Helen Fowler, and Pink Opal.

Among the best tropicals for cutting are the day-blooming Aviator Pring, Blue Beauty, William Stone, August Koch, Mrs. C. W. Ward, and Mrs. G. H. Pring; and the night-blooming *Nymphaea dentata* and its varieties, *N. Omarana*, and Emily Grant Hutchins.

Choosing Cut Flowers

Most water-lilies, growing normally in a pool, open their blooms for three consecutive days or nights. A few open four times, some only twice. But practically all water-lilies will extend their normal performance by a day or two when cut and taken into the house.

Both hardies and tropicals make good cut flowers. To get the best out of them, select newly opened blooms for cutting. If you have a small pool, this will not be much of a trick. If you have a large pool, with

Plate 31. This attractive center-piece consists of a shell bowl and the floating blooms of Pink Opal and the snowy-white *N. odorata gigantea.* An ice cube or two in the water helps keep the flowers open.

A. AUBREY BODINE PHOTO

Plate 32. This study in a black iron urn with the dark green of hosta foliage and evergreen branches features the blooms of Virginalis, *N. odorata gigantea,* and *N. Gladstoniana,* all gleaming white with centers of golden-yellow stamens. Arrangement by Helen L. Smith.

A. AUBREY BODINE PHOTO

several dozen water-lilies blooming at once, you will have to learn to recognize a newly borne flower. Look for a blossom in which stamens are not yet curled or tangled, but still spread cleanly apart. Look for plump, round anthers which have not yet begun to shed pollen, and for a stigma with the tiny basin still holding a droplet of nectar.

Usually the hardies and day-blooming tropicals, after being cut, will follow their normal habits and open their blossoms the same as if they were still in the pool. The night-blooming tropicals, when cut, usually follow their normal routine and stay open from about 7 p.m. until well into the following morning. But not always. Sometimes a combination of factors—temperature, humidity, and so on—causes blooms to fold up into buds again.

How to Keep Blooms Open

There are two sure ways of keeping blooms open. You can place stems in a vase of ice water, and store them in the refrigerator until time to use them as decorations. You will find that they will then remain open for a few hours. Or you can let the blooms unfold to their fullest before cutting them, and then put a drop of melted paraffin or wax from a lighted candle at the point where stamens, petals, and sepals join. Hardening, the paraffin or wax forms an unseen but sturdy cast which holds blooms open. Either procedure keeps flowers at their loveliest for three or four days, with no loss of luster or fragrance.

A word of caution: Water-lilies set out in this way as decoration bear up well under heat and even a bit of handling, but a strong, sustained draft of cold air will kill them. So don't set them directly in front of an air-conditioning unit.

How Many Plants for a Pool?

The best advice I can give you in the interests of an attractive pool is not to crowd it. This may be bad for business, but I am duty-bound to warn you that many new water gardeners overdo planting.

Here is a rule-of-thumb that may help. Figure your square-footage of water surface. An 8- by 10-foot pool, for example, gives you 80 square feet. Now remember that most water-lilies fall into one of three size classifications which I have indicated in the listings. Extensive growers cover about 10 to 12 square feet when mature; medium growers cover 8 to 10 square feet; small growers confine themselves to about 4 square feet or less.

Cover no more than half the pool surface with water-lilies. Leave room for some submerged, floating, and border aquatics. You also will want some free, clear-water space, for reflections on the surface are one of the principal charms of a water garden.

So, for your 8 by 10 pool, select only enough water-lilies to cover 40 square feet or thereabouts. This gives you more variety than you may imagine—four extensive growers, five or six medium growers, or as many as ten small growers.

As you will see in the water-lily listings, *Nymphaea tuberosa* and all its varieties, some of the odoratas, such as *gigantea*, and practically all of the tropicals are extensive spreaders. They quickly fill a large pool with a pretty pattern of foliage.

If you prefer small water-lilies, you will do well to consider *Nymphaea odorata minor*, *N. tetragona*, *N. mexicana*, *N. Laydekeri rosea*, and *N. pygmaea* and its varieties, particularly *helvola*. The day-flowering *N. elegans* and *N. Daubeniana* are among the very few tropicals with a small spread.

List of "Bests"

Hardly a day goes by at Three Spring Fisheries when we do not answer at least one letter from a customer who wants a water-lily with some specific and outstanding characteristic—the tallest, the widest, the reddest, the most fragrant, and so on. Here are recommendations in some of these groups.

Plate 33 Comanche, biggest and best of the Changeable water-lilies, opens a rich rose, overlaid with apricot, and passes to a deep, then deeper, coppery bronze as it matures.

A. AUBREY BODINE PHOTO

Plate 34. *Nymphaea gigantea hudsoniana* is a beautiful blue tropical, and one of the freest in growth and bloom. It is a rich, deep color, with inner petals somewhat lighter and a cluster of golden stamens. "Without a doubt," writes Bisset, "the best of the tropicals."

A. AUBREY BODINE PHOTO

Plate 35. Shell Pink, a most attractive tropical, clear pink with large flowers. Sparingly viviparous.

A. AUBREY BODINE PHOTO

EARLIEST

Nymphaea Gladstoniana, W. B. Shaw, *N. Marliacea chromatella,* James Brydon, *N. somptuosa, N. colossea,* Comanche, and *N. gloriosa* can be depended upon, just about anywhere in the country, to be among the first to bloom each season.

LARGEST

Nymphaea Gladstoniana, Escarboucle, William Doogue, *N. Andreana,* Mme. Julien Chifflot, and Sunrise among the hardies, *N. gigantea, N. capensis zanzibariensis,* Aviator Pring, Peach Blow, Pink Platter, Shell Pink, Talisman, and Wild Rose among the day-blooming tropicals, *N. dentata magnifica, N. Omarana,* Missouri, James Gurney, and B. C. Berry among night-blooming tropicals, with the latter two producing the very largest blooms.

Most Prolific

Nymphaea alba candidissima, W. B. Shaw, James Brydon, *N. Lay-dekeri rosea, purpurata* and *fulgens,* and *N. Marliaceą chromatella* and *carnea* for the hardies; the day-blooming *N. flavovirens,* William Stone, Mrs. C. W. Ward, August Koch, Director Moore, Henry Shaw, and Pink Pearl; and the night-blooming *N. dentata magnifica* and *N Omarana* among the tropicals are free blooming with a fine, long succession of flowers.

Most Fragrant

The most fragrant hardies are *Nymphaea odorata* and *N. tetragona* and their varieties, and I give a special personal recommendation for James Brydon, Helen Fowler, and Rose Arey. All the day-blooming tropicals are fragrant, most of them *very* fragrant.

With Double Blossoms

The double-flowered water-lilies with the most distinctive forms, in my opinion, include among hardies *Nymphaea tuberosa Richardsonii,* James Brydon, Gloire de Temple sur Lot, Gonnêre, and *N. Marliacea chromatella;* and among tropicals, those of *N. capensis zanzibariensis,* a day bloomer, and the night-blooming *N. dentata magnifica,* Missouri, James Gurney, and Sturtevant.

Plate 36. Persian Lilac, one of the prettiest and most delicate of the pink tropicals.
A. AUBREY BODINE PHOTO

For Deep or Shallow Pools

Water-lilies that flourish in deeper than ordinary pools include the *Nymphaea alba candidissima, N. odorata gigantea, N. tuberosa* and *N. Marliacea albida, rosea* and *carnea,* all hardies.

Hardies which do well in shallow pools, say a foot or even less of water, include *N. odorata minor, N. tetragona* and *helvola* and varieties, and Jo Ann Pring, *N. mexicana, N. Laydekeri rosea* and *fulgens, N. pygmaea* and varieties.

Practically all day- and night-blooming tropicals do well in shallow water.

For Tubs and Miniature Pools

The shallow water hardies listed above are all fine for tub culture and very small pools.

Best Lake Lilies

For lake and pond planting, most water gardeners favor, among the hardy water-lilies, the Marliac varieties. These varieties tend to stay put in clumps which do not spread widely. For those hobbyists who want the water-lilies to spread, the *Odorata* and *Tuberosa* varieties are recommended. Suggested hardies for shady sections of the lake or pond: *Chromatella,* Rose Arey, *Gloriosa,* Comanche.

Practically any of the tropical water-lilies are good for pond planting.

For Indoor Winter Culture

The *Daubeniana* and August Koch, tropical day-bloomers, do well through the winter in indoor pools for many water gardeners. For experimentation, try any other very free blooming tropicals which function in less than full sun. See WINTERING THE TROPICALS in chapter on PROPAGATION, CULTURE AND WINTER CARE.

For Aquarium Culture

Very good for aquarium culture inside in either summer or winter are two new water-lilies developed only recently in experimental tanks, at Three Springs Fisheries.

The Margaret Mary is a tiny, star-shaped tropical day-bloomer with baby-blue petals and a golden center. The bloom is about the size of a silver dollar. The small clear green pads are 3 to 4 inches in diameter. Viviparous.

The Dorothy Lamour is a miniature hardy water-lily bearing soft yellow blooms which resemble half-opened rosebuds. Three- to four-inch pads are bright green marked with chestnut brush strokes.

Both of these flowers grow in about half a pint of earth. Both do well under the artificial sunlight of a "Gro-Lux" or similar bulb, or in a sunny window. Both thrive in outdoor pools if set out in established warm weather.

IN LESS THAN FULL SUN

Direct sunlight is a necessary stimulant for flower production, and the more of it a water-lily gets the more profuse the blooming will be. However, there are a few varieties which are so free-blooming that even a few hours of sun will produce a satisfactory number of blossoms.

These tropical day-bloomers bloom with as little as 4 hours of sun:

Daubeniana, August Koch, Patricia, Panama Pacific, Blue Bird, Independence, Director Moore, Isabelle Pring, St. Louis.

Five to six hours of sun will give you rewarding blooms on these tropical day-bloomers:

King of the Blues, Persian Lilac, Mrs. G. H. Pring.

The Emily Hutchings, Mrs. George C. Hitchcock, and Juno (all night-blooming tropicals) also bloom with 5 to 6 hours of sun.

VIVIPAROUS

Strongly viviparous: Isabelle Pring, white; Peach Blow, pink; Talisman, tea-rose-pink.

Normally viviparous: Daisy, white; Bagdad, Blue Bird, Blue Beauty, Dauben, blues; Celeste, violet; Independence, Patricia, Pink Platter, Panama Pacific, Wild Rose, pinks.

Weakly viviparous: Shell Pink, Rio Rita, pinks.

BEST BY COLOR

New water gardeners frequently ask us to recommend the best water-lily in a certain color. To avoid argument, I want to stress that I give here my personal preferences. Describing a beautiful flower is like describing a beautiful woman—no two men agree.

RED. The hardy *Nymphaea Marliacea ignea,* James Brydon, Attraction (reddest), and *N. atropurpurea* (darkest); the tropical day-blooming *N. gracilis rubra,* B. C. Berry, and H. C. Haarstick, and the night-blooming *N. Omarana,* George Huster, Frank Trelease, and *N. columbiana.*

Plate 37. Midnight. Abundant deep rich purple flowers, small, with a few large petals and many smaller stamenlike petals toward the center. Small leaves.

YELLOW. *Nymphaea Marliacea chromatella, N. odorata sulphurea, N. pygmaea helvola,* and Sunrise among hardies, and these tropicals —the day-blooming St. Louis, St. Louis Gold, Aviator Pring, African Gold, and Sunbeam.

WHITE. The hardy *Nymphaea alba candidissima, N. Gladstoniana, N. Marliacea albida* and *N. Virginalis;* the tropical day-blooming *N. flavovirens,* and Mrs. G. H. Pring, and the night-blooming *N. dentata grandiflora* and *superba.*

PINK. The hardy Mrs. C. W. Thomas, Pink Opal, and Rose Arey; the tropical day-blooming General Pershing, Independence, Mrs. C. W. Ward, and Persian Lilac, and the night-blooming *Nymphaea Bissettii* and Mrs. George G. Hitchcock.

CHANGEABLES. The hardy *Nymphaea amibilis,* Paul Hariot, and Comanche.

BLUE. The day-blooming *Nymphaea capensis, N. zanzibariensis,* Blue Beauty, Midnight, William Stone, Bagdad, Director George T. Moore, and Mrs. Edwards Whitaker.

There are no blue hardies, nor are there any blue night-blooming tropicals.

Best Six

Probably the most thumbed page of our catalog every year, judging by the orders we receive, is that page devoted to a selection of six good water-lilies with which new gardeners can begin. We select with an eye to variety of color, flower form, and blooming habit. And, of course, we include only those water-lilies which we are sure will grow for amateurs.

We confine our selections to the hardies, because we feel new gardeners are interested mainly in first establishing perennial growers. Most water gardeners grow the tropicals only as annuals, and so select a few of them year by year, usually preferring to try different forms and colors each time. These are the six we have selected:

Nymphaea Marliacea albida, rosea, and *chromatella; N. Robinsonii,* Attraction, and Mrs. C. W. Thomas.

Best Dozen

For a somewhat larger pool, which will take twelve water-lilies, add these to the above six:

Nymphaea alba candidissima, N. tuberosa Richardsonii, W. B. Shaw, *N. Gladstoniana,* William Falconer, and Mrs. Richmond.

Best Eighteen

For the pool which will accommodate eighteen water-lilies, add these six, and then you will have a veritable social register of the finest, most beautiful hardies in cultivation:

Nymphaea lucida, N. odorata rosea, Dawn, *N. fulva,* William Doogue, and Rose Arey.

CHAPTER THIRTEEN

Accessory Aquatic Plants

The balance of life in a water garden is strong and natural, seldom requiring any adjustment it cannot make for itself. At the same time, it is intricate and interdependent. Water-lilies and other aquatic plants will grow in a pool that has no fish. Goldfish will live in a pond that has no plant life. But neither will flourish without the other. In a well-stocked pond the water seldom can take in enough oxygen by surface absorption to replace that utilized by the fish in their "breathing." And so submerged water plants, which exude oxygen constantly as a waste product, are necessary to keep oxygen content at healthful level. Fish, as they take oxygen from the water, throw off carbon dioxide, a product quickly assimilated and converted into plant tissue by water plants.

The plant life of a water garden grows at three levels. There are submerged or oxygenating plants beneath the surface; floating plants on the surface; and in the surrounding ground, slightly above water level, the marsh and bog plants.

Some submerged and some floating plants *must* go into your pool, since goldfish do very poorly without them. Border plants are necessary only to please the eye, but they are important, too, for water-lilies are twice as beautiful with a background of accessory aquatics.

SELECTING AQUATICS

The simplest way to select aquatics for the health and beauty of your pool is to leave it up to your water-lily dealer. Almost every one offers standard assortments of submerged, floating, and border plants. These are well balanced, in both variety and quantity, and you have only to order a large assortment or a small one, depending on the size of your pool. If your dealer does not advertise such assortments, you can give him the size of your pool and ask him to make a selection for you.

After you have tended your water garden for a season or two, you will have your own ideas, likes and dislikes, and will be able to order aquatics thereafter in more specific terms. If you have a neighbor with a water garden, you can enlarge your collections by trading cuttings.

WHAT IS AVAILABLE?

In assembling this list of aquatics to recommend to you, I drew from the catalogs of what I consider the twelve leading dealers in the United States. I omitted those few rare plants, which they have for sale only on occasion, as well as those which grow only in the cool waters of the northern United States and southern Canada, and the tropical and semitropical plants which thrive only in the hot and humid South. The aquatic plants which remain are those that you can order from practically any dealer, and those that will thrive in practically any section of the United States.

These plants keep pool water healthful by releasing oxygen into it and taking from it carbon dioxide, which, in strength, becomes poisonous to fish. These oxygenators can be seen at their work frequently in patches of strong sunlight, particularly when they are producing an overabundance of oxygen. Tiny, silvery bubbles form on the submerged foliage, break away, and rise to the surface.

Oxygenators contribute to the pool's welfare in other ways. Just by being there, they offer enough competition for sunlight and food to keep microscopic vegetable organisms from multiplying too rapidly. It is these tiny suspended vegetable organisms, in overabundance, that turn pool water a murky, unattractive green.

Foliage of the submerged plants also serves, to an extent, as a bed to receive the spawn of goldfish and provides a protective cover in which baby fish hide.

HOW TO PLANT THE OXYGENATORS

These plants, *Anacharis, Cabomba, Ludwigia* and *Myriophyllum,* will grow without planting. Merely twist a piece of wire around the base of the stems to serve as ballast and to hold the stalks upright. Then drop them into the pool. They will grow more luxuriantly, however, if the stem ends are stuck into a small flower pot of heavy loam. A 4- or 5-inch pot will accommodate up to half a dozen plants. *Vallisneria* and Mares-Tail should be planted in pots or boxes of loam and placed on the pool floor.

All of these submerged plants are perennials. If you live in a mild climate, you may never have to reorder them. You may have to replace

ARROWHEAD

WATER~ARUM

PICKEREL-WEED

PAPYRUS

IRIS

CAT-TAIL

UMBRELLA~PALM

LIZARDS TAIL

GREEN TARO

DRAWING 29. *Aquatic Plants.*

the more delicate, feathery plants, however, if your pool freezes over and if your goldfish tear them pretty well to pieces during the winter period of little or no growth. All are inexpensive.

Submerged Aquatics

Anacharis — (Elodea canadensis). Also called Ditch-Moss, Water-Pest, Water-Thyme, Babbington's-Curse. A fine oxygenator for outdoor pools. Located where there is plenty of sun, it is an extremely free grower, as some of its unflattering names imply. A wild form, somewhat smaller and sparsely foliated, grows throughout the United States and in southern Canada. This, if transplanted to your pool, will do very well, but the cultivated form is inexpensive and far superior. In an aquarium indoors, either form does poorly. A healthy, cultivated plant in an outdoor pool is about 6 inches long, with pliant stems bearing whorls of deep green, willowlike leaves. It spreads quickly by runner and, if it can find enough soil in which to root, will develop a plant chain several feet long on the bottom of the pool. At the plant extends itself, the growth at the older end of the chain becomes yellow. It has to be controlled by pinching off the old growth and keeping only a foot or so of the plant at the new end of the chain.

Cabomba — Also known as Washington Grass, Fanwort, Water-Shield. It probably was a sprig of this plant that the man at the pet store threw in free when you bought goldfish. A good oxygenator, and the fish eat parts of the tender foliage. Other virtues are the lacy appearance of the fanlike leaves and the fact that a piece of any needed size can be pulled from the growing mass and dropped into bowl or aquarium. *Cabomba* propogates principally by branching. Aquarium sprigs are usually 5 to 6 inches long, but left alone with plenty of room, stems grow several feet in a season.

*caroliniana—*Grows wild in ponds from Pennsylvania to North Carolina, the form usually sold or given away with goldfish.

*roseafolia—*Similar but with a reddish cast to stems and undersides of leaves.

*Ludwigia—*Also called Swamp Loosestrife. Basically a marsh grower, but this does quite well as a partially submerged aquatic if planted in shallow water at the edge of a pool where it can break the surface with its upper foliage. It grows from about 6 inches to 2 to 3 feet and bears round, glossy green leaves. It sends roots out horizontally, and new growths spring from them. To keep the plant under control, trim off the new end of the chain. When the old plant exhausts itself, propagate by planting a few cuttings in a 2-inch pot of wet soil with a top layer of sand. Keep the soil saturated. By the time the cuttings rot, they

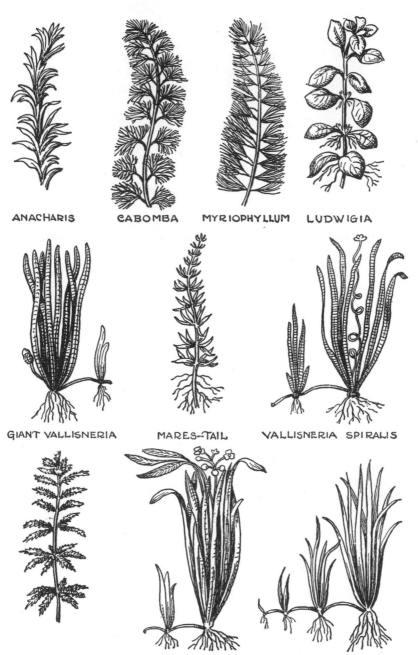

ANACHARIS   CABOMBA   MYRIOPHYLLUM   LUDWIGIA

GIANT VALLISNERIA   MARES-TAIL   VALLISNERIA SPIRALIS

PARROTS-FEATHER • SAGITTARIA NATANS • SAGITTARIA SUBULATA

DRAWING 30. *Submerged Oxygenating Plants.*

will have produced small new growths, which can then be set out where desired. If allowed to develop in strong sunlight, the leaves will take on a copperish tinge, bright red on the undersides. Grows wild at the edge of streams throughout North America, but the wild form is inferior to a cultivated South American form, which is the variety most dealers have.

MARES-TAIL — *(Hippuris vulgaris)*. A spikelike plant which grows from 6 to 8 inches to 2 to 3 feet, with groups of narrow, pointed leaves arranged around the stem in whorls. It grows wild in pools, ponds, and backwater throughout the northern part of the United States and is easy to find and transplant. It used to be a leading favorite with water gardeners, but has fallen off in popularity in recent years, probably because the plant thrusts itself above the water surface in dense patches if not kept trimmed. It is a fine oxygenator, and a little pruning now and then easily keeps it under control.

Myriophyllum—Also called Water-Milfoil. A feathery, dark-green plant much like *Cabomba* in size, manner of propagation, and appearance, but finer, bushier, and more delicate. A good oxygenator, and the fish eat it. The extremely fine, hairlike leaves are excellent to receive the spawn of goldfish. A number of forms grow wild throughout the country.

proserpinacoides—Also listed as Parrots-Feather, and quite aptly. This is a partially submerged form with a profusion of delicate, feathery, blue-green plumes that trail across the surface of the water. It is very pretty around the bases of other plants and is widely used in fountain basins.

verticillatum—Generally considered the best American species, thriving in both deep and shallow ponds of the United States and southern Canada.

Sagittaria—A fine oxygenator and a free, strong grower, used widely in commercial aquariums. The plant is dark green, with long, grasslike leaves. There are a number of species in the United States, several large enough to break the surface of the water. When they do, they produce tiny, cup-shaped white flowers with yellow centers. The plant reproduces principally by runners. It also develops small tubers among its roots, particularly when it is crowded, and these, too, produce new plants.

gigantea—The largest submerged form in popular usage, growing to 10 to 15 inches. Much used in large commercial aquariums, for it will stand up under rough treatment from fish nets.

natans—Sometimes called Ribbon Arrowhead. Perhaps the most important form of the group. Grows to 9 to 10 inches, and all year around, releasing a tremendous amount of oxygen. Has a purifying influence that endears it to aquarium owners. Like a scavenger, it feeds upon whatever waste settles to the bottom, and the soil or sand in which it is planted never turns sour.

subulata—A miniature form, 3 to 7 inches when full grown. A very free grower, spreading by runners. Eventually will cover an entire pond bottom, providing a good spawning ground for adult fish and a safe cover for the young.

Vallisneria spiralis—Also known as Channel-Grass, Eel-Grass, Tape-Grass. There isn't a better oxygenator. The long, ribbonlike foliage resembles that of *Sagittaria,* although of lighter green and semitransparent, also straighter, with less tendency to spread. Sometimes grows to 2 feet, the longer leaves trailing on the water. There are two sexes of the form, and each reproduces in two ways: by runners, producing small plants of its own sex; and by seed, through cross-fertilization. The female plant produces a small, cup-shaped white flower, which floats on the water at the end of a long, spiral stem. The flower of the male plant, which contains a case of pollen, develops on a short stem, only a few inches from the root crown. When the case splits, the pollen rises to the surface, and water action, wind, and insects carry it to the female blossom.

Floating Aquatics

The plants of this group are among the most fascinating to watch develop and propagate, and they require practically no care. They live on air, water, and microscopic matter suspended in water. The water gardener can easily control them by simply scooping up excess growth and throwing it away.

They also have their practical uses. By providing shade and competing for the pool's suspended food supply, they help hold down the growth of algae. The roots provide spawning beds for the adult fish and protective cover for the babies.

PLANTING

Like many of the submerged plants, they will grow quite well if merely dropped into the pool, but will do better if their dragging roots are allowed to touch soil. Most of them are annuals. They are inexpensive, and so it is practical to treat them as annuals and order new stock every year.

Azolla caroliniana—A mass plant, crinkly and mosslike, a single cluster being about as large as the eraser-end of a pencil. It spreads quickly,

Upper left: Needle Leaf Ludwigia. Upper right: Green Ludwigia. Lower left: Water Hedge. Lower right: Aquatic Baby Tears.

Upper left: Florida Dwarf Anacharis. Upper right: Another type of Dwarf Anacharis. Lower photo from left to right: Cabomba caroliniana and Cabomba aquatica.

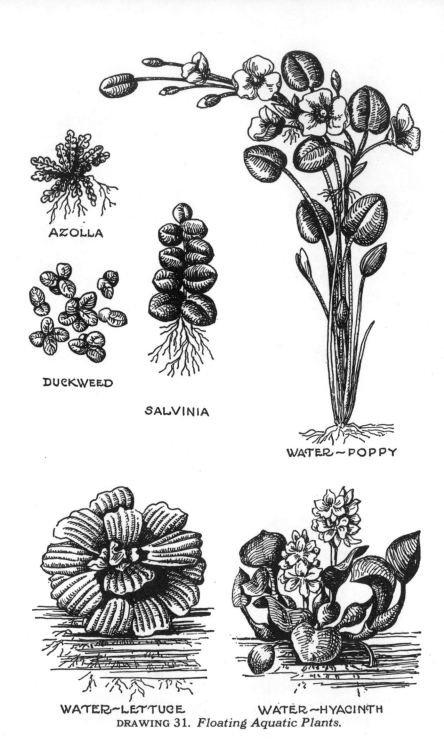

AZOLLA

DUCKWEED

SALVINIA

WATER~POPPY

WATER~LETTUCE

WATER~HYACINTH

DRAWING 31. *Floating Aquatic Plants.*

WATER~CHESTNUT   FROGS~BIT

FLOATING~HEART

WATER~SNOWFLAKE   WATER~FERN

DRAWING 32. *More Floating Aquatic Plants.*

and soon forms a carpet on the pool surface of dull sage green to dark red, depending on how much sun it gets. The more sun, the redder the plant. It is easy enough to control in a very small pool, where it can be scooped up and thrown away, but it can be a terrible nuisance in a larger pool. It is a pity the plant is such a pest, for goldfish love to feed on the roots.

DUCKWEED—*(Lemna minor)*. Another tiny, carpeting plant, even more of a pest than *Azolla*. The leaves are oval, about the size of a match head, and it propagates at an alarming speed by offshoots. It can truly be called the dandelion of the pool, for within a short time it will choke out other plants. The plant is fine for aquariums and very small pools, where it can be controlled. The small, tender roots, which are eaten by fish, have a laxative effect and serve nicely as fish tonic.

FLOATING HEART—*(Nymphoides peltatum)*. A yellow paperlike bloom which grows erect, a few inches above its 3- to 4-inch lilylike pads on the water. A perennial, it should be planted with the crown of the root 6 to 18 inches below the surface. Each bloom lasts only a day, but the plant is so prolific that it puts on a show all season. A word of warning: it reproduces in three ways—by surface runners, by runners at the pool bottom, and by pods of very fertile seeds. It will become a pest if not watched closely. Never plant it in the same container with a water-lily, and never allow it to grow freely on an earth-covered pool floor. Keep it in check by careful pruning at the pool surface and on the pool bottom.

FROGS-BIT—*(Hydrocharis morsus-ranae)*. An attractive floating plant, introduced from Europe, with bluntly triangular leaves the size of silver dollars and small white blooms shaped like primroses. Terminal buds form in the fall, and then the plant decays and the buds drop off and sink to the bottom. The following spring they rise to the surface again and start new plants. This plant has one serious drawback. Snails are attracted to it, and if not checked they feed on the soft, spongy leaves and quickly ruin its appearance.

SALVINIA—A very small plant, consisting of pea-sized, heart-shaped leaves covered with a nap of tiny hairs. It reproduces generously and soon covers sections of the pool with a velvety carpet. The plant will not become a pest, however, for goldfish keep it under control. They feed on the roots, after which leaves fail to reach full development. It will be wise to keep a replenishing stock of *Salvinia* on hand by protecting one clump from the fish with wire screening.

SHELL-FLOWER—*(Pistia stratiotes)*. Also called Water-Lettuce. A pale bluish-green floating plant with velvety, fluted leaves the size and shape of garden lettuce. It grows in a saucer-sized rosette and trails a beard of long (sometimes 18-inch) wavy roots, which are not nearly so good as those of Water-Hyacinth for spawning, being much sparser, but they are one of the best substitutes, now that the use of Water-Hyacinth is restricted by conservationists. The shell-flower does best in hot summers, but it will grow in a partially shaded area of the pool. It needs a lot of moisture to attain best growth and should be sprayed with the garden hose now and then. It will anchor itself and do even better if roots are allowed to touch a soil bottom or a container of soil. It produces new growths in chainlike formation.

WATER-CHESTNUT—(*Trapa natans*). A floating annual herb with foliage and fruit somewhat like that of the chestnut tree. The toothed, triangular leaves are not much larger than postage stamps, and the cluster making up each plant is about the size of a saucer. The plant is kept afloat by swollen, hollow sections of stem 2 to 4 inches long. The flowers are small, white, and inconspicuous. The seeds are somewhat smaller than chestnuts, black and hard, each with four curving hornlike spikes.

WATER-FERN—(*Ceratopteris thalictroides*). This is a true fern although the plant does not look much like a fern, but rather like dark-green garden lettuce, floating in clusters 6 to 12 inches in diameter and a foot or more high. It does better in an indoor than an outdoor pool, although it grows quite freely outside. New growths spring up from the edges of the leaves, break off, and float away to establish themselves as separate plants.

WATER-HYACINTH—(*Eichhornia crassipes*). Each plant is a floating island of dark green leaves, with pale lavender-blue blooms that resemble those of the Easter hyacinth. In the pool each cluster can be anchored into a fixed position, if the water gardener so desires, by tying a weighted string to the roots.

The plant provides an attractive indoor interest, and it winters well inside. Simply float it in a container of water which has 3 to 4 inches of soil in the bottom, and give it a sunny window position. Replace the water from time to time to keep it fresh.

But, alas, dealers can no longer ship to customers out of state, for this is now unlawful. If you cannot find a dealer in your own state with a supply of Water-Hyacinth you will have to do without it, but you can make (as many water gardeners have) some other provision for the goldfish spawn. This can be done by constructing a wooden frame, say of one-inch material, 6 inches wide and 30 inches long. Cover the frame with chicken wire, and this, in turn, with a 1- to 2-inch layer of dried Spanish moss. Place this rack in the pool; it will float and hold the moss about 6 inches below the surface. As a spawning ground, it will be as efficient as the root systems of several plants of Water-Hyacinth.

AZURE WATER-HYACINTH—*(Eichhornia azurea)*. Also called Purple Water-Hyacinth, Creeping Water-Hyacinth. A plant with runners which creep across the water surface, and ride prettily upon it, but without the aid of the air-filled bulbs which keep the more common form of Water-Hyacinth afloat. Flowers, similar in shape, are of a richer purple hue.

WATER-POPPY—*(Limnocharis Humboldtii)*. A three-petaled yellow flower, resembling the California poppy, with a brown eye. Root of the parent plant must be embedded in a container of soil, much as a water-lily is planted. Runners are sent to the water surface, producing new plants which then send strong runners down to the pool bottom in an effort to obtain fresh rooting. It produces a profusion of bloom and smooth, deep-green foliage, which floats prettily among the water-lilies.

WATER-SNOWFLAKE—*(Limnathemum indicum)*. A small, attention-getting plant with smooth leaves like those of a miniature water-lily. Blooms, which appear at the junction of leaf and stem, are held a few inches above the water. They are white, five-petaled, with a white, lacy covering, making the flower look exactly like its namesake. This is not truly a floating plant, for the parent should be rooted in a container of soil 6 to 8 inches below the surface. It reproduces through leaves, which break, float away, and re-establish themselves as new plants in shallow water.

Marsh and Bog Plants for the Pool Border

These plants cover the harsh line where pool and earth meet, and also provide a varied setting for your water-lilies, making your pool a more beautiful place in general. Even in a formal pool, it is a good idea to plant the corners and the center with a variety of graceful accessory plants. Some of the taller border plants are a *must* for the informal pool, too. As I have said, one of the charms of an informal pool is that of seeing half a dozen different views as you approach from half a dozen different paths. This can be accomplished only by planting natural, attractive screens here and there about it.

PLANTING

Because the border plants do not produce the tremendous amount of foliage and bloom the water-lilies do, they do not need the rich fertilizer in their soil. Any good, heavy loam will suffice.

Three general levels of planting are employed for the plants listed in this section.

Those with submerged roots can be planted in 6-, 8-, or 10-inch pots, or in boxes, and set on a ledge or shelf in the pool at the water depth prescribed for them.

Those plants which do best with root crowns at, or just slightly above, water level must be planted in boxes or in built-in receptacles filled with earth to the proper level.

The third group includes plants which come from fairly dry land, but not so high above water level that roots cannot grow in marshy, saturated earth. I have indicated the proper level for each plant in the listing which follows.

The size of the plant mass which develops depends, of course, on the size of the container in which it is planted. If you want a plant to reproduce itself until it forms a sizable clump, allow for expansion by providing a large receptacle. If you want to restrict the plant to an individual growth or a very small clump, supply a smaller receptacle.

ARROWHEAD—*(Sagittaria)*. From the standpoint of use and decorative form, the *Sagittaria* which we discussed earlier among oxygenating plants is very different from Arrowhead. Botanically, however, they spring from the same genus, *Sagittaria*. I listed the submerged form as popular usage identifies it. Botanically, it would also be proper to list these bog and shallow-water plants as *Sagittaria*, but they are popularly referred to as Arrowhead.

COMMON ARROWHEAD—*(Sagittaria latifolia)*. The plant takes its name, of course, from the shape of the dark-green leaves. Height is variable, from a few inches to 2 feet or more. The spikes of small white flowers suggest apple blossoms with yellow centers. Will grow in wet soil or in water up to 6 inches. Propagates by runner and must be controlled by occasional thinning.

GIANT ARROWHEAD—*(Sagittaria sagittifolia)*. Similar, but larger, from 1 to 4 feet.

JAPANESE, OR DOUBLE-FLOWERING ARROWHEAD—*(Sagittaria japonica flore-pleno)*. Similar, but with double-petaled spikes.

BOGBEAN—*(Menyanthes trifoliata)*. Also called Buckbean, Marsh Trefoil. Low-growing, creeping perennial with glossy, olive-green leaves borne in threes. Star-shaped flowers, white inside and pink outside, with conspicuous red stamens, come in fragrant clusters. Each petal is fringed. Hardy when planted in mud under no more than 6 inches of water. Foliage soon scrambles out of the water to cover whatever pool-side space there is. Propagated by seed and by root division.

BULRUSH—*(Scirpus)*. Grasslike leaves and flowers in small spikes. Perennial, grows in bog mud or under an inch or so of water, and propagates by root division, seeds and suckers. Spreads rapidly and must be controlled. A number of forms offer a range of sizes.

cernuus—Grows to about a foot, with slender hair-grass stems some-times erect, sometimes drooping. At the end of the stems, it bears small, yellowish-white blooms. Grows indoors as well as in a pool.

lacustris—A mass of fat, dark-green rushes 3 to 9 feet high, bearing umbels of chocolate-brown blooms at the tips of the stems. This is the form aptly called Bulrush, a term which is a corruption of Pool Rush, the original name for this species. Also listed as Great Rush.

Tabernaemontani—Similar to the lacustris but grows only to 2 feet, and stems are covered with bluish-green fuzz.

> var. *zebrinus*—Also called Zebra Rush, Porcupine Quill Rush. Grows 4 to 5 feet and produces handsome green- and white-banded foliage. Grows best with roots under a few inches of water.

CARDINAL FLOWER—*(Lobelia cardinalis)*. Excellent and widely used border plant, about 2 feet high, with deep-green, mint-shaped leaves and spikes of fiery-red blossoms. Does well in an inch or so of water. Perennial blooming from July well into September.

CAT-TAIL—*(Typha latifolia)*. One of the most common of all bog plants. This species, when well established, may grow a 5- to 6-foot wall of foliage, with dark-brown "tails" taller by another foot or so. Grows best in 1 to 6 inches of water, and reproduces by creeping rootstocks. Is best controlled by restricting roots in a planting container.

GRACEFUL CAT-TAIL—*(T. angustifolia)*. Similar, but with shorter, narrower foliage, and thinner, more graceful tails. If planted un-restrained in a natural pond they will take it over in two to three years.

PYGMY CAT-TAIL—*(T. minima)*. Dwarf of the family, with rushes only 12 to 18 inches, the tails not much thicker than lead pencils. A type often used in dried-flower decorations. Foliage develops well the first year, but the tails do not appear until the second year.

CREEPING PRIMROSE—*(Jussiaea diffusa)*. A fast-growing vine with waxy, deep-green, narrow, pointed leaves and many bright-yellow blooms which look like primroses. Does best in a inch or so of water, but will also grow in any saturated soil. Strong stems lie above ground or water, frequently turning up 6- to 8-inch lengths to sprout blooms and new leaves.

EGYPTIAN PAPER PLANT—*(Cyperus papyrus)*. A graceful species of the sedge family which produces palm-shaped tufts of thready, green-ish-brown inflorescence at the ends of graceful, triangular, bending stems. Well situated, with roots under 2 to 3 inches of water and with plenty of sun, it can reach 10 to 12 feet. By pruning, it is easily kept to

4 to 6 feet. It reproduces by seed, by root division, and through small plants which sprout from the tops of the arching stems. There is a dwarf variety which grows only to 2 feet, but it is not yet commercially available on any appreciable scale.

FLOWERING-RUSH—*(Butomus umbellatus)*. An erect plant with three-sided, sword-shaped leaves 2 to 3 inches high, much like iris. It bears funnel-shaped umbels of rose-pink blossoms at the top of long, thin stems. It is propagated by root division, and does well in either saturated soil or an inch or so of water.

FORGET-ME-NOT—*(Myosotis palustris)*. Aquatic variety of the old American favorite. The bright-blue florets on thin, hairlike stems become quite dense when the plant is grown in an inch or two of water. Clumps of bloom and foliage sometimes become a foot high.

HORSE-TAIL RUSH—*(Equisetum)*. Thin, leafless, graceful rush, with evergreen stems that grow to height of about four feet. Considered among prettiest of the rushes. The plant's creeping rootstocks make it valuable for holding watery banks firm, and covering waste areas at the water's edge.

IRIS—*(Iridaceae)*. A genus of one of the largest and most important flower families under cultivation. The genus divides into the bearded or "dry iris," which thrives in well-drained soil, and the beardless or "wet iris," which grows in heavy, moist soil. Most of the water-loving species and varieties placed for decoration at the edge of the pool do best with the root crowns under an inch or two of water. Flowers begin to open in the latter part of May and early June—while hardy water-lilies in the pool are just stretching themselves after their long winter sleep—and thus iris fills in that bloomless gap which begins with pretty weather and continues until the hardies open in June.

WATER IRIS—*(Iris versicolor)*. Also called Marsh Iris, Blue Flag, Violet-blue flowers with streaks of yellow, green, and white are borne on stems about 2 feet tall. Foliage, which is thick and free growing, is only slightly shorter. Does well in either plashy mud at water level or under an inch or two of water, and will reproduce rapidly in either location. There are many similar variegated forms, but this is the classic form, and year after year a top favorite.

YELLOW FLAG—*(Iris pseudacorus)*. The royal flower of France and the national emblem. The fleur-de-lis is a stylized reproduction of it. This iris might be called a bright yellow counterpart of the Blue Flag, except that it usually grows half again as large and its sword-shaped leaves are somewhat broader.

LIZARD'S TAIL—*(Saururus cernuus)*. Also called American Swamp

Lily. A 2½- to 5- and 6-foot shallow-water or bog plant with bright-green, heart-shaped leaves as big as a man's mitten. The fragrant flowers, which begin to appear in midsummer, are slender, nodding spikes of feathery white. The plant takes its name from the shape of the tail-like bloom. Grows wild in swamps almost everywhere in the United States.

MARSH-MARIGOLD—(*Caltha palustris*). Sometimes called Cowslip or Buttercup. A low-growing pond-edge plant with rounded, deeply notched leaves and waxy yellow blooms which look like giant buttercups. Propagates by runners, and tends to spread sparsely over a sizable area instead of crowding, but runners can easily be guided to fill a particular space. Plants ordered in spring usually arrive too late to bloom before the next year, since this is about the earliest of the bog plants to blossom, often in March. Does best with the root crown barely under water.

PICKEREL RUSH—(*Pontederia cordata*). Also called Pickerel-Weed, Pond-Weed. One of the finest of the pond-edge plants, growing to 18 to 24 inches, with large, arrow-shaped, olive-green leaves carried well above the water. Spikes of closely packed, violet-blue flowers are attractive and produce freely. Grows best in 3 to 4 inches of water and propagates freely, principally by division of roots; requires little or no control. Even when crowded, the smooth, shining foliage looks neat and precise. This is a North American aquatic, much prized by European water gardeners, who import a great deal of it.

PRIMROSE-WILLOW—(*Jussiaea longifolia*). An attractive pool-edge plant from 3 to 4 feet high, with graceful, woody stems, willowlike foliage, and a profusion of yellow blooms resembling primrose. Grows well with roots in either wet soil or in muddy bottom under an inch or two of water.

SWEET FLAG—(*Acorus calamus*). Also called Beewort. A hardy marsh perennial herb, at home in shallow water or in saturated earth, with broad, dark-green straplike leaves which grow 2 to 3 feet high. Foliage is similar to that of iris. The flower, a conical spike 2 to 3 inches long of small greenish bloom, is borne on a long stem. The plant is as old as any other in cultivation. All parts emit a pleasant scent when crushed and have a warm, pungent taste suggestive of cinnamon. In the early days it was used as medicine for a variety of ills, from diseases of the eye to stomach disorders. More recently it has been used to scent hair pomades and flavor tooth pastes and cough sirups. It propagates by root division.

var. *variegatus*—More popular in the United States, with foliage an attractive combination of green and cream and the same aromatic characteristics.

TARO—(*Colocasia esculenta*). Also called Elephants-Ear. A genus of tuberous herbs, various forms of which range from 1½ to 3 feet, grown for the showy foliage. Elephants-Ear is an apt name in view of the shape of the leaves, which are no larger than a human hand on some of the smaller forms, but as large as the ear of an elephant on larger species and varieties. Planted with the root crown at water level, Taro thrives and spreads by root division. Grown indoors in winter, in a tub or bucket of soil, and kept well watered, it also does quite well as a house plant.

This is an edible plant. The foliage in various tropical countries is prepared like asparagus, and tastes rather like it. In Japan, the starchy rhizomes are boiled—to get rid of the bitter, toxic acridity—and eaten like potatoes. The Hawaiian dish, *poi,* is from this plant. Rhizomes are crushed, cooked, allowed to ferment for a few days, and served as thick, pasty gruel.

Some of the larger dealers in aquatics carry as many as half a dozen forms, and nearly all have these three forms:

GREEN TARO—(*C. indica*). Only 1½ to 2 feet high with dark-green, shiny foliage. One of the strongest-growing forms.

IMPERIAL TARO—(*C. antiquorum illustris*). Sometimes called Black Caladium. Grows 3 to 4 feet with foliage of bluish-green, splotched violet-black in an artistic pattern.

VIOLET-STEM TARO—(*C. multiflora*). Grows 2 to 4 feet with large, bluish-green leaves in pretty contrast to violet stems, midribs, and veins. Leaf edges are stained an attractive lavender.

TURTLE-HEAD—(*Chelone*). A hardy perennial herb which grows wild to 2 to 6 feet in wet meadows, swamps, along the edges of rivers, and in roadside ditches throughout most of eastern North America. The narrow, toothed leaves are spear-shaped and the bloom does look like the head of a turtle, with mouth open and ready for business. Flowers appear in midsummer and continue until frost. This propagates readily by seed, root division, and cuttings.

glabra—Also called Cod-Head, Snake-Head. A smaller form with white or pale-pink blooms.

Lyonii—A taller species, with dense, heart-shaped leaves and reddish-purple blooms.

obliqua—Also called Red Turtle-Head. Similar in form to the *C. glabra,* but with reddish-purple flowers. Earliest blooming of the group.

UMBRELLA-PALM—(*Cyperus alternifolius*). Also called Umbrella Plant. An attractive sedge, 1 to 3 feet high, with flat, grassy, umbrella-like leaf heads borne at the end of slender stems. Like the Egyptian

Paper Plant, to which it is related, this spreads by seed, root division, and from young plants which form at the ends of the grasslike leaves. Grows well in a bog or in 2 to 3 inches of water. Transferred to a jardiniere of moist soil, which must be kept that way, it makes a splendid house plant.

WATER-ARUM—*(Calla palustris)*. Also Wild Calla or Bog-Arum. A modified version of the calla lily, growing to about a foot. Does well with roots in mud slightly above or below water level. This is a perennial that need never be moved in milder climates. Where there are killing frosts, rootstocks must be taken indoors for the winter. The first year the plant bears a profusion of small, shiny, heart-shaped leaves; the second it develops creamy-white blooms of classical lily form—a trumpet-like spathe, or sheath, surrounding a yellow spadix, or flower spike. The spadix becomes a cluster of red berries in autumn. Water-Arum is interesting in that it is one of the very few plants fertilized by snails. The offensive odor (to humans) of the bloom attracts the snails, which make their way painstakingly up and down the stems to visit first one blossom, then another. The plant also propagates by root division.

WATER CANNA—*(Thalia)*. A perennial herb similar to the canna. Grows well under a few inches of water at the pool edge or in a large flower pot resting on the pool floor. Propagates by root division. Leaves are shaped like broad spear points, attractive in form and arrangement. Flowers are deep purple, and borne on graceful spikes held aloft on long, arching stems. These are the two most popular forms:

dealbata—Grows 3 to 4 feet with leaves 6 to 9 inches long, covered with a fine dusting of white powder which gives a unique blue-green cast. If left on the pool floor, well below the freezing line, the plant will survive the winter along with the hardy water-lilies. Roots left in shallow water or in pond-edge mud will be frozen to death. Moved indoors for the winter, this form makes a nice house plant. A single planting will produce a dense clump of bold, attractive foliage.

divaricata—The larger form, sometimes 5 to 10 feet tall. Leaves are dark and shiny, not with the mealy look of the *T. dealbata*.

WATER CLOVER—*(Marsilea)*. A favorite for decorating odd corners of the pond and covering sloping mud banks with an attractive blanket of foliage like field clover, except that stalks and leaves are covered with silky down.

Drummondii—The floating variety, which does best in fairly deep water where clumps sometimes grow 1½ to 2 feet thick.

quadrifolia—Much smaller and does well on a bank or in water. The four-leaved foliage forms a covering only 3 to 6 inches thick. Like

M. Drummondii, it reproduces by wind-borne spores and by root division.

WATER-CRESS—(*Radicula nasturtium-aquaticum*). Also Water Nasturtium. The familiar hardy perennial which is gathered at the edges of cold, spring-fed streams and eaten as a crisp, piquant salad. The small, round, dark-green leaves, tiny white flowers, and succulent stems are also relished by fish. The dark, waxy look of the 2- and 3-foot branching stems contrasts prettily with the feathery foliage of other floating and submerged greenery. The plant has certain oxygenating characteristics which also make it beneficial. Does best when rooted under 2 to 3 inches of water. Is propagated by seeds and cuttings.

WATER-PLANTAIN—(*Alisma plantago-aquatica*). Also called Mad Dog Weed. A free-flowering plant growing 2 to 3 feet high with broad, heart-shaped leaves, somewhat like those of common plantain, and pyramidal clusters of small, delicate-white or pale-pink blooms. Grows in deep water, but blooms most freely when roots are embedded in mud under only an inch or so of water. Propagates by seed and root division.

WILD RICE—(*Zizania palustris*). Also called Indian Rice, Water Rice, Water Oats. An annual aquatic grass with broad, flat leaves, reedy stems, and large, branching terminal flowers. Planted in 5 to 6 inches of water, it soon provides a handsome backdrop of foliage 8 to 10 feet high. An excellent pond border for bird-lovers, for the seeds attract ducks and other game birds. Must be grown from seed which is well soaked before planting.

Plate 38. The water garden supports not only the submerged and floating plants in the pool, but also a great variety of land plants which thrive around the border. Iris alone presents the pool owner with a choice of many varied colors and forms.

SINGER PHOTO

CHAPTER FOURTEEN

Repairs, Maintenance, Pest and Disease Control

If you are enough of a craftsman to build a water-lily pool, you probably have achieved a perfectly level structure. Sometimes, however, pools tilt, either because they were constructed to conform to the level of the surrounding ground instead of to the water level, or they have settled unevenly on part-soft, part-hard foundation. Water may be lapping at the brim at one end of such a pool, but be 6 to 8 inches below the brim at the other end.

THE TILTING POOL

There is nothing you can do to correct a pool that tilts. I have seen people try to build the rim higher here and there with bricks or concrete, but I have never seen anyone do it successfully. Tilting is not really as serious as you imagine. Just try to accept the situation as it is. By strategic placement of shallow-water and border plants, you can cover your mistake pretty well—even attractively.

SMALL LEAKS

Small leaks caused by hairlike cracks in the pool floor or walls can be annoying, but they also are not much of a problem. Frequently they pass unnoticed, for pools consistently lose a certain amount of water through evaporation. If you add water now and then to make up for evaporation, it may be weeks before you realize the pool is leaking.

Put off the repair of such cracks, if at all possible, until the pool has been drained for cleaning in spring. Thick, heavy clay, rubbed into the cracks, makes good temporary patching. Once you have drained the pool, the size of the cracks will dictate your procedure.

If the cracks are very fine, a coat or two of special pool paint, available from most dealers, will probably seal cracks nicely. Or you can cover them two or three times with a heavy coat of waterproof varnish or artificial resin, which most paint stores carry.

If the cracks are somewhat larger, and there are many of them, coat the interior of the pool to a thickness of ⅛ inch with a mixture of one part cement and three parts fine sand, adding just enough water to give the mixture the consistency of wet plaster. Apply with a trowel, and smooth with a wooden float. Be sure to cure the pool before you put plants or goldfish into it.

Some gardeners have done very well by thinning the above mixture and "painting" the pool surfaces with it, applying it with a broom. Give the pool two paintings. Again neutralize with the vinegar and water treatment as described in Chapter 4.

If there are only a few cracks to seal, your paint store probably will be able to provide a mastic or caulking compound which will seal them.

BIG CRACKS

If you have a large crack in the shell of your pool, you are in for trouble. Big cracks, which seldom occur in pools made of reinforced concrete, are caused by uneven settling of the pool shell or by ice pressure in winter. If cracks would get no larger, they would be repairable. But they do get larger. Once a major crack occurs, it usually continues to widen a bit with each passing season, making any patch in it worthless.

But you can try. Some do manage successfully to apply patches to such cracks, and you may be one of the lucky ones. Drain the pool, clean it out, and then chisel out the inside surfaces of the big crack to give your patching material something to hold on to. Prepare a half-and-half mixture of sand and cement, making it just wet enough to be plastic and easily applied. Give the patch plenty of time to set before curing it, preparatory to refilling the pool.

Pool Maintenance

Unless you are an old hand at water gardening, the horrible looking layer of scum which undoubtedly will form on top of your pool shortly after you fill and plant it for the first time will break your heart. Have courage, for this is the most natural situation in the world.

223

SCUM AND ALGAE

A goodly part of the scum is dust and bits of organic material which have escaped from your planting boxes. Once the earth and fertilizer in the boxes become thoroughly saturated, they will not release further clutter.

Scum consists also of countless millions of tiny suspended vegetable organisms, thriving on the manure, in solution, which has been let loose in the water. These organisms, to a large extent, are various forms of algae. They will be ever-present—and welcome—in your pool. Part of the scum quite possibly may be fish food. If you are a new water gardener, you probably will feed your fish too much, and excess food will remain in the pool to decompose.

Surprisingly enough, one of the principal factors contributing to the scum will be plenty of sunlight. The foliage of water-lilies and of floating and submerged plants in a newly planted pool takes a few days to spread. As it spreads, it kills out the microscopic plant life in two ways: First, it competes for food in suspension in the pool water; second, it produces more and more shade as it spreads, and in shade the microscopic plants cannot multiply or even hold their own.

So you must remind yourself that within the course of the few weeks it took you to set up your water garden, you have been aiming at a balance of life which it takes nature months and years to establish. If you have goldfish and submerged plants in the pool, in addition to the showy plants, the pool will soon find its own balance and hold to it.

Now that you know what causes the scum, it is an easy matter to get rid of it. Simply raise the water level of the pool by a quarter of an inch. The floating scum, with a little guidance from you, will run off down the overflow drain. If the pool does not have an overflow drain, sweep the scum to one corner with a folded newspaper or a broom and dip it out.

GREEN WATER

Healthy pool water is not crystal clear, but has a slightly cloudy, greenish tinge. This green cast is due to the millions of suspended microscopic algae, plankton, and similar plants, which are necessary for the health of the goldfish. It is easy to determine the proper balance of these plants in the pool water. Roll up your sleeve and hold your hand about 12 inches below the surface. If your hand is barely discernible at that depth, the balance is perfect.

As for crystal clearness, remember that you will not see the water of a pool as you see water in an aquarium. At the vantage points from which you will enjoy your pool, you will not see into the water at all, save for glimpses of the darting goldfish. What you will see will be reflections of water-lilies, of border plants, and of the sky.

MURKY WATER

At times minute plant life in your pool, particularly forms of algae, will grow in superabundance. When it does, there are means of thinning the water. One popular way is to drop a few fresh-water mussels into the pool. I must admit they do a remarkable job of clearing up the water, but many gardeners feel they are more trouble than they are worth. Watch out for dead ones which have to be removed immediately; for they decompose quickly.

Another way is to treat the pool with potassium permanganate (obtainable at your drugstore). Figure out the water volume in cubic feet. Then multiply the number of cubic feet by 7.48 (or 7 ½ is close enough) to get the water volume in gallons. For each 2,000 gallons of water, throw into the pool one ounce of fined (not crystallized) potassium permanganate. The "fines" dissolve more quickly. Keep them in a tightly stoppered jar and mix only when the solution is needed.

For a day or two the pool will look like diluted grape juice. However, the pool will regain its natural pale-green color after two or three days —and the excess plant life, particularly the stringy, unwanted forms of algae, will have been killed off. Potassium permanganate, used in this manner, kills off lesser organisms, both plant and animal, which might be annoying or hampering to goldfish and water-lilies, and it is a sort of general, all-round tonic for the fish.

A word of warning: Measure as carefully as you can for this treatment. If the potassium solution is too strong, it will kill the goldfish. If too weak, it will not kill off the objectionable plant and animal life.

COPPER SULFATE TREATMENT

There is an alternate treatment for murky water, effected with copper sulfate, 23 grains for every 1,000 gallons of water. I do not recommend it for various reasons. First, the potassium permanganate treatment works out quite well, and so an additional treatment is not needed. Secondly, it takes only a slight overdose of copper sulfate to kill plants and goldfish. Thirdly, copper sulfate does the job *too* well, killing every bit of algae in the pool, including desirable forms of it, too. Moreover, traces of the chemical remain in the pool water for two or three days after the treatment, and I think they hamper plant and fish growth.

Pest and Disease Control

Water-lilies probably suffer less from diseases and insects than any other ornamental plants. Perhaps this is because they are extremely healthy in their watery beds, and therefore vigorous enough to throw off ailments that cause many earth-borne plants to fail. Perhaps they have little trouble with insects because goldfish in the pool eat insect eggs and larvae as soon as they appear. However, various harmful insects and two forms of fungi do make their appearance on rare occasions, so it is wise to be able to recognize them.

APHIDS (*Rhopalosiphum nymphaeae*). These reddish-black pests will appear fairly early in the summer, particularly if the season is hot with little rainfall. In the water garden, you will see them first on leaf stems of lilies which hold bloom and leaf above the water. If aphids are not checked on stems, they will move on to the leaves. They live by sucking plant juices, and, if not eliminated, will cause leaves to discolor and eventually decay.

Aphids are easy to get rid of. Twist the nozzle of your garden hose down to a fine, businesslike spray. Wash the aphids off stems and foliage into the pool. The fish will do the rest.

BROWN CHINA MARKS MOTH (*Hydrocampa proprialis*). A small moth with 1- to 1¼-inch spread, the orange-brown wings patterned with white. It lays small clusters of eggs close to the edge of leaves, and the eggs soon hatch small white larvae.

The insect is worst in the larvae stage. It cuts pieces from leaves and attaches itself between them to make a floating home in which to travel from one plant to another, borne by wind and water motion, eating around the leaf edges as it goes.

Fortunately, the pest is rare, for it is hard to kill. Destroy the larvae by removing any floating, stuck-together bits of debris. Dip them from the pool and destroy.

Kill the insect in the moth stage with a lamp trap—a lantern or other light set out at night over a dishpan of water on which a film of kerosene floats. The light will attract the moths to their doom in the kerosene.

Kill the eggs and newly hatched larvae by dislodging them from the leaves. Just push the leaves under water for a moment, and the fish will do the rest of the job for you.

CADDIS FLIES (Trichoptera). Potential pests, for they feed on roots, buds, and leaves of just about anything they can find growing in the water. They cannot get a start in a pool with goldfish, however, for their larvae are aquatic—and a favorite fish food.

Leaf Miner (*Chironomus modestus*). A slender, streamlined larva, ¼ inch or less long, which eats its way over the surfaces of leaves, leaving unsightly channels which resemble Chinese ideographs. If insects appear in small numbers, remove them individually from the leaves. If they appear in greater strength—which is seldom—spray infested leaves with a fine film of kerosene. Three daily sprayings should suffice. Bordeaux mixture, Slug Shot, and powdered DDT are also effective.

Leaf Roller (*Botis nelumbialis*). An early summer larval pest which attacks the leaf edges, rolling the leaves over upon themselves and gumming them down to form shelters. The larva is a heavy eater and will soon destroy a whole leaf, working from edge to center. When it reaches the center, it burrows into the stem.

Luckily, this pest is rare, for about the only way to get rid of it is to pinch the rolled-up leaf edges or remove the infested leaves.

Water-Lily Leaf Beetle (*Galerucella nymphaeae*). This ovate beetle emerges from winter hibernation in pool-side vegetation, attacks leaves and blooms of water-lilies, and spoils the appearance of both. Beginning in June, it lays from 6 to 20 bright-yellow, ovate eggs in clusters on leaf surfaces. The larvae, which hatch in a week, are blue-black on top, yellow on the underside, and somewhat longer than the parent. Clustering in colonies, they feed hungrily upon foliage and soon strip a leaf.

The beetle produces several broods a year. It is the most destructive pest known to water-lily fanciers—but it also is one of the rarest. Rid the pool of it by trimming pool-side vegetation in the winter and by submerging infested leaves so that fish can eat larvae and eggs.

Fungi

There are two forms of fungi which affect water-lilies, but they are so rare I have never been able to find a popular name for either of them. The names under which they are listed here I gave myself in order to differentiate them in my own mind.

Leaf Fungus (probably a form of *Ovularia nymphaerum*). This one makes infrequent appearances in hot, humid weather. It shows up in dark patches on the leaves, which disintegrate shortly thereafter. The few water gardeners I know who have seen it say it is easily controlled by quick removal and burning of the first leaves on which it is seen.

Leaf Spot (probably some species of the *Cercosporae genus*). This fungus shows up as scattered spots on water-lily leaves, and causes edges to dry and turn up. Bordeaux mixture, thrown in a fine, misty spray on the lily pads every other day for a week, usually kills it. Leaves on which it has already made appreciable progress should be removed and burned.

OTHER ENEMIES

Pools near a house or larger natural ponds some distance away are seldom bothered by animal pests. Under unusual circumstances, however, any of the following could conceivably become plentiful enough to be a nuisance. There are quick and simple remedies for all of them.

CRAWFISH. They cut off young leaves and sometimes small buds. They are no trouble in the back-yard pool, for they can easily be removed whenever the pool is drained for cleaning. It is seldom that an annoying number of adults find their way into a concrete pool anyway. And they are not much trouble in an open, natural pond, for these are usually stocked with enough game or large goldfish to gobble up each new brood of crawfish babies.

DUCKS. Never a problem in the backyard pool, but both wild and domestic ducks have been known to catch fish and pick at water-lily foliage and roots in farm ponds.

MUSKRATS. These have an expensive taste for lotus and water-lily rootstocks. If there are enough muskrats to cause real trouble, perhaps you can interest a young man in your neighborhood in making himself some money by trapping them. Their runs are easy to spot, and they are not hard to trap. If there is only one muskrat, or possibly two or three, you might get a grim enjoyment out of potting them yourself with a rifle.

RATS AND MICE. If you have any of these in your house, they will discover your water-lily roots and eat them. Store roots either out of reach or in ventilated metal containers.

SNAILS. These are not much trouble in a natural pond, since sunfish and goldfish feed on them. In a small pool, the snails you dropped in to serve as scavengers may reproduce to such an extent as to become unsightly. Then they are easily removed. At night put a section of cabbage or lettuce, perhaps half a head, tied to a floating piece of board, in the center of the pool. Next morning it will be covered with snails. Destroy them. Repeat the process until the snail population is reduced enough to suit you.

Snails sold as pool scavengers do not feed on aquatic foliage. However, your pool may attract the large, black-shelled variety which does eat leaves and blooms. They are easily differentiated from the others and can be attracted by the cabbage lure and destroyed accordingly.

SNAPPING TURTLES. These are a problem only in the natural pond and a real headache until you get rid of them. The snapping turtle feeds on young leaves and flowers, and if you get a really hungry one, he will snap off water-lily buds as fast as they form. Set a few hooks for him, baited with spoiled meat. Or, once again, you may enjoy oiling up the rifle and settling with him in person.

Snapping Turtle will destroy plants, and slow-moving fish too.

M. F. ROBERTS PHOTO

CHAPTER FIFTEEN

Building and Stocking the Farm Pond

A farm pond is comparatively simple and inexpensive to develop, but it is hardly in the do-it-yourself field. It requires professional help, and, in some instances, governmental sanction. You can satisfy yourself as to whether you have a good natural site, but you should not start building before consulting someone who has at least the rudiments of topographic engineering.

Building the Pond

Ordinarily, ten to thirty acres of watershed are considered a sufficient source of water for a small farm pond. So is a stream or spring capable of filling the proposed pond basin in a year's time or less. But too much water can be as much of a problem as too little, and such a problem may entail special provisions. These are best worked out by a professional.

The type and formation of the soil in which the basin of the pond will be made are other basic considerations dependent on borings and soil tests. There are also legal aspects, for government permission is frequently involved when the course of a stream is to be dammed or diverted.

You may be able to work out the design of your dam and spillways yourself, if you are a fair amateur engineer, but free consultation and other help are available to you, and you will do well to take advantage of it. Help will also be available to you in the stocking of your pond with game fish.

The government offers two excellent publications which will give you a wealth of general information on farm ponds. You can order "How to Build a Farm Pond," Department of Agriculture Leaflet No. 259, five cents, and "Managing Farm Fishponds for Bass and Bluegills,"

Farmers' Bulletin No. 2094, fifteen cents (with the money enclosed) from the Superintendent of Documents, U. S. Government Printing Office, Washington, D.C.

For specific consultation on building and stocking a farm pond, get in touch with your nearest representatives of Soil Conservation and Fish and Wildlife. Your county agent will tell you where to find them.

Proper Planting

Farm ponds are built to provide water for livestock when other sources dry up during drought, for fire protection, to provide swimming, boating, and year-round fishing, to attract waterfowl, and for numerous other reasons. The use for which a pond is intended will influence, of course, the size, shape, and design. There is no type of farm pond, regardless of its utilitarian service, which hasn't magnificent possibilities for water-lilies and shore-line plants.

There is a mistaken idea that decorative plants in a farm pond constitute a nuisance, however pretty they may be, the objection being based on the idea that they will quickly spread and cover the entire pond. Another objection comes from farmers who stock their ponds with game fish. In my part of the country, which is western Maryland, such stocking is frequently done with bass and bluegills. It is a nicely balanced combination, for the bluegills multiply just fast enough to support a good bass population, but not so fast that they can crowd out the bass. In a pond overgrown with greenery, say the pond owners, the bluegills have too much protective cover in which to hide from the bass, their population soon increases disproportionately, and the balance is upset.

Planted indiscriminately with decorative aquatics, a pond undoubtedly would be overtaken by these problems, but planted with a variety of *carefully chosen* water-lilies and aquatics, it will not be spoiled for its intended use. At the same time, it will be a most beautiful aspect of the landscape.

WATER-LILIES

All of the Marliac water-lilies are excellent for farm ponds. They offer a complete range of colors, forms, and sizes, and need no attention from year to year. Although they will produce a few more blooms and leaves each season, they will not spread. In a three- to four-year period, a single planting will have developed a tangle of roots and stems as big as a bushel basket. If desired, such a mass can be broken down to provide growing points for other parts of the pond.

Set the sections directly on the bottom. They will flourish on almost any fertilizer you have at hand. Water-lilies of the *odorata* and *tuberosa* species will spread if planted directly in the bottom, and within a few years will cover a pond. This can easily be prevented, however, by planting them in boxes or tubs which will restrict roots and prevent spreading. But when so planted, they require new soil and fertilizer every other year.

Tropical water-lilies are splendid for a pond. They do not spread. They can be planted directly in the pond in shallow water along the shore, but they must be propped up to a point where they can break the surface of the water if planted in the deep areas of the pond. They will die in the winter unless cared for as suggested in Chapter 9.

LOTUS

The huge blooms and leaves of the lotus are especially beautiful in the open, semiwild setting of a farm pond. Some species are difficult to get started in a pond but, once established, they are even more difficult to curb. For this reason, plant lotus tubers in boxes and tubs which will restrict spreading.

BORDER PLANTS

Many tall sedges and rushes (as described in Chapter 13) are spreaders, but need not be ruled out as a means of beautifying a farm pond. Indeed, it would be a pity to overlook some of the spectacular effects they can provide. Some of these will spread only along the edge of the pond, where they can easily be controlled by cutting. Others will move only into the very shallow water along the shore. All can be kept under close control, if you wish, by planting in containers.

Fertilizing

If you are to have a productive pond for fish or plants or both, you must use fertilizer. Fertilizer, in addition to feeding major plants, also supports the growth of algae and other suspended growths. These, in turn, support a variety of minute animal life, on which fish feed.

A commercial mineral fertilizer is much to be preferred to manure, blood meal, or other organic fertilizer, which encourage the development of unsightly scum. For the best fertilizer for your pond, seek advice from your local Soil Conservation representative. It will depend on what you want to grow, what section of the country you live in, and various other factors.

At Three Springs Fisheries, we satisfactorily support both plant and fish in our ponds with a 10 (nitrogen)-10 (superphosphate)-10 (potash) mixture, using 1,000 pounds to the acre. When we have drained a pond for cleaning or repair, we broadcast this fertilizer directly on the pond floor and then work it into the soil before refilling the pond.

Fertilizer can also be broadcast on the surface of the water from a rowboat. This is best done, of course, at a time when the runoff is not heavy enough to carry away most of the nourishment you have scattered.

Stocking with Fish

If you want to add goldfish to a farm pond for decorative effect, you must stock heavily so there will be enough of them to see, also enough to reproduce fast enough to replace the hundreds of small fish lost through the spillways after every rainstorm heavy enough to cause a runoff.

Goldfish, in the freedom of large, seminatural ponds, often grow to the length of a foot or more. They can be attracted close enough to the shore line to be seen and enjoyed by establishing a few of the prettier spots as feeding locations.

The pond owner will have to make up his mind, however, whether he wants goldfish or game fish, for the goldfish are soon devoured if the two are put in together.

PART II *GOLDFISH, TROPICALS*
AND
AQUARIUMS

CHAPTER SIXTEEN

All About Goldfish

Goldfish, as we know them today, are not merely normal life forms, nor accidents of nature, nor achievements of man, but a very old combination of all three. Nature did the initial work with the creation of *Carassius auratus,* goldfish from which today's many forms, colors, and variations have been developed.

At birth the color is silvery olive-gray, but there is a strong tendency to revert to an inherent albinism and also to various forms and peculiarities. Through these—bulging eyes, odd tail and fin formations, patches of red, yellow, silver, or black on the bodies—the great variety of goldfish have been developed, especially by the Chinese, Japanese, and Koreans, who have worked with the mutant forms for hundreds of years and through thousands of fish generations. It was the Oriental breeders who segregated them and interbred them again and again and again. They exaggerated the mutations until bulging eyes developed into spectacular, telescopic eyes; slightly enlarged fins and tails became magnificent, sweeping veils; patches of red were extended until bodies were covered entirely with beautiful red-gold scales. And these mutations were fixed so that succeeding generations continued to produce true to form.

EARLY HISTORY

China is generally considered the ancestral home of the goldfish. There is one Chinese fairy tale about their magical appearance in a lake near the mountain called Ch'ien-ch'ing, in the ancient Province of Chekiang, back in the misty days of the world's beginning. There is another fairy tale about the early years of the Chou Dynasty, more than seven and a half centuries before Christ, when for one hundred days the world was without rain. While sacrifices were being made to the gods, a sparkling, bubbling well suddenly appeared. A goldfish, the world's first, leaped from the well, and then the rain began to fall.

In any case, goldfish were kept as pets during the Sung Dynasty from the late tenth well into the thirteenth century. There are old references to breeders "who can change the color of fish to gold," and recommendations on feeding and the treatment of ills. By the end of the thirteenth century, red, gold, black, and mottled fish seem to have been comparatively easy to buy as pets, having become an accepted part of Chinese culture. Goldfish were pets in Japan by 1500, but it was not until 200 years or so later that the Japanese breeders began cultivating goldfish on such a scale as to make them available to any except the wealthy.

The influence of the Chinese and the Japanese on goldfish forms can readily be seen in the illustrations in this book. The Chinese bred them in the same sort of "beautifully ugly" forms as we see in their grotesque ceremonial dragons, temple dogs, and other native works of art. The Japanese preferred a gentler beauty, the sort exemplified in their carvings and paintings, and so they produced many forms with graceful, flowing, veil-like fin and tail formations.

Seafaring travelers in the seventeenth century brought goldfish into England and France as expensive curios from the Orient. If one story is true, they were first offered as a unique gift to amuse Madame de Pompadour.

In 1878, the first goldfish were brought to the United States by Rear Admiral Daniel Ammen in a sizable shipment for the United States Fish Commissioner. On display in Washington, they created an overnight sensation. Private fanciers and a few farsighted dealers ordered shipments of their own immediately, and the goldfish was well on the way to becoming one of the most widely owned house pets in America.

"AMERICAN GOLDFISH"

There are no native American goldfish. Those seen or caught in American lakes, ponds, and streams were undoubtedly escaped or released pets. However, the United States leads the world in mass production, and the output of three or four fair-sized American fisheries easily exceeds the national production of Japan. The fixed species and varieties of goldfish now in America are as outstanding in quality as in quantity, and no fish surpasses them physically or artistically. Several fisheries, including our own, still order stock from Japan now and then, but we do this only to hold our quality by adding new blood.

Being concerned with the business all my life, it has been pleasant for me to see goldfish develop from a comparatively expensive oddity to a simple joy that everyone can afford. There is hardly a town today in which a youngster cannot walk into a dime store and, for a little

Plate 39. Common goldfish, Comets, Fantails, Shubunkins, Calico Fantails, Nymphs, and other ornamental fish fill this fifty-gallon tank at our fisheries headquarters and draw a steady crowd of observers. Some of the livelier Comets leap out of the aquarium from time to time, to the delight of the watcher in the picture.

A. AUBREY BODINE PHOTO

small change, walk out with a couple of goldfish in a glass bowl or in one of the new plastic goldfish sacks.

In Japan goldfish are as popular as in America. Old men, with two buckets of goldfish hanging from a pole balanced across their shoulders, are familiar sights on the streets. The goldfish sell for the equivalent of a penny or two, depending on the size and kind, and, as in America, children are the best customers. And though speaking a different language, they make the same noises and smile the same smile as American children when they run home with a couple of new goldfish.

Vital Statistics

There are two basic types of goldfish—scaled and "scaleless." The scaled fishes, the common goldfish, Comets, Fantails, and others, as we have said, are silvery olive-gray for three to six months. Then irregular spots of black, white, and gold appear, and in a few more weeks the black and white disappears, and the fish are covered with opaque, red-gold scales, bright and metallic. They will, that is, if they are going to color up at all. A small percentage of goldfish never do, and we sell hundreds of thousands of these uncolored ones every year as bait fish.

The so-called scaleless fish actually have transparent scales which look like a delicate skin. This makes beautiful glowing, but not shining, colors possible among forms like the Shubunkins and Calicos. Their colors, including blues and lavenders, appear in many combinations. Like human fingerprints, no two fish are alike. Scaleless fish are white at first, but begin to color up about the same time as the scaled varieties do, and the first patches of color which form stay as long as the fish live.

Age

Determining age by size cannot be reduced to a formula, for some varieties grow more quickly than others. However, a fairly accurate rule-of-thumb can be applied. At six months, most goldfish are 1 to 2 inches long. A 3- to 4-inch length indicates one to two years' growth. After that, growth slows down and progresses to a large extent according to surroundings. In an aquarium, a goldfish may grow to 4 or 5 inches in eight or ten years. In an outdoor pond, in the same time, it

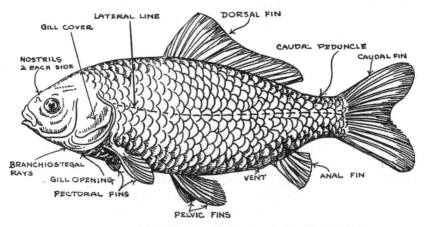

DRAWING 33. *External Parts of the Goldfish.*

may grow to 10 to 12 inches. A specialist with a microscope can determine age by the rings in the scales which are growth-marks similar to the rings in the trunk of a tree.

BREEDING

The average water gardener probably does not want to take the trouble to set up elaborate facilities for goldfish breeding, but some understanding of the life cycle in his pool will certainly increase his enjoyment of it. Healthy fish begin to breed when they are about a year old. In an aquarium, breeding usually takes place in late winter or early spring. Outdoors, goldfish breed in spring and early summer. The female, her body swollen with eggs, will swim rapidly over and through root or leaf masses of submerged plants, rubbing against them as she goes and leaving a mass of perhaps several dozen eggs at each place. Eggs are pale amber, about the size of pinheads.

A male goldfish can be distinguished from a female during the breeding season by the series of white dots which then appear along the side of gill plates. Also the male can be seen scurrying after the female to fertilize the eggs as she lays them. This process—the female flitting about laying eggs, the male in pursuit—is the well known "fish circus" which can often be observed in aquarium or pool. The circus usually begins early in the morning and lasts until around noon.

Nothing will come of the egg laying if the eggs are left alone, for the young fish usually will eat them. But if an egg drops into a crack and hatches, adults will not eat the baby fish as it ventures forth.

HATCHING

If you want to see more of the life cycle, you will have to assist it. Remove the aquatic plants with the fertilized egg masses clinging to them to a tub of warm (about 70-degree) water and leave them alone. Fish will hatch in five to six days, the original brood consisting of perhaps 300 tiny fish.

Powdery rice flour or Red Dog sifted lightly on the water makes excellent food for the babies, but the first three or four days they are better fed hard-cooked egg yolk forced through coarse cheesecloth. After two or three weeks the fish can eat the soupy, pasty part of boiled oatmeal. A few snails should be dropped into the tub to consume any excess food as soon as the fish have hatched. Put in before hatching, however, the snails will eat the eggs.

You must do a steady job of eliminating the smaller and weaker fish of the brood during the summer. Of the original 300, less than twenty of the biggest and healthiest should remain by midsummer. At the end of summer, the new brood can be moved into the pool with the other fish. The larger fish in the pool will not eat the smaller new arrivals, for most of them will be able to take care of temselves.

Male Goldfish showing nuptual tubercles on gill plate. Photo by Laurence Perkins.

CHAPTER SEVENTEEN

Species and Varieties of Goldfish

The common goldfish (*Carassius auratus*) are the patriarchs of orna-mental fish for, excepting the tropicals, these are the fish from which most of the fancy breeds have been developed. A healthy specimen has a short, wide head, small mouth, bright eyes, a long, flat body arched in both belly and back, with a stiff dorsal fin rising from the middle of the back arch. The scales are bright, the tail stiff and moderately forked, and the fins stiff and of moderate size.

The common goldfish is hardier than most of its descendants, remains healthy under a wider range of temperatures, and will even survive a few hours out of water, if kept moist. It breeds prolifically, and it will eat practically anything. It is a favorite for its hardy nature and be-cause it can be trained to eat from the hand. The various colorations sometimes go by special names. The silvery albinos are called Pearls. Those which color up to yellow instead of red-gold are called Canaries. Those with red-gold scales, with patches of black, are frequently sold as Orioles.

COMET

The Comet was developed in the late 1880's, first by accident and later by selective breeding, in the ponds of the Fish Commission in Washington, D.C. The body is more elongated and there is much more elaborate fin and tail development than in the parent.

The extensive fins and tail make the Comet one of the fastest and most graceful of all goldfish. It swims with smooth, darting movements often too fast for the eye to follow. It is particularly active in the spring, when it frequently will leap out of the water. For this reason, aquar-iums containing Comets should be covered with a screen during the fish's lively season. Like the parent species, the Comet is very hardy and simple to feed.

243

A Comet Goldfish. Photo by Dr. Herbert R. Axelrod.

JAPANESE FANTAIL

Another strain of the common goldfish, and a beautiful addition to any pool, is the Fantail, whose movements are as slow, deliberate, and stately as the Comet's are swift. The appearance of *any* Fantail in a water garden is a beautiful sight, but serious fanciers often prefer the type with double tails and double anal fins. A tail joined at the top is called a web-tail and looked upon as a blemish by those who breed fish for show competition. A single instead of a double anal fin is also considered undesirable. To all but the experts, one type is as pretty as another.

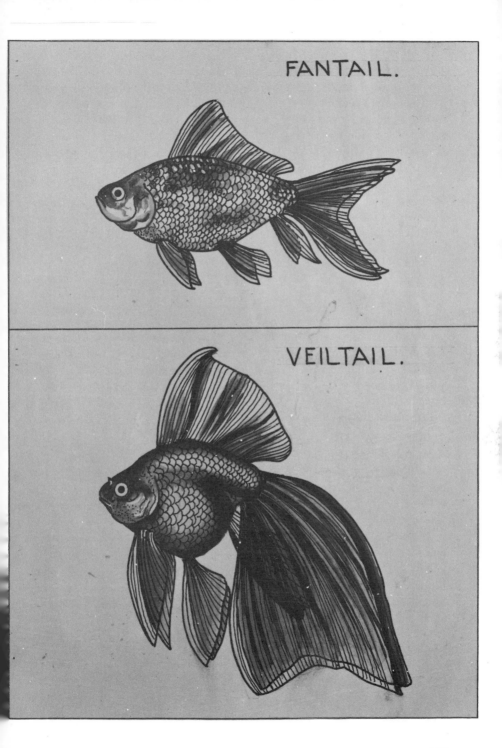

FANTAIL.

VEILTAIL.

VEILTAIL

Also called Fringetail, Ribbontail, Gauzetail, Lacetail, and Muslin-tail, this is an extended development of the Fantail and something of a prima donna. The body is shorter and chunkier than that of the Fantail, and fins and tail grow so long they drape gracefully in filmy folds, far out of proportion to the size of the body. It takes two years, or longer, for the Veiltail to reach full development and beauty, and once it does, feeding must be watched closely. If fed too much, fins and tail will continue to develop, becoming thick, and finally split and ragged.

This type is judged to have attained perfect form when the dorsal fin is as wide as the body and when the flowing double tail is twice the length. At this stage, reduce the food supply to about half of what the fish ate previously.

NYMPH

A modified Veiltail with a single, instead of double, tail and anal fin, the Nymph is very seldom bred as such. Usually it appears as a sport, turning up in broods of Veiltail stock. Nymphs are not as glamorous as the Veiltails but quite pretty and very active. The shape of the body is similar to that of the Veiltail, but neither fins nor the single tail is as well developed.

SHUBUNKIN

In view of the long history of ornamental fish, the Shubunkin is a comparative newcomer, being introduced by the Japanese about the beginning of this century. It is a scaleless hybrid, one parent being the common goldfish, the other a Demekin, a pop-eyed fish with scales usually uniform black, pale-red, or pale reddish-yellow, but sometimes variegated.

In form and size, the Shubunkin resembles the common goldfish, the coloring usually in patches of red, black, blue, yellow, brown, and lavender upon a pearl or pale-blue background, but often bright-red Shubunkins, attractively spotted black, will show up. On rare occasions a new brood will contain Shubunkins which are uniformly purple or lavender.

Like the common goldfish, the Shubunkin is hardy and quite active in either pool or aquarium.

CALICO TELESCOPE

There are three principal types of scaleless Chinese fish—Calico Telescope, Calico Fantail, and Plain Scaleless. The Calico Telescope, with

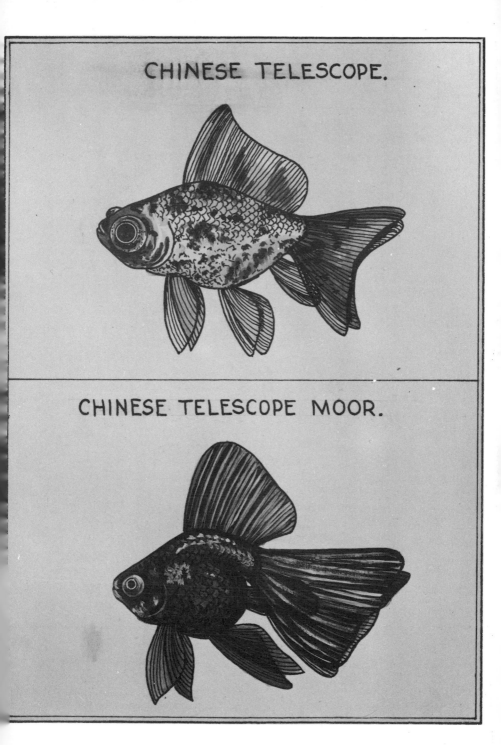

CHINESE TELESCOPE.

CHINESE TELESCOPE MOOR.

SHUBUNKIN.

COMET.

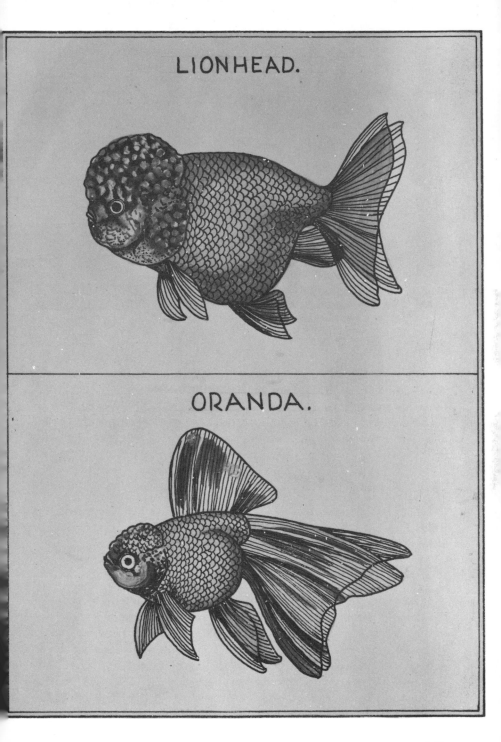

LIONHEAD.

ORANDA.

Young Common Goldfish. Photo by G. J. M. Timmerman.

pop-eyes and the short, squat form peculiar to all telescope fish, is the best known. Its mottled coloring is that of the Shubunkin. Most fish fanciers, myself included, agree that with the possible exception of Esther Williams, the Calico Telescope is the most beautiful thing that swims. In competition, it wins more best-of-show awards than any other fish.

Calico Fantail

In shape and coloring, the Calico Fantail is exactly like the Calico Telescope, but it lacks the telescopic eye development. It is, in short, a Calico Telescope which did not develop according to form.

Plain Scaleless

In form, the Plain Scaleless is identical with the Calico Telescope or the Calico Fantail—occurring both with and without the abnormal eye development—but there is a striking difference in color. It is red or white, or a mottled pattern of the two. The red of a scaleless fish is velvety oxblood red, and lacks the metallic shine of the red-gold scaled fish. Fins and tail are white, sometimes spotted black. The skin of both Calico and Plain Scaleless fishes is so transparent that the eggs of the female may be seen in her body when she swims in front of a light.

A Black Telescope Goldfish. Photo by Guenter Senfft.

TELESCOPE

A number of forms and colors come under the classification of Telescope. In fact, this includes practically all fish with protruding eyes. They are better known individually by such commercial names as Calico, Plain Scaleless, Moor, and so on.

But the Chinese Telescope might be called the basic telescope type. This fish, as a baby, looks like a golden Veiltail—as well it might be. Telescope fish do not begin to show the abnormal eyes until from two months to two years. Once the eyes begin to develop, they continue to do so as long as the fish lives.

Usually whatever development is going to take place begins when the fish is three to five months old. If it lives as long as a year without showing it, then it probably never will. The Chinese Telescope without special eyes should not be called so, but be identified as a Veiltail.

The term telescope, incidentally, is misleading. The eyes in no way give telescopic vision to the fish. In fact, the opposite is true; the more telescopic the eyes, the more myopic the fish seems to be.

MOOR

An extremely pretty fish, on the small side, usually a sooty, velvety black, and of short, chunky telescope form. Although most popular as blacks, pale-red and pale reddish-yellow Moors do occur now and then. A uniformly black Moor may shade off to blue-gray or a golden cast along the underside of the belly. Those with blue-gray casts usually retain their black color. Those with a golden cast sometimes turn gold.

The Moor is a tricky fish to breed, especially with a good black coloring in mind. The best black offspring come not from two black parents, but from one black- and one red-scaled fish.

CELESTIAL

This is a remarkable fish, with a body shaped like that of the Chinese Telescope. The coloring is a uniform black or pale orange, or a combination of the two in mottled pattern. Most striking is the eye formation, the pupils being situated on top of the eyeballs, so that the fish seems to be gazing heavenward—hence the name Celestial.

There is a story to the effect that Celestials acquire their peculiar eyes from being placed in special jars when they are very young, the jars letting light in only from slits in the top. Not so. They are bred like other varieties.

This one is a feeble swimmer and spends most of its time on the bottom, resting on its belly. It is also delicate and so not very good for aquarium display, and no good at all in an outdoor pool.

LIONHEAD

A strange and grotesquely beautiful fish—and an unfortunate one—by reason of certain malformations—the smooth, humped back, nearly globular body, and no dorsal fin. This makes it an extremely poor swimmer. Unable to maintain balance, it often swims upside down or vertically with head down. It is the head growth which gives the Lionhead

A male Lionhead. Notice the missing dorsal fin. Photo by Laurence Perkins.

An Oranda, which looks like a Lionhead, but this variety has a dorsal. Photo by Dr. Herbert R. Axelrod.

its name. It is also called Buffalohead, which is even more descriptive of the shape of the odd growth.

The malformation on the head begins to take shape fairly late in the first year and becomes larger and larger. As the fish ages, the growth begins to form thickly over the gill plates, which makes breathing difficult.

The Lionhead will then seek cooler water which is well oxygenated. Even in the best surroundings possible, the fish may suddenly die, presumably of suffocation. Some Lionheads fail to develop the head growth, and these remain quite hardy.

The coloring is usually the conventional goldfish red and white, although smoke-colored bodies and yellow heads are not uncommon.

254

A Bubble-eye Goldfish. Photo by Tachbrook Tropicals.

ORANDA

This is a modification of the Lionhead and far superior to it, although the coloring of the two is similar. The shape of the Oranda tends more toward that of the Veiltail, including tail and fin development. There is a dorsal fin, so this is not the clumsy, bungling swimmer the Lionhead is. The head growth is also modified, being confined principally to the top of the head. It does not spread so as to hamper the fish. This is a comparatively fragile fish which does best in aquariums.

This Veiltail Goldfish has such long fins it can hardly swim. Photo by Marcuse.

*Colorful Japanese Carp, or Koi, are brilliant additions to the clear
shallow lily pond. Photo by Dr. Herbert R. Axelrod in Hawaii.*

Shubunkin.

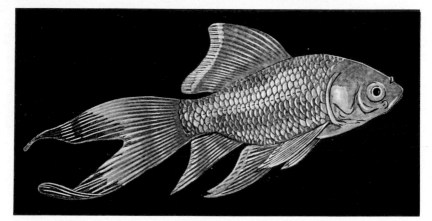

Comet.

Common.

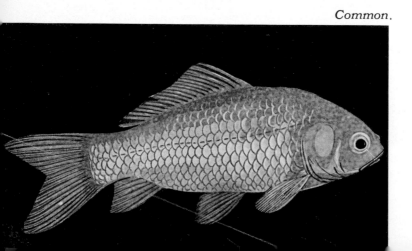

Calico Telescope.

GOLDEN ORFE

A new attraction for the pool or aquarium, a fish of European extraction which is becoming more and more popular with fanciers. The Golden Orfe is a slender fish, orange-gold on its topside, a paler yellow-gold color on its underbelly. It is extremely graceful as it darts about, and is said to be one of the fastest of all living things. Often, in an outdoor pool, it will leap from the water in pursuit of an insect on the wing.

OTHER FORMS

By crossbreeding the various species and varieties, fanciers have produced many forms, such as the Veiltail-Moor, the Veiltail-Calico, and others. I am not listing them here, for few will thrive in an outdoor pool for the water gardener.

WORD OF WARNING

The fish I usually recommend to my customers for an outdoor pool are the common goldfish, Comets, Shubunkins, Moors, and both Calico and Japanese Fantails. All others, with the exception of the European Tenches and Orfes, do better in indoor aquariums. However, at one time or another I have heard of all the leading ornamental fishes—extremely fancy ones included—doing quite well in outdoor pools, particularly in the milder sections of the country. So let your own judgment guide you in where to "plant" your fish. As the man at the carnival says: "You pays your money and you takes your choice."

Giant Golden Carp. Photo by Dr. Herbert R. Axelrod.

The most valuable colors of Koi are the tri-colored ones. A metallic gold Koi has been developed and is also highly prized. Photo by Dr. Herbert R. Axelrod.

Japanese Fantail.

Celestial.

Oranda.

Lionhead.

CHAPTER EIGHTEEN *Tropical Fish*

This chapter is intended as a general, primary introduction of the tropical aquarium fishes to the amateur.

As the amateur's particular interest takes shape—small fishes, large fishes, live-bearers, egg-layers, fishes of some specific variety—he will want to consult larger, more specialized books which deal with his special interest in thorough, informative detail. Many fine books of this sort are easily available, and they are not expensive.

Specialization seems the most practical approach, especially in the beginning, for there are hundreds of species and varieties of tropical fish, and there is a great deal to be learned about each one of them.

Fishes from different parts of the world, like people from different areas, are accustomed to different environments, climates, and foods, and must have a close approximation of these necessary things if they are to thrive away from home.

Fishes taken from slow-moving jungle creeks, where drainage over rotting wood and leaves lends acidity to the water, must have aquarium water similar to that slightly acid river water. Other species taken from brackish waters along the seacoasts cannot thrive without a touch of salt in the aquarium water. Duplicating these natural surroundings is a challenging and fascinating phase of keeping tropical fish.

Foods—the types, amounts, frequency of feeding—vary widely from one family of fish to another, and often there are widely different requirements among species of the same fish family.

Feeding requirements for fish also change as they grow from the newly hatched small fry stage to adulthood.

Ailments which sometimes beset tropical fish, special problems encountered in trying to achieve some particular form by cross-breeding and selective breeding, and other developments all require special instruction.

This instruction is easily found.

A magnificent specimen of a Sailfin Red Wag Platy developed by Dr. Joanne Norton. Photo by Dr. Norton.

One of the aquarist's best sources of information is his bookshelf. A bit of browsing in a good bookstore or petshop will turn up half a dozen dependable, well illustrated works on tropical fish. So will the public library. These, coupled with a collection of the different commercial catalogs which the aquarist will soon acquire, will give him a pretty good background before he knows it.

The dealer from whom the hobbyist buys tropical fish, whether he is the operator of the petstore on the corner or a grower who does most of his business by mail order, is usually a fount of information. Don't hesitate to see or write a dealer for information. Most of them are glad to recommend instructive books and help with special problems.

One of the most informative sources, and one of the most pleasant, is another hobbyist. Exchange of information between hobbyists is always rewarding, and frequently the old-timer learns something from the upstart. Such friendships usually begin with the trading of information, and wind up with the trading of fish.

Of the tropical fish discussed in this book, only the fresh and brackish water varieties are considered.

We divide them, for discussion, into two groups—live-bearers and egg-layers.

LIVE-BEARERS

All aquarists, newcomers and veterans alike, love the live-bearing tropical fishes. They run a full range of interesting shapes and bright colors. They are active, and provide an endless fascination to the watcher. They are especially good pets for beginners, for they thrive with a minimum of care. Most important, they are immediately rewarding. They breed easily. The broods of young they produce on a monthly schedule emerge into this world as active babies, much more advanced than the small fry of the egg-laying breeds.

Sexes of the live-bearers are easy to distinguish. The anal fin of the female is rounded, fan-shaped, fully developed. Instead of a fan-shaped anal fin, the male has a rounded, pointed anal fin modified into an intromittent organ called a *gonopodium* through which he internally fertilizes the female's eggs.

Breeding requirements are few and simple. The mothers, as they become swollen with young, require a bit of extra food and sometimes a warmer aquarium. The young, until they become large enough to fend for themselves, often need protection from their parents. One of the common traits of the live-bearers is cannibalism; both parents are guilty.

There are safeguards. Mothers-to-be can be transferred to aquariums of their own and confined to a spawning trap, a plastic enclosure which gives her freedom of movement, but allows her babies to escape.

Another good protection for smaller fishes, if there are adults in the aquarium with them, is a plentiful planting of aquatic greenery in which the small fish can hide if pursued.

The most common forms of aquarium live-bearers are the Platies, Swordtails, Mollies and Guppies.

PLATY MOONS

Older reference books list these fishes in the genus *Platypoecilus* hence the popular name Platy. Another common name for them is Moon, for the earlier breeds brought into this country from lower Mexico and Central America showed distinct dark crescent shapes on the caudal peduncle. In the many varieties which have since evolved, this marking has disappeared entirely, and is of such modified colors in others that it is scarcely distinguishable.

The Bleeding Heart Wagtail Platy, developed by Joseph Cooley and marketed by Gulf Fish Farms, Palmetto, Florida. Photo by Dr. Herbert R. Axelrod.

The Platyfish have more recently been classified as members of the genus *Xiphophorus* which also includes the Swordtails.

Platies run to an average aquarium size of 2 inches. They are active and cheerful as they explore all levels of the aquarium, nibbling at the algae. Their basic hues include red, gold, blue, black, sunset shades, and different varieties bear striking markings over these colors. Some varieties are designated as *tuxedos,* which indicates a dress suit pattern. Some are designated *wags* or *wagtails.* This indicates a fish with a colored body and contrasting black tail and dorsal fin. The moving tail becomes especially noticeable as the fish swims, hence the popular term *wag.*

The Platies are prolific, producing about 25 small fry in each brood. The parents are benevolent in most cases, but now and then a mother will eat some of the young if given the chance.

Popular dealer varieties include: Blue, Red, Black, Leopard, Gold Crescent, Bleeding Heart, Milk-and-Ink, Gold Wag, Red Wag, Red Tuxedo, Gold and Black Tuxedo, Black, Marigold, Red Tail, Sunset Variatus, and Bleeding Heart Wagtail. New varieties with long dorsals are also available.

SWORDTAILS

Fish of this species (*Xiphophorus helleri*) are often identified as Helleries after the collector, Carl Heller, for whom they were named. They are Mexican and Central American fishes.

The Swordtail, usually running from 2½ to 3½ inches, cuts a dashing figure in the aquarium. It needs more room than some of the other tropicals. Even in the freedom of a large aquarium, the male may become something of a bully among smaller males of his own or other species. When this occurs, aquarists usually give him a tank of his own or transfer him into an aquarium with larger fish.

Base colors include greens, reds, golds, blacks, albinos and varicolor, and many of the fish are marked with a variety of tuxedo, wag and other overlaying patterns.

They are active fish, graceful and darting, constantly foraging on the algae that grows in the aquarium. They demand quite a bit of salad in their diet. When they clean the aquarium of algae, aquarists drop in greenery in the form of finely shredded lettuce or cooked spinach.

Swordtails are very prolific breeders. The young are robust, about a quarter-inch long at birth, and a big, healthy female may produce 75 in a brood.

Popular dealer varieties include: Albino, Brick Red, Velvet Red, Green, Gold, Painted, Black; Gold and Red Tuxedo Swordtail; Brick

Above: A female Wagtail Platy. Below: A female Sailfin or Hitop Platy. This variety is also known as a "Mickey Mouse" because of the design in the tail of the fish. Compare the anal fin of these females with the photo of the two male lower fish on page 267. Note the tiny white spots. This is ichthyophthirius, and is curable.

Above: A pair of Green Swordtails. The male is the lower fish. Below: Black Berlin Swordtails. Photos by Dr. Herbert R. Axelrod.

Sailfin Molly males. The Green Sailfin Molly is a natural fish. The Black Sailfin Molly has been inbred and produced from some sports which occur now and then in natural populations. Photo by Dr. Herbert R. Axelrod.

Red, Green, Velvet Red Wag Swordtail. New varieties with long dorsals and double lyre tails are also available.

MOLLIES

A much loved aquarium favorite. Mollies are cheap, hardy, and beautiful.

The genus *Mollienisia* covers several species and varieties found in waters off the lower eastern coast of the United States and as far south as Venezuela, along the Gulf Coast and eastern Mexico. They have been found in inland fresh water and far out in the ocean, but they prefer brackish water. Aquarists provide this by adding a bit of salt to the aquarium.

Mollies are shaped prettily, with a pronounced dorsal fin providing an added touch of glamor to many varieties. They occur in a variety

A magnificent male Guppy, developed by Paul Hahnel. Photo by Dr. Herbert R. Axelrod.

of colors—green, black, albino, marbled and chocolate, and in many varieties these colors carry striking marbled and spotted overlaying patterns. In the aquarium they attain lengths of 2 to 3½ inches.

Females, in a comfortable, uncrowded aquarium, produce about 25 offspring in a brood, and will eat them if given the chance.

The adults are friendly community fish. The males constantly court the females. Given plenty of light to reflect, they add considerable color to an aquarium as they move slowly but ceaselessly about.

Popular dealer varieties include: Albino, Lyretail, Green Sailfin, Sphenops, Yucatan, Black, Marble Molly.

GUPPIES

The Guppies *(Lebistes reticulatus)* have been called "Missionary Fish," for without a doubt they have converted more people to the tropical fish hobby than any other aquarium pet. We get them from waters along the coasts of Guiana and Venezuela and the Island of Trinidad.

They are tiny fish from 1 to 1½ inches in length, with mixed colors of silver, reds, golds, blues, greens. Like fingerprints, no two are exactly alike.

The Guppies are among the best of all tropical fishes for beginners. They are hardy, easily bred (broods from 30 to 100), can stand temperature changes, close confinement and even foul water. They eat practically any kind of food.

Their charm is their pretty form, their brilliant colors and their ceaseless activity. They flit around an aquarium like flying sparks. The especially active males have been called "the playboys of the aquarium."

Popular dealer varieties include: Red, Gold, English, Deluxe, Rainbow, Trinidad Guppy, Blue Tail, Red Tail, Black Veil Tail Guppy.

EGG-LAYERS

Most of the tropical aquarium fishes reproduce by laying eggs, which they may scatter loosely across the bottom or attach to plants or rocks.

The hobbyist has more of a problem determining the sex of the egg-layers, for it is sometimes difficult to tell them apart. Usually the males are more slender, with longer anal or dorsal fins, and show brighter colors. Usually the females are larger and heavier in body. *Usually!*

In this chapter we will discuss the more popular aquarium egg-layer groups—Barbs, Tetras, Rasboras, Panchax, Danios, Cichlids and the Bubble Nest Builders, Bettas, Gouramis and Paradise Fish.

A pair of Rosy Barbs. Photo by G. J. M. Timmerman.

BARBS

The Barbs (along with Danios, Rasboras, White Cloud Mountain Fish, Carps, Minnows and Goldfish) belong to the family Cyprindae, one of the biggest families of fish in the world. Branches of the family range in size from a few inches to several feet, and are found in North America, Europe, Asia and Africa.

Barbs were for many years classified in the genus *Barbus,* which explains the popular name Barb. More recently they have been placed in the genus *Puntius,* and other genera.

Their shape resembles that of the common goldfish. In their many varieties they range in length from a little more than an inch to 6 inches. Most of them come to us from Ceylon, Java, Thailand, Sumatra, Malasia and India, although there are many varieties in China and Africa.

A pair of Tiger Barbs. Photo by G. J. M. Timmerman.

Barbs like a sunny spot, perhaps because it shows them off to best advantage. Their bodies are covered with mirror-like scales, splashed handsomely with brilliant colors. They are playful fish, and as they move about their scales catch and reflect the sun. Many of them become beloved pets, for they live 4 to 8 years.

In that part of the summer when there is no danger of cold nights, Barbs can be transferred to an outdoor pool.

Popular dealer varieties include: Sumatranus, Shuberti, Cherry, Rosy, Clown, Black Spot, "T" Barb.

DANIOS

The Danios are ideal aquarium fish. They are active, but not nervously so. Their horizontal stripes show beautifully to advantage when they move about in small schools. They like the upper part of the aquarium. They thrive on practically any kind of food.

They are streamlined fish, some of them rather like miniature tuna in shape. Colors run from pale golds to blues, blue-greens, violet, blue-blacks, most of them with contrasting horizontal markings.

A pair of Spotted Danios. Photo by G. J. M. Timmerman.

We import them from India, Ceylon, Indonesia and Thailand.

There are two groups. The genus *Danio* includes the larger species. The genus *Brachydanio* covers the smaller varieties. (From the Greek *brachys,* meaning short.)

All are prolific breeders, but quick to eat the spawn if preventative steps are not taken by the aquarist.

Popular dealer varieties include: Giant, Pearl, Zebra, Gold, Leopard, Spotted Danio.

RASBORA

There are close to four dozen species of the genus *Rasbora* known, but less than a quarter of them work out in aquariums. Those varieties which can adapt do adapt very well, and are among the long-lived aquarium fishes.

A pair of Pearl Danios. Photo by Timmerman.

Rasbora heteromorpha, *the most popular of Rasboras. Photo by Timmerman.*

They are streamlined, ranging in aquarium lengths from 1 to 5 inches. Basic colors are silver, salmon, olive and golden browns, with bold markings in brilliant colors.

Don't expect to breed them successfully if you are an amateur.

Popular dealer varieties include: Rasbora Het, Lantern Eye, Scissortail, *R. maculata.*

WHITE CLOUD MOUNTAIN FISH

This fish, *Tanichthys albonubes,* is named for Tan, the Chinese Boy Scout who found it.

It is one of the most popular of aquarium fish. Some dealers list it with their Danios, for the two have much in common. Both come from flowing streams and thus do well in lower temperatures than many other tropical fish can stand. It also bears up very well in higher temperatures.

Other dealers group it with their Tetras. It resembles the Neon Tetra in shape, has equally brilliant colors. The tail and fin markings of the White Cloud are brilliant red. Its body is golden brown, marked with horizontal stripes of red-gold and iridescent blue-green. In the early days when Neon Tetras were scarce and expensive, this fish became widely popular as "the poor man's Neon."

The fish breeds freely.

TETRAS

Some years back several aquarium fish of the family Characidae, or Characins, as they are called, were included in the genus *Tetragonopterus*. This genus actually is a small one which applies correctly to a comparative few of those fish now listed in it. Such names as "Black Tetra," "Tet from Rio," "Neon Tetra" and so on have no scientific standing at all, but the terms have become so widely accepted in popular usage they are undoubtedly here to stay.

Most aquarists consider Tetras among the aristocrats of the aquarium. Their symmetrical shapes and gorgeous coloring make them individually beautiful, and they form striking contrasts when they swim in schools. Their movements are graceful and serene.

Some species breed freely in the aquarium; most do not.

White Cloud Mountain Fish. Photo by Timmerman.

Popular dealer varieties include: Neon, Glowlight, Red Eye, Blood-fin, Black, Bleeding Heart, Gold, Head and Tail Light, Von Rio, Cardinal, Rosaceus Tetras; Tetra pulcher, *Copeina arnoldi*, Red Ruby, Serpae and Red Phantom.

PANCHAX

The fishes of this group, which come from Africa, India, Ceylon and Indonesia, are unusual in shape and brilliant in color. Their bodies are long and tubular, with unusual fin and tail development in males. With their large, pointed jaws they can swallow some of the smaller aquarium inhabitants. They show all the brilliant colors in bold patterns on body, fin and tail.

They like the upper part of the aquarium, just under the water surface. They are jumpers, and so require a covered aquarium.

This group of fish had a dramatic introduction to the public about 25 years ago when the form *Aplocheilichthys macrophthalmus* became available. Some dealer gave the fish the popular name of Lamp-Eye, and the rush was on. The popular name is descriptive, for the upper part of the fish's eye is a pale, metallic green. Under reflected light from above, the fish appears to have the lamp-like eyes of some of the deep sea fishes.

Most fishes of the Panchax group breed easily. Parents will ignore the spawn, but may eat the hatched fry. They rarely grow over 1¾ inches and are short-lived.

Popular dealer varieties include: Gold Medaka, Lyretail, Blue Gularis, Lamp-Eye.

CICHLIDS

The Cichlids (family Cichlidae), most of which resemble the sunfish in shape, are the big fish of the aquarium. Different species found in Africa, Central and South America and India range in size from 2 inches or so to a foot.

Most of them are highly colored, especially the males. Most of them have unusual fin and tail development. Often the males are fighters, scrapping among themselves, even attacking their own mates at times. In fact, a male and female in courtship appear to be scrapping, rough play which has been known to result in the female's death.

At the same time, fishes of this group are among the most conscientious parents in the aquarium world. They guard their spawn by turn, and as the small fry emerge they are herded together and guarded carefully by the parents, a delightful aquarium sight.

Cardinal Tetras, Cheirodon axelrodi. *Photo by Dr. Herbert R. Axelrod.*

Above: A trio of Rosy Tetras. Below: The Bleeding Heart Tetra. Photo by Kremser.

Above: The African Lampeye. Below: The beautiful Dwarf Cichlid from Colombia and Venezuela, Apistogramma ramirezi. Photo by G. J. M. Timmerman.

Gulf Fish Farms have produced many magnificent fish, but the Golden Convict Cichlid is one of the most popular. Photo by Dr. Herbert R. Axelrod.

Popular dealer varieties include: Angels, Orange Chromide, Egyptian Mouthbreeder, Firemouth, Keyhole Fish, Jack Dempsy, Jewel Fish, Ramirezi, Golden Convict.

Bubble-Nest Builders

The popular aquarium bubble nest builders—Bettas, Gouramis and Paradise Fish—belong to the order Labyrinthici, the fish of which are distinguished by a labyrinthine chamber. It serves as an auxiliary breathing apparatus. This chamber is roughly comparable to the lungs of a mammal.

To supplement the oxygen these fish utilize by gill action, they frequently move to the surface for a gulp of air. They force this air into their labyrinthine chamber, where the oxygen is absorbed by the bloodstream. At times the fish releases the used air in a bubble of saliva, which rises to the surface and floats. In the course of a few hours the fish can build a floating nest half an inch thick and as big as a saucer.

Above: A pair of Dwarf Gouramis, the male being the most colorful. Below: Kissing Gouramis. Photo by Hansen.

Above: A wild Angelfish found by Dr. Axelrod in British Guiana. Below: Tank-raised Angelfish from Denmark's Charlottenlund Aquarium.

*The largest of Siamese Fighting Fish is the Libby Strain. Photo by
Dr. Herbert R. Axelrod.*

In breeding, the male maneuvers the female to a position beneath
the bubble nest, siezes her in a nuptial embrace, squeezes some eggs out
of her, and promptly fertilizes them. As these eggs drop to the bottom,
the male (sometimes the female assists) picks up each egg, and guides
it to the nest. There the eggs stick until the small fry hatch.

Fishes of the family Anabantidae, to which these three popular
aquarium forms belong, come to us from Africa and southern Asia.

Above: *Marble Hatchetfish.* Below: *Blind Cave Fish. Photos by Dr. Herbert R. Axelrod.*

BETTAS

The Bettas, known also as Siamese Fighting Fish, are of subdued colors in their wild state. Aquarium breeding has produced many forms of high color—cornflower blue, bright greens, sooty blacks, vivid reds, cream-colored fish with brightly colored fins. Selective breeding has also produced long, graceful fins and tails.

The males are rough customers. Two of them put into one aquarium will fight. In their native land they were often fought in this manner for sport.

Popular dealer varieties include: Red, Blue, Green, Lavender, Blue-and-Red, Red-Green-Blue Betta.

GOURAMIS

Gouramis, although closely related to the Bettas, do not have their fighting dispositions. Under good conditions, they are friendly community fish.

Their shapes are box-like, for the most part, and their striped, spotted and speckled patterns occur in a variety of lovely hues, from pastel to the brilliant shades.

Most popular form, probably, is the Kissing Gourami. These fish, with pale pink bodies and large black eyes, frequently pair off nose to nose and kiss.

Popular dealer varieties include: Dwarf, Blue, Kissing, Pearl, Opaline, Chocolate Gourami.

PARADISE FISH

This one is a native of the rice fields of China, and is sold by some dealers as the Rice Fish.

It is similar in form to the Betta, but with brighter, more metallic hues. It is similar to the Betta, also, in fighting temperament.

Dealers sell three forms. The Red Paradise Fish has a pale brown body broken by bright green vertical bands. The White Paradise Fish is an albino form with a pale yellow body marked with pink bands. The Black Paradise is very dark.

SCAVENGERS

Scavengers serve a double purpose in the aquarium. Some of them are interesting to watch, and they help keep the tank clean of leftover food and other decomposing material.

A pair of Glassfish. Photo by Timmerman.

Catfishes form the bulk of most scavenger lists. They do their work well and are easy to breed. Some of them are nocturnal, hiding in the daylight hours, moving about at night. This disturbs some varieties of tropical fish, which prefer to rest undisturbed through the night.

There are other forms of scavengers. Ask your dealer, or check your catalog, for loaches, miniature flounders, snails, shrimp, and crawfish.

RARE, UNUSUAL AND SPECIAL VARIETIES

The broad, sweeping groupings of the more common tropical fish discussed in this chapter cover only those which are best known and available with most dealers.

By no means should you overlook such fascinating aquarium pets as Pencil Fish, Glass Fish, Bumble Bee Fish, Hatchet Fish, Head Standers, Blind Cave Fish, Butterfly Fish, Mosquito fish.

Dealer catalogs are one of your best sources of information on these off-beat varieties. Your dealer can be extremely helpful. Usually he can tell you where to order some special variety if he does not himself have it in stock.

CHAPTER NINETEEN

Care and Feeding of Goldfish and Tropicals

The hardy breeds of goldfish are so rugged that few die from lack of attention, but you can pamper practically any of them to death in a week. Most goldfish that die before their time do so by reason of three leading forms of overkindness.

The greatest cause of trouble is overfeeding. Few amateur fish fanciers seem to realize that important adjustments must be made for fish kept in unnatural surroundings, particularly in bowls and aquariums. Living wild, fish eat practically all the time. That is because food is not too plentiful, and fish must scurry around the livelong day in an effort to find enough. It is disastrous to reverse this natural order of things by giving fish plenty to eat and at the same time depriving them of space in which to work the food off by exercise. If allowed, fish confined to an aquarium will literally eat themselves to death. Fish in outdoor pools live under more natural conditions, it is true, but the rule of sparse feeding also applies to them.

Another danger is crowding. Six or eight goldfish is an aquarium designed for three or four, or overcrowding in the same proportion in an outdoor pool, will soon separate the strong from the weak, and the weak will die.

Too much sun and improper water temperatures, along with too frequent changing of the water, are also harmful. In a large bowl or average-sized aquarium properly placed and not overcrowded, the water need not—should not—be changed more often than once a week, and I have kept goldfish healthy in an aquarium for as long as two and three months without changing the water.

For the cold-water fishes:

Most aquarium pets are able to adjust fairly quickly to the type of water it is easiest to provide for them.

If the public water system in your community draws upon water which is so hard in its natural state that housewives have trouble getting soap to form suds, this natural water would be difficult for aquarium fish. Usually such water goes through a softening plant, however, and the softened water is fine for fish.

Unless the water in your community is extremely highly chlorinated, it can be made acceptable.

The addition of fluorine in some water systems to prevent tooth decay of the people who use it is, as far as I have been able to see, quite harmless to fishes. Who knows? Perhaps it is as good for fish as it is for humans.

Deep well water may have too heavy a mineral content. Swamp water, or any similar water which contains decomposing vegetation, is too acid. Fresh rain water is not acceptable.

Natural, clear water dipped from a free-flowing stream or a pond in which fish and greenery live would be close to perfect water for the aquarium.

Most hobbyists, however, will draw upon the household taps for aquarium and pool. Do it this way:

If you are setting up a new aquarium, set it up two or three days before you bring in the new fish.

At the household tap, put your thumb over the spigot to make the water emerge in a spray. This aerates the water, and it will release most of its chlorine. If filling an outdoor pool, fill it from the garden hose, with the nozzle set to form a spray.

Go ahead and plant any aquatic greenery you like, and allow the aquarium or pool 24 hours or more before you add the fish. This time allows the water to release most of its remaining chlorination. It also gives the water a chance to settle to a temperature between 60 and 70 degrees (F.), which is the level it will find in most homes, and the temperature in which goldfish do best.

IMPORTANT: Get away from the all-too-popular idea that aquarium fish like a nice, fresh, cold change of water every few days.

A filter system in the aquarium adds to the health of the fish, but is not necessary. In a filtering system the aquarium water is pumped by way of a tiny, quiet motor through a chamber containing sand, activated charcoal, glass wool and other filtering materials. It changes the water

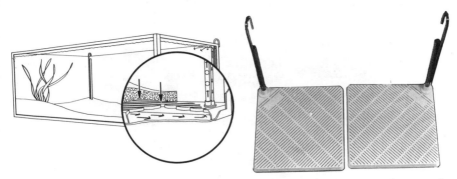

For your home aquarium as well as your pool, use an undergravel filter. This provides circulation of water through the gravel and helps maintain crystal clarity. Photos courtesy of Miracle Plastics Corp., Long Beach, California.

in no way, except to keep it very clear.

An aerator helps, too. This is a simple hose extension from the pump and it releases a small and constant stream of air bubbles at the bottom of the aquarium. The aquarium water absorbs considerable oxygen from this air stream.

An automatic electric heater, which controls the aquarium temperature through a thermostat, is seldom needed for the cold-water fishes, unless the aquarium occupies some especially cold part of the house.

For the tropical fishes:

The same water requirements met for the cold-water fishes apply to the tropicals, with a bit of added attention. Tropical fishes are somewhat more demanding than the hardy goldfish varieties.

Some of them can do very well without the filtering system, but do better in an aquarium equipped with one. With many tropical species the filter is a necessity. So is the aerator. So is the heating unit, for most tropical fish demand a temperature ranging from 70 to 80 degrees at all times.

The tropical fish need added attention, too, in the maintenance of an acid-alkaline balance in their water. This is called the pH factor.

Water is seldom chemically neutral, being slightly acid or slightly alkaline. Some tropicals prefer it one way, some another. In a scale set up for aquarists, the designation 7.0 is considered neutral.

Using the popular type of testing kit, the aquarist adds to a specimen of aquarium water a few drops of an indicator solution, an extremely sensitive dye. He then compares the specimen color to a color chart, and by matching specimen color to numbered colors of the chart he can get a reading on the extent of acidity or alkalinity in the water.

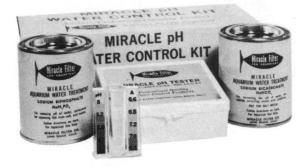

The pH of your aquarium water is important. Buy a reliable test kit at your petshop, along with chemicals to adjust the pH if it is necessary. Photo courtesy of Miracle Plastic Corp., Long Beach, California.

Bromthymol blue is used widely as an indicative dye. It registers acidity (readings below 7.0) or alkalinity (readings above 7.0) from 6.0 to 7.6. This range is usually much wider than that needed in general aquarium treatments. Once he has a reading, the aquarist can adjust the chemical balance of the water by adding corrective solutions.

All aquarium fishes are sensitive to odors, especially the tropicals. Move them out of the rooms in which you plan to do any painting, for some varieties have been killed by fresh paint fumes.

For specific varieties of tropicals, check your dealer as to foods, aquarium size, aquarium greenery, pH factor and temperature.

Feeding

Goldfish will eat practically anything, but you will find it convenient to buy a prepared fish food. There are a number of excellent brands with a perfectly balanced content of food, salts, and minerals. Ask your dealer to recommend one.

What you feed goldfish is not nearly so important as *how much* you feed them. You cannot rear them properly if you feed them when they seem hungry, because they are *always* hungry, even hungry enough to beg. Indulge them occasionally, if you like, but infrequently and only with tidbits.

Whatever fish food you buy will have a printed label telling you how much to allow for a certain number of fish of a given size. Follow directions only at the start. Observe the fish as they eat what you throw to them. After a few days of watching, limit them to only as much food as they will consume in five minutes. Remove the surplus, for it becomes waterlogged, decomposes, fouls the water, and kills some of your fish.

Feed goldfish lightly and only once a day. If they become torpid and slow moving, try feeding them every other day, or every third day, and see if they don't become livelier. If they do, hold them to the lighter diet. I know fanciers who feed their fish only every fifth or sixth day, and theirs are among the finest I have seen. This is not unkind. By keeping fish hungry you keep them lively and comfortable, and prolong their lifespan by several years.

It is far worse to overfeed than to underfeed, and the worst thing you can possibly do is to load up your aquarium or pool with extra food when you go away for a weekend. It is better to let the goldfish miss a few meals. Do not feed them any heavier than usual when you return and resume the feeding schedule.

Food Variety

Goldfish thrive on variety in their diet from time to time. Feed them scraped or finely chopped oyster, clam, or shrimp—preferably raw—or earthworms, if you want to go to the trouble of digging and chopping them. Fish will nibble at cooked spinach, and it is good for them. And they like salad as well as you do, for they will pick frequently at the greenery growing around them. The larger fish—3 to 4 inches or longer —seem to consider freshly swatted flies a delicacy. Any of these things, however, are to be given *instead* of the regular food, *not* in addition to it.

Space to Live

Goldfish hovering near the surface of the water, "blowing bubbles," "playing," or "just being friendly," are a pretty sight to anyone who knows nothing about them. All of these "cute" doings have been reported to me by customers now and then. However, all indicate a cruel situation, for they are sure signs of suffocation.

Plenty of room for living is vitally important to goldfish, for living room is also "breathing" room. As fish breathe water and extract oxygen from it, the water absorbs more oxygen from the air. This absorption is not rapid, and considerable water surface must be exposed to provide enough absorption to sustain life properly. I use the expression "considerable water surface" in a relative sense. To illustrate, a 2½-inch goldfish needs all the oxygen that can be absorbed in about 50 square inches of water surface; that means the entire water surface of a 7- by 7-inch square bowl or of a circular bowl 8 inches in diameter at the water level.

Fanciers long ago reduced this business of pool, bowl, and aquarium capacity to formulas, and these are easily applied.

First figure the area of water surface. Most pools and aquariums are straight-sided and can therefore be filled to any suitable depth. Most bowls taper in at the top, so fill these only to the point of widest dimension, thus providing the greatest possible water surface.

Figure out the water-surface area in square inches. For square or oblong pools and aquariums, multiply width by length. In round bowls and pools, multiply pi (3.1416 or 22/7ths) by the square of the radius. Simply estimate the surface area of irregular pools (unless you remember a lot more plane geometry than I ever knew) and, to be on the safe side, make your estimate low.

With the area of the water surface determined, stock the pool or aquarium with no more than 1 inch of fish (not counting the tail) for every 20 square inches of water surface. As an example, a 10- by 12-inch aquarium would present 120 square inches of water surface. That would allow comfortably for 6 inches of fish—one 6-inch fish, six 1-inch fish, three 2-inch fish, or any other length combinations you want.

Fanciers disagree somewhat on the amount of surface to allow for each inch of fish. Some allow 24 square inches, others feel 18 square inches is enough, especially for the rugged common goldfish. In my experience, I have found that a 20 square-inch allowance works out well, and that is the recommendation I make to you.

Now let us modify this capacity rule in two ways. First, let it apply only to the hardier goldfish—common goldfish, Comets, Japanese Fantails, and other forms rugged enough to spend the winter under ice in an outdoor pool. Allow the more elaborate forms—Veiltails, Moors, and so on—25 square inches of water surface to every inch of fish.

Then consider that the larger the fish, the more oxygen it requires per inch of length. A 5- or 6-inch goldfish, for example, uses more oxygen than five or six 1-inch fish. This does not amount to a very great increase in oxygen needed, but in an aquarium full of fish it is an appreciable factor. So, once again, play safe by keeping your estimate low and tend to understock rather than overstock. (Heaven only knows how much potential business I am throwing out the window with this advice, but I would rather have a dozen well pleased new customers than twice that many disappointed ones.)

These rules apply to both cold-water and tropical fish.

Estimating Capacity by Volume

Only the area of water surface is pertinent in figuring the capacity of a pool or aquarium for fish; depth does not count at all. Goldfish in a 10- by 12-inch aquarium will be quite as well off in a 1-foot depth as in a depth of 3 or 4 feet.

At one time the water capacity was figured by volume, and fish were stocked at the rate of 1 inch of fish for 1 gallon of water. This has not proved to be a practical system.

Effect of Aquatic Plants

Water gardeners, applying the capacity rule, often inquire whether they should count the entire water surface or deduct the area covered by water-lily leaves and other foliage. Do not deduct. It is true that foliage does cover a great deal of water surface in outdoor pools, but it does not seem to affect the surface absorption of oxygen. Turn over a floating water-lily pad, and you usually find the underside covered by air bubbles, bubbles released by water when it had an overabundance of oxygen. It stands to reason that these bubbles will be reabsorbed if and when the oxygen content of the water lowers a little.

The beneficial effects of oxygenating plants are not to be considered when figuring capacities. Their healthful influence should be provided *in addition* to plenty of living space. Also remember that oxygenating plants do their good work only under the influence of light. At night, unless very strong artificial illumination is provided, pool and aquarium water must have the oxygen content replenished entirely by surface absorption.

Temperature

Goldfish do their best in water temperatures of 50 to 80 degrees. If the range can be narrowed to 60 to 70 degrees, so much the better. Whatever the temperature in which fish live, it is important to keep it constant, with no sudden changes.

In Pools

You need not worry about the temperature of an outdoor pool, for in summer it will fall within the proper range. When the water cools off in fall and finally freezes over in the winter, the temperature change will be gradual enough for the fish to adjust easily to it. Don't worry if the fish slow up a bit as the water gets colder; just cut down on their food supply. The colder the water, the less active the fish. Their metabolic rate dwindles proportionately, and hence the need for less food.

Goldfish can winter safely and comfortably in a pool 2 feet or more in depth, for this puts them below the freezing line. Be sure to rake dead leaves out of the pool before the first freeze, for decomposing leaves—especially those of maple and oak—produce a situation poisonous to fish.

The fish will be practically motionless by the time the pool freezes over, and will need no food at all while the pool remains ice-locked. A very sparse feeding is in order when the ice melts and the fish begin to move around again.

Don't fear, either, that the fish will smother under the ice. The colder the water, the more oxygen it can hold. The fish, in their near motionless state, use only a small percentage of what is available. Water gardeners sometimes make small air holes in the ice and sprinkle occasional sparse feedings into it. This is not necessary. There is some harm in it, actually, for uneaten food decomposes and fouls the water.

IN AQUARIUMS

The water temperature in an aquarium requires more consideration, but it is easy to maintain at a safe point, too. Goldfish do well in winter in a room comfortable for human beings. Except for unheated corners of the basement, extremely cold bedrooms, and southern windows which get sun all day, almost any place in the house will do for an aquarium, as long as it has about two hours of direct sunlight daily.

Word of warning: A spot above a radiator is out of the question. The warmer the water, the more oxygen it releases, and there is no surer death for goldfish than warm water.

Amount of Sun

Ideally, an aquarium should be placed where there is two hours of direct sunlight daily. This much light playing upon the oxygenating plants will enable them to do their good work efficiently, and yet it is not enough to make the water dangerously warm.

Sunlight is harmful if it causes too much plant action in the aquarium, resulting in an overabundance of algae and other microscopic green growth. This can be controlled to an extent by smearing the sunny side of an aquarium (on the outside) with a coating of Bon Ami or other household cleanser. If this doesn't check excess growth, try covering the sunny side of the aquarium with colored cellophane or with colored or white paper.

As for sunlight on the outdoor pool, a minimum of four hours a day was—or should have been—one of the prerequisites for the pool site. The more sun above and beyond this minimum, the better.

Avoiding Shock

An insidious cause of death among goldfish is shock, the effect of which is often not noticeable right away. Just as a bad cold or extreme fatigue can weaken the resistance of a human being and make him susceptible to various ills that he might be strong enough to resist otherwise, so shock weakens goldfish.

They suffer shock most often while being transferred from the pet store to their new home, or while the pool or aquarium water is being changed. The shock in the first instance is slight and necessary; in the second instance, it is unnecessary and can be fatal. When you clean an aquarium, don't draw a bucket or huge jar of cold water from the tap, gather the goldfish in a net, dump them into it, and leave them there for two or three hours while you scrub and refill the aquarium, and then dump the fish back into fresh, clean, cold water. This is shocking treatment because it is completely different from anything fish might encounter under natural conditions. For fish, there is no such thing as a sudden *natural* change. Air temperature may soar or drop alarmingly, to the intense discomfort of human beings and other air-breathing animals, but change of environment for fish is always very gradual.

Fish subjected to such shock probably won't show the ill effects immediately. A day or two afterwards, however, a dozen different goldfish may display a dozen different ailments, all results of shock—sluggishness, congested fins and tails, a dull, filmy covering on the scales, and so on. Most of them will probably recover in time, particularly if doctored. Such continued shocks, however, will keep them in poor condition, and drastically reduce their normal lifespan.

How to Change Aquarium Water

Changing aquarium water can be a simple and safe business. The easiest procedure is to transfer the fish *in the old water* into another container. Then clean the aquarium, refill it, and let it stand for two or three hours before you move the fish back into it. This allows the fresh water to approach proper temperature and also permits the release of any unnatural gases—an important consideration if you live in a community where water is heavily chlorinated.

As a short cut, when drawing new water for the fish, press your thumb against the tap so that the water comes out in a fine spray (or attach a spray gadget to your faucet). This aeration gets rid of chlorine. Then bring the water to proper temperature with a few cups from the hot-water tap.

The same procedure should be followed when changing water in an outdoor pool. Transfer the goldfish, in the old water, to some used wash tubs or other suitable vessels, and set them where sunlight will not fall directly on them. Normally, the greater amount of the pool water would require more time to warm up and release chlorine, but the same short cut can be used. Fill the pool with the nozzle of the garden hose adjusted to throw a spray. Filling of the pool this way may take a little longer, but the aerating of the water is worth the extra time. As for temperature, warm up the water with a few buckets of hot water.

Take care as to the kind of container you select to hold the fish while the pool is being refilled. New wooden tubs (unless of white cedar or cypress) and new zinc tubs may poison fish, as will any kind of container made of copper. A well-used zinc washtub, a crock, or stone jar will do very well.

CHAPTER TWENTY *All About Aquariums*

Many an interested amateur might have installed an aquarium of gold-fish in the living room long ago if he had not been frightened by the idea that it entails a lot of expense, particularly the cost of an air pump which he has been told is necessary. Not so. Air pumps are used advantageously by pet-store operators who must crowd a lot of fish into limited quarters. Such pumps, however, certainly are not necessary for aquariums that are not overcrowded. Follow the capacity rule in stocking an aquarium, add a few oxygenating plants, place the aquarium where it can get the required sunlight, and you will have no need for a pump. Neither will you need a trickle of running water, another pet-store device. In fact, either an air pump or running water can keep in constant turmoil an aquarium which otherwise would soon become well balanced.

SIZE AND STYLE

Make your own choice. Personally, I have an aversion to most goldfish bowls because it annoys me to see the fish kept in small containers which are little more than prisons. If you buy a bowl, buy a big one, 10 or 12 inches in diameter, and do not overcrowd it. The keystone and the flat-sided types illustrated here are the most efficient designs you will find. If you chose a small container, do stock it accordingly, perhaps with only one fish.

Flat-sided, plate-glass aquariums are the easiest to keep clean, give you the best show, and are inexpensive, particularly if you can find one second-hand. Being fragile, they do not travel as safely as other household effects when a family moves. For this reason, aquariums show up frequently as used, but still usable, merchandise in second-hand stores, junk shops, and at auctions of household goods.

DRAWING 34. *Containers for Ornamental Fish.*

Keep your fish in a stainless-steel framed aquarium. Be sure that the frame of the aquarium is tapered so it is stronger on the bottom where the water pressure is greater.

However, new aquariums of standard shapes and sizes are not expensive. Even aquariums which are custom built for some special scheme of decoration are reasonable enough.

How to Fix a Leaky Aquarium

An aquarium out of use for a long time will often leak when first filled again. If seepage at the seams is slight, throw a handful of mud into the water and stir it up. Then let it set overnight. If this fails, empty the aquarium and apply stiff, clean clay as caulking around the inside seams. Finally, if the aquarium continues to leak, empty it, wash it thoroughly, dry it, and then cover all cracks along the inside seams with a good grade of waterproof varnish or fill with plastic cement.

Don't try to repair a leaky aquarium while it is full by applying waterproofing solutions to the outside seams. This has never been known to work.

The Aquarium Floor

Covering for the floor of the aquarium is far more important than you might suppose. The ideal covering is sand of medium coarseness, the grade used for making concrete. This remains loose enough at all times for the roots of aquatic plants to spread and draw sustenance from it. Use a 1- to 2-inch layer of it.

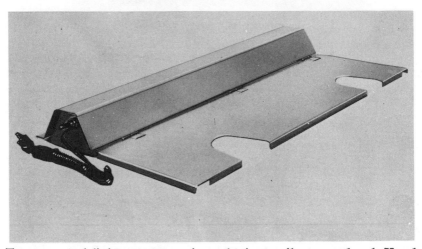

To cover and light your aquarium obtain a reflector or hood. Hoods like this one are recommended because they are made of non-magnetic stainless steel, and have no sharp edges.

Fine sand packs down and becomes too hard for roots to penetrate. Coarse sand is to be avoided if the particles are large enough to hide fish droppings and bits of food. Such tiny scraps, if the snails or fish can't find them, decompose and foul the water. For this same reason, pebbles, small stones, and marbles—regardless of how pretty they look —are to be avoided.

Now and then the sand will become dark and foul-smelling, for no apparent reason. More often than not, I suspect, this is a result of insufficient sunlight. Aquarium plants which get the required two hours usually do a good job of drawing enough food material from the aquarium floor to kep the sand sweet. Try giving the aquarium a little more sun if this trouble develops. In the meantime, the sand can be sweetened quickly by rinsing to remove all foreign matter, and then spreading it out on a newspaper to dry in the sunshine.

PLANTING AQUATICS

Dressing up the aquarium with a bit of greenery is the next step, and oxygenating plants for this purpose are discussed in Chapter 12. Some fanciers advise a plant for every square inch of aquarium floor. The plants need not be dispersed over the entire floor, of course, but can be arranged artistically in clumps and borders, much as marginal plants are arranged around an outdoor pool.

Others maintain that one aquatic plant for every 4 square inches of aquarium floor is enough. In my own aquariums, I plant at a rate about halfway between these two schools of thought, and mine are so balanced that they do not need frequent changes of water.

Disinfecting Aquatics

Before planting any aquatics in aquarium or pool, trim off all dead leaves and branches and examine each plant carefully for insects or eggs. You can play doubly safe, as I do, by immersing all new plantings of aquatics in disinfectant before introducing them to your pool or aquarium. I use household ammonia and water in a 1 to 50 mixture (4 teaspoons to 1 quart or 1 cup to 3 gallons) and let the plants soak in this for two hours.

Selecting and Disinfecting Goldfish

Buy any of the hardy breeds of goldfish at any time of year. Select them for beauty and generally healthy appearance. Age is not much of a factor with these breeds, for in an aquarium the lifespan ranges from 10 to 20 years. In outdoor pools, they often live beyond the age of 30 years.

The size of the hardy goldfish you select will also be a matter of personal choice. Remember that goldfish have the characteristic of adapting growth to surroundings. They grow slowly, if at all, in a small aquarium. The larger the aquarium or pool, the larger they will grow.

The fancy breeds require a little shopping. Age *is* a factor with these fish, for their lifespan in an aquarium (few are considered hardy enough for outdoor pools) ranges from only 6 to 12 years.

Early or mid-autumn is a good time to buy these fancy breeds. A fancy fish 1½ to 2 inches long (excluding tail) at that time will probably have been hatched only the preceding spring. At this age, they are ideal stock with which to start, big enough to stand the shock of being moved into a new aquarium, still so young that they do not yet show their distinctive tail and fin developments. If you are interested in fancy fish at all, you will undoubtedly want to see their growth from the very beginning.

Buy a fully developed fancy fish, by all means, if one catches your eye. But remember that once a fancy fish has achieved its most beautiful fin and tail forms, the remaining years will be declining years.

Disinfect new goldfish, too, as you did the aquatics, before putting them into their new home. A two-hour swim in a solution of potassium permanganate, ⅛-grain tablet (from the drugstore) to 1 gallon of water, will kill almost any bacteria they may have brought along and also help them recover from the shock of moving.

Tropical fish do not need and should not be given this treatment.

Aquarium Maintenance

Scrub your aquarium with practically any preparation that cuts dirt well for you in other household jobs, and rinse it thoroughly before putting it back into service. Accumulated dirt and algae on the sides are best removed by scraping with a razor blade, then scrubbing with soap or detergent and water, with or without ammonia added.

Use a plastic or copper sponge on the stubborn spots. Do *not* scour with sand or other abrasive, as this in time will dull the glass with hundreds of minute scratches.

GREEN WATER

Whatever kind of an aquarium you have and wherever you place it, the water will eventually take on a greenish color, the result of the growth of millions of tiny aquatic plants, mostly algae. How did the algae get there? They could have come in the front door, through the screen of an upstairs window, or ridden in on your shoulder.

The air around you at this moment contains countless suspended spores of many kinds of plant life, each searching, as it were, for a combination of circumstances which will allow it to settle down and raise a family. The spores that fall and grow upon the moist face of a rock in dark, damp woods become moss. Those that settle on damp clothing and raise blotchy looking colonies we know as mildew. Others form mold on unprotected food. Some of the spores that fall into your aquarium and pool are those of algae, one of the more spectacular growers among spore-borne plants.

A certain greenness in the water is desirable. In an outdoor pool you can test the water for proper coloration, as I have suggested, by holding your hand about 12 inches below the surface. If the outline is barely discernible at that depth, the color of the water is perfect, indicating a good balance.

An excellent excess algae preventive is an abundance of aquatic plants in the aquarium. By their shade they hold down algae growth.

Algae can develop to a point where they cease to be a blessing and become a nuisance. However, too much algae become unsightly before they are dangerous to fish, so if you ever have to deal with them there will be plenty of time to do so. When the aquarium water becomes practically opaque, try to find the cause.

An overcrowded aquarium is often the answer. Double-check the number and size of fish you have, and make sure your capacity calculations were correct. If overcrowding is the cause, the situation will right itself soon after a few fish have been removed.

Too much sunlight is another cause. Remember that the aquarium should get direct sun for only two hours a day. If it is getting more than two hours, and algae are too numerous, try cutting down the strength of the light by pasting white or colored tissue paper over the sunny side of the aquarium.

To kill algae, remove snails and *tropical* fish from the aquarium and drop in a bit of "fines" potassium permanganate. Figure the capacity of the aquarium water in cubic inches, divide by 231 to get the capacity in gallons, and allow ⅛ grain tablet to 1 gallon of water. Leave aquatic plants and goldfish in the aquarium during the treatment. It will do them good. The potassium permanganate will color the water purple. This will fade to lavender, to pale brown, but finally the water will clear. Excess algae will be gone, but will return if the situation which caused them has not been corrected.

Dying Algae

Keep your eye on any aquarium with an exceptionally heavy growth of algae, for under such circumstances the water will often undergo a chemical change which will kill off the whole algae mass. Once they begin to die, turning brownish yellow in the process, there is no stopping the process. Change the water immediately, for decomposing algae generate gases that kill goldfish.

If the chemical change takes place during the night, the goldfish will be pretty sick by the time you spot trouble in the morning. The change to fresh water will soon revive them.

Cloudy Water

Cloudy water in an aquarium, unless it is extremely overcrowded, is caused by only one process—decomposition. There may be a dead fish or snail, or accumulated bits of food. If cloudy water doesn't smell sour by the time you notice it, it soon will. There is only one way to correct it and that is to change the water.

CHAPTER TWENTY-ONE *Scavengers for Pools and Aquariums*

Scavengers are the Sanitation Department of pool and aquarium. They keep them tidy and the water sweet by consuming excess algae as it forms on plants and on the sides of pool or aquarium, and by consuming fish offal, scraps of food, or even dead fish that sink to the bottom unobserved.

Snails

The term scavenger is practically synonymous with snail, for snails do the bulk of the work. There are other scavengers which do fairly well, but they are insufficient without snails.

Snails also serve as a living meter which indicates any drastic chemical changes taking place in pool or aquarium. A slightly acid condition of water, healthy for goldfish, causes the shell of a snail to become pitted and scored. That will be your indication of a healthy pool. Extremely acid water, dangerous to fish, will first kill snails.

If snails cling to the surface rim of pool or aquarium for as long as a day, the water may be out of balance. If you investigate and find the water foul, change it. If the water is not cloudy and has no odor, assume that the snails are objecting to acidity or to an exceptionally high oxygen content. Neither of these developments is dangerous to fish.

BREEDING OF SNAILS

Even though snail breeding is a quick and simple procedure, few find is worth doing since snails seldom need replacement and are quite inexpensive. If you want to breed a few, however, set aside an aquarium

RED RAMSHORN

JAPANESE

POND

AUSTRALIAN

AFRICAN EARHORN

FOUR HORNED

SPIRAL TRUMPET

BLACK RAMSHORN

DRAWING 35. *Snails for Aquarium and Pool.*

or bowl which has been used long enough to acquire a pretty good growth of algae. If you must use a new container, transfer to it some of the water and algae from pool or aquarium.

Snails deposit eggs on plants and on the walls in gelatinous masses about as large as a thumbnail. Start a brood by plucking the egg-bearing plants and dropping them into the container you have prepared or by transferring a few adult snails. Eggs left where fish can get them will usually be eaten. If the fish do not get the eggs, then they will eat the young snails of most species as soon as they appear.

Eggs hatch in three weeks. Sprinkle flour or pulverized fish food into the brood container, and remove the adults at that time so they won't eat all the food. When the young snails are large enough to move around (after a week or two), feed them lettuce, cabbage, melon rinds, tomato peelings, bananas, cooked spinach, or practically any other fruit or vegetable scraps you have.

Species and Varieties

AFRICAN PAPER SHELL SNAIL. A prettily formed snail of medium size, of somewhat flattened shape, with attractive brown markings on a horn-colored background. One of the better ones, a good scavenger and one that won't attack aquatic plants. If you breed snails, include this one, for it is easy and quite useful. Every time you clean your pool you will find empty shells of this species, for it is comparatively short-lived.

AUSTRALIAN RED SNAIL. One of the smaller species, with a conch-shaped shell, bright orange-red. Very useful, of average hardiness, and reproduces in pool or aquarium without special conditions.

JAPANESE SNAIL. Also called Great Japanese Snail, Trapdoor Snail. One of the largest and one of the best scavengers, often grows to the size of a golf ball, is very hardy, and has a long life. The pea-sized progeny are born alive, too big for fish to eat.

POTOMAC SNAILS. Resembles the Japanese Snail except for three brown stripes running parallel to the spiral of the shell, and sometimes sold as such, but is far inferior. Practically inactive, and does little good.

LIMPET. Small snail about the size of a match head, with flat, semi-transparent shell, rather attractive. Turns up occasionally in pools and aquariums, sometimes in considerable number, having apparently gotten there as a stowaway on some newly purchased aquatic plant. Do what you like with limpets, for they are as harmless as they are useless.

POND SNAIL. Small, dark snail hardly as large as the end of a little finger. Easily identified because the spiral of the shell is the reverse of that of most other snails, might be called "the snail with the left-hand thread." Breeds prolifically, and the hard shells of the very young protect them from fish. Called the best of all the scavengers, a busy and thorough feeder. The small size enables it to move easily among the more slender plant stems in search of algae, feeding locations that other snails are usually too large and too heavy for.

RED RAMSHORN. Also called Coral Snail, Copenhagen Red Snail. An excellent scavenger with a large, flattened, orange-red shell shaped like the horn for which it is named. Does quite well in pools, but is particularly popular for aquariums, where it can be seen. Considered the most handsome snail.

BLACK RAMSHORN. Black-shelled, medium-sized snail, similar in shape to the Red Ramshorn and just as good a scavenger. Quite common in European water gardens and aquariums, but somewhat scarce in the United States.

WHITE RAMSHORN. Similar to the Black Ramshorn, but with a white shell. Common in Europe, comparatively rare in the United States.

Other Scavengers

FRESHWATER MUSSEL. Two or three of these to every 10 gallons of water in an aquarium can do a great deal of good, for they live by extracting algae and other bits of living matter from the water around them. In an outdoor pool their use is questionable, for they die easily, and as they decompose they foul the water unless quickly consumed by snails. Dead mussels can quickly be spotted in an aquarium and removed, but in a pool, where several dozen of them would be required to do any good, they can easily decompose unnoticed. Even in an aquarium they are subject to some criticism, for they move ponderously, roiling the water and often uprooting aquatic plants.

Mussels can be ordered from practically any dealer, or you can dig your own. Find a stretch of river shore strewn with mussel shells, and draw a rake through the mud and sand of the nearby shallows until you turn up as many as you want.

FROG. I enjoy the sound of a frog in a pool, although many water gardeners consider them dangerous to fish. It is true that a frog can eat a fish almost as large as itself, but this possible danger is not necessarily serious. First the frog has to catch the fish, and that is a difficult feat unless the fish is one of the extremely slow-moving fancy breeds. We have thousands of frogs living in our commercial ponds, and don't feel that we lose any appreciable amount of livestock to them. Frogs are worthless as scavengers, though often sold as such.

311

DRAWING 36. *Scavengers.*

Whatever their shortcomings, frogs add a lot of interest to a pool. They like to sit on the floating water-lily pads, and often you find them on the lotus leaves. This does not harm the plants.

SALAMANDER. Another pool pet frequently cataloged as a scavenger, which it is not. It lives principally on insects and insect eggs. Its quick, darting movements around the border of a pool add a certain interest, and it does no harm.

TADPOLE. As aquarium scavengers, tadpoles have doubtful value. It doesn't take them long to learn to eat food thrown to the fish, and then they are scavengers no longer. They are active and keep the sand bottom in constant turmoil. If they amuse you, have them, for they do no real harm.

WEATHERFISH. An interesting aquarium scavenger and a very good one, which inhabits the bottom of the aquarium, frequently burrowing into the sand as it feeds on matter that settles there. This constant burrowing makes it valuable in larger aquariums, where the sand might otherwise pack down too tight for plant roots to penetrate it easily. Although they grow several inches long, a 3- to 4-inch size is best, for they roil the water less and do not uproot the aquatics. They do their good work in pools, too, but, being bottom dwellers, cannot be seen.

CHAPTER TWENTY-TWO *Ailments and Enemies of Goldfish*

At the very beginning of this discussion I want to say that none of the diseases or parasites which sometimes plague goldfish affect human beings. Hygienic precautions should be taken by anyone handling sick goldfish, but only against transferring trouble from one fish to another. There are, indeed, many types of misfortune which can befall goldfish, but take heart, for all of these things are not going to happen to your goldfish. In fact, if you keep a pool or an aquarium for the next fifty years, you probably won't run into more than a very small percentage of them.

As in any health program, prevention is far more effective than remedial treatment. Here are a few measures which will keep the health of your pool or aquarium at the highest possible level.

It should be pointed out that few of the following treatments are to be applied to tropical fish. The tropicals, in their hundreds of species and varieties, sometimes require a special, more delicate handling. Consult a tropical fish dealer, either in person or by mail, for advice on the treatment of ailing tropicals.

To Keep Goldfish Healthy

1. Observe at all times the advice given as to capacity of container, temperature of water, and feeding of fish.

2. Before introducing new aquatic plants, sterilize them as outlined in Chapter 20.

3. Before adding new goldfish to pool or aquarium, regardless of where you bought them, sterilize them, too, for an hour or two in a potassium permanganate solution, $\frac{1}{8}$ grain per gallon of water. Like other dealers, I sell a prepared fish dip, which is also an effective sterilizing agent.

314

4. Watch for drooping dorsal fins (on fish which normally hold them stiff), for sluggishness, congested fins, and excrement containing slime or bubbles. Isolate ailing fish immediately and treat according to symptoms.

5. Also sterilize dip-nets and containers used for treating fish with the potassium permanganate solution mentioned above.

SICK BAY

Ailing fish removed for treatment should be kept in a broad, shallow receptacle in only 2 to 3 inches of water. A dishpan makes an excellent sick bay, and so does a used washtub or partially filled goldfish bowl. Have the water in the treatment receptacle of the same temperature, as closely as you can judge, as that in which the fish have been living. Keep ailing fish out of strong light, and suspend feeding unless otherwise specified, while they are being treated.

GREEN WATER TREATMENT

Any tired, sluggish fish seem to revive immediately upon transfer to different water. This water, if green, is all the more beneficial. A good provision to make for treatment is a spare aquarium planted with a few oxygenating plants and kept ready for use. Otherwise, obtain green water from your own or from a neighbor's pool, or from a stream where fish are known to live.

MUD-BOTTOM TREATMENT

For the lesser ills, as a run-down condition, transfer the fish for a few days to shallow temporary quarters, such as an old washtub, with 2 to 3 inches of mud in the bottom. This is wonderfully invigorating. Put a few sprigs of oxygenating plants and a snail or two in the tub to make it more livable.

DRIPPING WATER TREATMENT

For some reason which nobody can yet explain, run-down goldfish perk up amazingly when placed in a container fed by a drip or trickle of water. Ailing fish, apparently on the verge of breakdown with something serious, can often be brought back to perfect health in two or three days of this treatment. Kept there long enough, fish show appreciable increase in growth.

The drip-fed container, incidentally, is a fine device for tapering down gradually any strong salt solution (given below) in which a fish has been placed.

SALT TREATMENT

Sea water, 1 part to 5 parts of fresh water, makes the best salt solution. If this is unavailable, use rock salt, 2 heaping teaspoons to 1 gallon of water. Table salt can be used, in the same proportion, but use a pure brand that has no cornstarch or other inert matter added to prevent caking.

Change the salt water daily during the treatment. A common procedure is to increase the strength of the solution daily, over a period of three to four days, until it is twice as strong as it was originally.

After two days, or when the fish show improvement, begin weakening the solution and taper it down gradually to the original strength before returning the fish to pool or aquarium. Remove fish from the solution immediately if they show signs of exhaustion by rolling over. One treatment suffices for most ills.

There is a quicker salt treatment used for some fanciers. They double the strength of the solution at the beginning—1 part of sea water to 2½ of fresh water, or 4 heaping teaspoons of dry salt to 1 gallon. They put ailing fish into the strong solution for a minute or more, or until they appear exhausted. Such treatment does cure fish, but I don't think it cures them as thoroughly as the milder, longer treatment. The harsher treatment also involves the risk of killing the fish by shock.

POTASSIUM PERMANGANATE TREATMENT

We treat whole ponds of goldfish with potassium permanganate, allowing 22 grains (by weight from the druggist) to 100 gallons of water. For a smaller volume of water, allow approximately ¼ grain to 1 gallon. This is on the strong side, but when we treat huge ponds of fish, we take into consideration the great amount of algae and other plant growth on which the chemical will expend part of its strength.

From ⅛ to ¼ grain per gallon is a good solution strength for treatment of fish in smaller receptacles. Leave them in the solution for two days, or until they show signs of exhaustion.

You can drop the potassium permanganate directly into pond or aquarium, if you like, for it will act as a tonic to aquatic plants and other goldfish there. Be sure to remove snails, for the solution may kill them. Also remember that potassium permanganate will kill off most of the algae.

Some ailments require repeated treatments with potassium permanganate, but such treatments should not be given more often than every ten days. The water need not be changed between treatments, for the chemical expends its energy in two to three days, and the strength is not cumulative.

Ask the druggist for the "fines" potassium permanganate, for it dissolves much more quickly than the crystals. Keep the chemical dry until ready for use; it weakens in solution.

AMMONIA TREATMENT

The effects of an ammonia solution—10 drops of household ammonia to 1 gallon of water—are sometimes beneficial. Leave the ailing fish in the solution 5 minutes, or until there are signs of distress. I have not personally experimented with this solution. Until I do, I would not advise it except as a last resort to rid fish of some extremely stubborn parasite.

Ailments and Diseases

It is a wonder that the short, squat bodies developed in various breeds have not crowded the internal organs into unnatural arrangements that produce more stomach trouble than they do. As it is, almost the only disorders due entirely to cramped body formations are constipation and swimming bladder trouble.

CONSTIPATION

The excrement of a healthy fish is brown, usually in long sections, and without bubbles or slime. Any departure from this norm, particularly if coupled with sluggish behavior, indicates constipation. There are several easy cures. You can sprinkle a pinch of Epsom salts into the water every week as prevention, or give scrambled eggs (sprinkled with Epsom salts), chopped lettuce leaves, spinach, or chopped earthworms (smeared with castor oil) as laxative foods.

For more drastic cases, transfer the fish for two days to a solution consisting of ½ ounce of salt and ½ ounce of Epsom salts to 1 gallon of water.

Since overfeeding is a common cause of constipation, reduce the diet a bit after recovery.

DROPSY

This ailment, which seems to be confined mostly to tropical and fancier breeds, is one of the worst, but comparatively rare. The affected fish seem well except that the body swells and the scales stand out at an angle, like the seeds of a pine cone. Fish may live several days with dropsy, but there is no known cure for it.

FIN CONGESTION

This is a common ill, especially among fancier breeds, for blood circulation is poor in filmy fin and tail surfaces, rendering them highly susceptible to ailment. Fins and tails become bloodshot, and in extreme cases split and fray.

This usually develops from overfeeding, cold water, sudden chill or other shock, or overcrowding.

The salt-water treatment for a couple of days is best. Two days in the potassium permanganate solution is also good. A third treatment consists of grasping the fish between folds of damp cheesecloth and swabbing the affected surfaces with cotton soaked in kerosene.

Don't feed the ailing fish at all during treatment, and reduce the diet somewhat after recovery.

GILL CONGESTION

This seems to be an advanced stage of gill fever which tends to attack fish about a year old and approximately 2 inches long. Gills swell, and the infection covers the throat with a grayish-white discoloration.

Drop the fish into a strong salt solution—6 or 7 heaping teaspoons to 1 gallon—and leave it there until it collapses. Revive it in a receptacle in which running water will carry away the germs loosened by the salt treatment.

This is drastic treatment and does not insure recovery, but it is the only approach known. Repeat treatment daily until a kill or a cure is effected.

GILL FEVER

This illness does not affect the amateur's fish, but rather those of the commercial fish grower. It is prevalent among small fry up to five or six weeks old. Gills swell and become inflamed, and the fever kills within a few days. It is so contagious that when a commercial grower finds one fish affected he destroys all other fish living with it without further investigation.

SWIMMING BLADDER TROUBLE

Fish affected with swimming bladder trouble rest on the bottom of pool or aquarium, or hang upside-down, or at an angle near the surface, and move only with apparent effort. When the bladder is affected, they lose all sense of balance. Scaleless fish and fish with shortened bodies are the most susceptible.

These symptoms may also be caused by stomach gases formed by indigestion. Treat any fish with such symptoms for constipation. If that treatment does not cure, it is best to destroy the fish.

TAIL CONGESTION

The most common cause of this ailment is the shock experienced by fish when taken from the dealer's aquarium to a new home. The base of the tail becomes densely bloodshot, and the congestion moves forward to other areas of the body. It is fatal unless checked.

A cure can be effected quickly by the salt-water treatment.

TAIL ROT

This manifests itself in a splitting and ragged disintegration beginning at the end of tail and fins and moving toward the body. If it reaches the body it will be fatal.

Tail rot is quickly cured by the salt-water treatment. If the fins and tail of the recovered fish are unsightly, hold the fish down on a wet board and trim them with a sharp knife. Swab the trimmed edges with a potassium permanganate solution, ½ teaspoon of the chemical to an 8-ounce glass of water.

TUBERCULOSIS

This is serious and difficult to cure. Unless you are especially fond of the affected fish, it is best to destroy them. When so affected, a fish stops moving around, stops eating, and wastes away until the body has shrunken far out of proportion to the head. Consumptive fish, however, have been saved in various ways—by transferring them to green water with ½ ounce of salt per gallon, by moving them to a mud-bottom aquarium, or by putting them on a diet of scraped oyster, chopped earthworms, and scraped shrimp.

Injuries

EYE INFLAMMATION

Goldfish with telescopic eyes are more prone than others to injuries about the eye, and these injuries sometimes cause the whole eye to become inflamed.

Swab the inflammation with boric-acid solution, mixed at the same strength as prescribed on the box for human beings. Or use 1 part iodine and 9 parts glycerine. Usually a single application of either solution is sufficient.

Cuts, abrasions, and infections on goldfish are best treated by swabbing with kerosene, with the iodine-glycerine mixture, or with household Mercurochrome. Apply daily, and give the fish the salt-water treatment until it begins to recover.

The salt-water treatment alone usually helps a goldfish recover quickly from bruises.

LOST SCALES

A goldfish which loses scales in a fight or an accident will grow new ones in time, unless other injuries are too severe. The salt-water treatment for a day or so will give it a good start toward recovery.

Parasites

ANCHOR WORM

This threadlike parasite is about half an inch long, and attaches itself with a firm grip on the bodies of goldfish. It is more annoying than dangerous to fish.

Treat the whole aquarium or pool with potassium permanganate, ⅛ grain per gallon in the aquarium, ¼ grain per gallon in the pool. It is necessary to repeat the treatment three times at ten-day intervals. Do not be discouraged if the treatment seems to have no immediate effect, for it is the eggs of the parasite you want to kill. The worm itself must be pulled or clipped from the goldfish for immediate relief. The head or anchor, if not removed from the fish by hand, will drop off in time.

FLUKES

Flukes are microscopic parasite worms which attach themselves to the gills, causing the fish to breathe rapidly and to come to the surface frequently for gulps of air. It must be terribly painful, for goldfish so infested jerk and dart about spasmodically. If not treated, fish stop eating, waste away, and die of starvation and exhaustion.

If the fish are in an aquarium, treat all of them. Disinfect the aquarium and refill it with clean water. If they are in an outdoor pool, examine all the fish and dip out the affected ones for treatment.

Prepare a solution of 5 drops of formaldehyde (which you can buy at the drugstore) to 1 quart of water. Put the fish in the solution, and then every minute, add 1 drop of formaldehyde for every quart of water, until the solution is built up to ten drops to every quart. Leave the fish in the solution for a total of ten minutes. Repeat daily until a cure is effected. Three treatments usually suffice.

ICHTHYOPHTHIRIUS

This white parasite is less than half as large as the head of a pin, but when several hundred attach themselves to a goldfish it seems to be covered by a grayish white mantle.

There are several treatments. For every gallon of water in the aquarium, add 4 drops of household Mercurochrome. (This solution will not harm aquatic plants.) Put the aquarium where it will warm up to 80 or 85 degrees. After a cure is achieved, usually in about a week, change the aquarium water. Before returning the fish to the aquarium, swab affected parts with Mercurochrome, full strength, or with kerosene.

A strong salt-water solution, 2 heaping teaspoons of salt to every gallon of water, is used by some fanciers. Raise the salt water to the same 80- to 85-degree temperature.

Others have cured goldfish of *Ichthyophthirius* by swabbing affected parts with kerosene daily and keeping the fish in a warmed aquarium. Two or three treatments usually suffice.

Aquariums should be cleaned and disinfected after a cure, for eggs of the parasite may settle to the bottom, hatch, and begin the process all over again.

The potassium permanganate treatment is also effective, and this is the only practical treatment for outdoor pools in which *Ichthyophthirius* has been discovered.

Your petshop will have special Ich medicine to help you.

ITCH

A fish that spends an appreciable amount of time rubbing against plant stems and other solid objects, or "scratching" himself along the sandy bottom of the aquarium, probably has an itch caused by one of several forms of parasites.

This ailment seldom occurs in an outdoor pool. Give all the fish in the aquarium the salt treatment, give the affected fish the progressive salt treatment, clean the aquarium thoroughly, and disinfect the aquatic plants before refilling the aquarium with fresh water.

LEECHES

These are more of an annoyance than a danger to larger fish, but

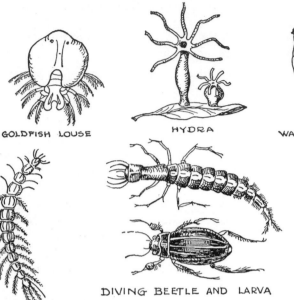

GOLDFISH LOUSE

HYDRA

WATER BOATMAN

DIVING BEETLE AND LARVA

WHIRLIGIG BEETLE LARVA

SILVER BEETLE LARVA

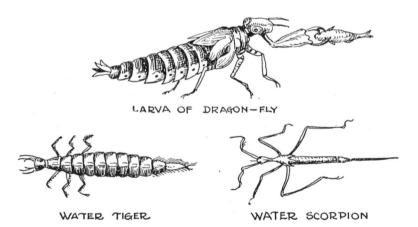

LARVA OF DRAGON—FLY

WATER TIGER

WATER SCORPION

DRAWING 37. *Pests and Enemies.*

leeches can kill small fry. The white aquatic leech, about ½ inch long and slender, attaches itself to the bodies and gills of goldfish.

Give all affected fish the progressive salt-water treatment. Scrub the aquarium, disinfect it with a solution of 1 teaspoon of ammonia for every 5 gallons of water, and disinfect aquatic plants in the same solution.

LICE

Fish lice are flat, transparent, and about the size of a pinhead. If enough attach themselves to the body they can be fatal. Fish with lice will rub vigorously against any solid object they can find. The parasite's blood-sucking, much like that of a mosquito's, creates a red spot on the fish.

Treat the whole aquarium or the whole pool with potassium permanganate when lice are detected—the aquarium with ⅛ grain to the gallon, the pool at twice that strength. Two or three treatments, ten days apart, are necessary.

WHITE FUNGUS

This is a parasitic fungus present in almost all aquarium or pool water, but one which healthy fish easily resist. A run-down fish overcome by the fungus is marked by a white scum which appears first on tail and fins, and then spreads to the body. When it enters the gills, it kills the fish. Often goldfish die before the fungus gets to the gills.

White fungus is very contagious, for when a fish is overcome by it the pool or aquarium is soon filled with fungoid bacteria.

Remove all affected fish immediately and subject them to the salt-water treatment.

Insect and Other Enemies

DRAGON FLY LARVA

Dragon flies hovering over the water, darting here and there in the sun as they run down and eat tiny insects on the wing, add a touch of beauty to a pool. They are harmless, in themselves, but their larvae are vicious enemies of goldfish, particularly the small ones. They are equipped with a terribly efficient combination. First, they move by the expulsion of water from the rear ends of their bodies, which gives them lightning-fast, jetlike maneuverability. Secondly, they have sharp, pincerlike mandibles which kill quickly.

As with most insect pests, there is not much that can be done except to kill them—both adults and larvae—on sight.

GIANT WATER BUG

This fierce predator among goldfish is large, often 2 inches or more in length, and sometimes hard to find, for the dull red or olive-brown coloring blends in with surroundings. It also can live under water for long periods, as it submerges with a supply of air bubbles sticking to its body and need not surface until they are exhausted. It is capable of inflicting a bite that causes severe swelling, so exterminate it with care.

HYDRA

A transparent polyp, the hydra is ½ inch long when fully extended, a fraction of that when it contracts its body, which it does when disturbed. It anchors itself to something solid and waits for prey. It is a menace only to newly hatched fish, but disastrous among them. The hydra, with a cylindrical body, and with up to a dozen tentacles surrounding a mouth at the free end of the body, stupefies its prey with poison, then draws nourishment from it at leisure. To rid an aquarium of hydra, remove goldfish and snails, and fill with a solution of household ammonia and water, 1 teaspoon to every 5 gallons. Clean and refill the aquarium after two hours.

PREDACEOUS DIVING BEETLE

This pest is ferocious and destructive to a degree out of all proportion to its size, which is seldom more than 1¼ inches long. Sometimes this beetle is solid brownish-black; sometimes it has a narrow border of brownish-yellow.

It is dangerous, for it is as agile as it is ferocious, and successfully attacks goldfish many times its size. It is as much at home under water as on the surface because it submerges with a bubble of air which it holds at the tip of the abdomen, a supply which lasts a long time.

The life cycle is a difficult one to fight, too. Whereas most water beetles lay their eggs on water plants, where the fish eat them, the Predaceous Diving Beetle deposits eggs within the tissues of the plants. The larvae that hatch from them are fish killers, too.

Fortunately, these beetles are easily spotted, even in very large pools. Dip them out as you see them and destroy them.

SPEARMOUTH

This is the larva of the Water Scavenger Beetle, and it is as deadly an enemy to goldfish as the Water Tiger. The body is round and plump, ofter 3 inches long. It stalks, pounces, and sucks blood with the same hunting technique as the Water Tiger.

WATER BOATMEN AND BACK SWIMMERS

A couple of aquatic bugs which look alike in size, brown color, and shape, range in length between ¼ and ½ inch. Look at the bug carefully if you see one in your pool. If there are two pairs of legs, one pair of which is held out like a pair of oars, you need not bother. It is a Water Boatman, which the fish will eventually catch and eat. If the bug has three pairs of legs, destroy it. It is a Back Swimmer, which attacks snails and small fish and can even bite human beings. A small amount of kerosene added to the water will kill the Back Swimmer when it surfaces to breathe.

WATER MITE

This is a bright red, globe-shaped parasite which sometimes attaches itself to goldfish. It is not dangerous but a nuisance.

WATER SCAVENGER BEETLE

This has a fierce-looking pair of mandibles and short antennae and is often mistaken for the Predaceous Diving Beetle, which has long antennae. The two are similar in size, shape, and color. Although the scavenger is said to attack goldfish, it lives principally on decomposed plant and animal matter.

The larvae are definitely predatory. It is a good policy to destroy on sight any beetle found in the pool, and ask questions later if you wish.

WATER STRIDER

This is a predator, no more than an inch long, but nevertheless one that takes its toll. It rides the surface of the water and attacks snails and small fish as they expose themselves.

WATER TIGER

The Water Tiger, larva of the Predaceous Diving Beetle, is as predatory and savage as the adult. The larva is flat, spindle-shaped, brownish-gray, and semitransparent, from ¼ inch to nearly 3 inches long. It is dangerous at every stage of growth, a never ceasing hunter, stalking goldfish many times its size, pouncing, killing with mandibles, and then moving off in search of other victims. It lives and grows by the blood of its quarry.

To rid a pool of such pests, try trapping them in an umbrella-type minnow seine baited with a piece of red meat.

WHIRLIGIG BEETLE

Sometimes called Coffee Bug because it is the size and shape of a coffee bean; also known as Perfume Bug because of the faint but pleasant (to some) odor it emits. The shell is black. It is not much of an annoyance, but both bug and larvae are predaceous among small goldfish and snails, and it can bite painfully.

GENERAL THREATS

If any goldfish in your pool are struck down or removed in some mysterious way, do not overlook the obvious in your search for the culprit. Remember that there are always small boys with powerful curiosity and pet cats with powerful appetites. Crawfish and frogs may find their way into your pool and live there unnoticed until some of the fish begin to disappear. The fancy, slow-moving fish are the easiest prey. Rats have a taste for goldfish, and they know how to catch them. All pool owners know that kingfishers, herons, and sandpipers catch and eat fish, but many have to learn the hard way that blackbirds often attack goldfish, too.

INDEX

331

335